LITERARY MAPS FOR YOUNG ADULT LITERATURE

LITERARY MAPS FOR YOUNG ADULT LITERATURE

MARY ELLEN SNODGRASS

CARTOGRAPHY BY
RAYMOND M. BARRETT, JR.

1995

Libraries Unlimited, Inc.
Englewood, Colorado

For Hugh, my fellow voyager

LIBRARIES UNLIMITED, INC.
P.O. Box 6633
Englewood, CO 80155-6633
1-800-237-6124

Project Editor: Tama J. Serfoss
Copy Editor: D. A. Rothschild
Proofreader: Ann Marie Damian
Interior Design and Type Selection: Alan Livingston

Library of Congress Cataloging-in-Publication Data

Snodgrass, Mary Ellen.
    Literary maps for young adult literature / Mary Ellen Snodgrass ; cartography by Raymond M. Barrett, Jr.
    xi, 223 p. 22x28 cm.
    Includes index.
    ISBN: 1-56308-164-4
    1. Literary landmarks--Maps. 2. Geography in literature.
I. Barrett, Raymond M. II. Title.
G1046.A65S6   1994 <G&M>
809'.0022'3--dc20

                            94-29795
                                CIP
                              MAP

Contents

Acknowledgments

The search for maps both past and present has taken me through books, encyclopedias, atlases, databases, and reference works, particularly *The Atlas of the North American Indian* and *The Atlas of American History*, both from Facts on File. I owe a great deal of my success at locating historically and topographically accurate information to the assistance of these agencies, libraries, and individuals:

American Automobile Association

Aruba Tourist Board

Lynne Bolick, Catawba County Library, Newton, North Carolina

Carlisle, Pennsylvania, Chamber of Commerce

Los Angeles, California, Chamber of Commerce

Charles and Susan Mason, Point Hope school system, Point Hope, Alaska

Janey Deal, Corki Miller, and Steve Johnson, Elbert Ivey Library, Hickory, North Carolina

Mohamed Bashir Sani, Nigeria Embassy

Santa Barbara Public Library, Santa Barbara, California

Taos, New Mexico, Chamber of Commerce

United States Information Service

Introduction

Much of classic and current literature pictures journeys. Youngsters demonstrate their maturity and responsibility by leaving home; warriors go off to distant battlefields; families uproot and resettle; adventurers and drifters explore promising settings; and the most daring seekers journey to unexplored lands. *Literary Maps* is intended to assist the reader, student, teacher, and librarian in more clearly envisioning the locations of these journeys and the landmarks that figure in their settings. Each book entry pairs a plot summary with a geographic overview; a detailed itinerary; and maps, each with illustrative labels, abbreviations, and arrows. Among the 35 titles selected are works suited to a varied audience, from middle school readers to more sophisticated needs and tastes. Each entry bears a distinguishing feature: the movement of characters over identifiable terrain.

The subjects of these works range wide. There are stories about animals, sports figures, runaways, sailors, soldiers, translators, truck and taxi drivers, mail carriers, teachers, rodeo riders, clergy, and law officers, as well as extraordinary families, some separated by disasters and tragedy, others impelled by hope or wanderlust. Look to, for example:

- Huck in *The Adventures of Huckleberry Finn*, who travels with an escaped slave down the Mississippi River on a raft;

- Mary and Peter in *Walkabout*, who wander the Australian desert on their way from a plane crash to their uncle's house in Adelaide;

- Reverend Stephen Kumolo of *Cry, the Beloved Country*, who visits Johannesburg, South Africa, in search of his sister and son;

- Maya Johnson in *I Know Why the Caged Bird Sings*, who reestablishes herself in new homes in St. Louis and San Francisco;

- Hugh Conway, who is kidnapped by plane in India and lands hundreds of miles to the north in a utopian monastery in Tibet, which becomes his *Lost Horizon*;

- Robin, the teenage mariner in *Dove*, who passes through many islands, countries, and oceans on his solo sail west around the world;

- Phileas Fogg and his servant Passepartout, who traverse the globe in an easterly direction as they attempt to win a bet by journeying *Around the World in Eighty Days*.

In each literary work, the reader will come upon new and different cultures, languages, and customs. Imagine Pago Pago island feasts and steamers churning out of Yokohama harbor, an Indian *suttee* ceremony, cooked wallaby for dinner, dining with wolves and lions, tending sheep, playing piano for a Louisiana circus, or leading a pet bear through the streets of Pagosa, Colorado.

Many of these titles are fictional depictions of historical events. For instance:

- Kit, the heroine of *The Witch of Blackbird Pond*, learns how it feels to be jailed for witchcraft in seventeenth-century Puritan Connecticut;

- Bright Morning, a Navajo native of Canyon de Chelly, Arizona, takes part in the Long Walk, a forced resettlement of Native Americans led by Kit Carson in *Sing Down the Moon*;

- Richard Wright, the central figure of *Black Boy*, observes soldiers marching home from World War I and joins the movement of southern blacks in search of equality in northern U.S. cities;

- Four nonfiction works—*Hiroshima, Night, Farewell to Manzanar,* and *The Endless Steppe*—describe the struggle to survive of people caught up in different aspects of World War II.

Fictional histories, particularly *Streams to the River, River to the Sea; The Light in the Forest; Jubilee; Their Eyes Were Watching God;* and *No Promises in the Wind*, depict characters who respond to such significant historical events as the Depression, the American Civil War and Reconstruction, the Emancipation Proclamation, the Indian wars, the World's Fair, Josef Stalin's regime in Soviet Russia, and Lewis and Clark's expedition across the American Northwest.

As you read the summaries and follow the characters' movements on the maps,

- commiserate with Ishi on how it feels to emerge from a dying Yahi Indian culture into an anthropological museum in the city of San Francisco;

- taste with Julie of the Wolves the wild berries that keep her alive on Alaska's North Slope as she runs from Barrow to Point Hope;

- flee with Karana across the Island of the Blue Dolphins toward a rescue ship bound for Santa Barbara, California;

- walk with Jessie Bollier from Mississippi to the Vieux Carré in New Orleans, Louisiana, on your way home from a voyage aboard *The Moonlight*, a doomed slave ship;

- observe how Ray Kinsella defies detractors and accommodates the ghost of Shoeless Joe Jackson by setting up his own baseball stadium in an Iowa cornfield.

Most important, select a character and involve yourself in movement. Search out borders, rivers, and mountains. Learn your way around. Get a feel for the land.

The experiences of Mattie Ross in Indian Territory, Buck in the Yukon wild, Elsa on the Kenyan plains, True Son on the road from Lenni Lenape territory to Paxton Township in Pennsylvania, and Mr. Braithwaite teaching at an East End London school will introduce you to new ways of reading and perceiving literature—as events set in real places that can be found in an atlas or on a map or globe.

- A day with Holden Caulfield will take you across New York City in the bittersweet confusion that accompanies adolescence;

- An afternoon in the sun on a cay will give you an ambiguous sense of panic and idyllic escape on an uncharted Caribbean isle;

- A stroll through Lima, Peru, will introduce you to the tinsel world of Perichole, the beautiful actress ruined by smallpox and restored to faith;

- A drive across California will acquaint you with the Wakatsukis' incarceration at a desert internment camp in the shadow of Mt. Whitney;

- A season on the rodeo circuit with Tom Black will prove to you that falling from a bucking bronco takes its toll in bruises and broken bones.

As you peruse these summaries and follow the treks recorded on the maps, select some titles you haven't read. Pack your bags and join the character. Along your way, get to know the countryside, its people and animals, and the excitement of unanticipated encounters. Expect to be entertained and informed every minute—and for a lot less than the cost of a ticket to some of the world's most intriguing corners.

The Adventures of Huckleberry Finn

BY MARK TWAIN

Young adult adventure novel, 1884

Geographical Summary: This classic Twain adventure story utilizes a wide segment of the Mississippi River as a setting. Kidnapped from Pike County on the upper eastern shore of Missouri, Huckleberry Finn escapes his abusive father on the Illinois shore and teams up with Jim, a runaway slave, on an island in the Mississippi River. Their adventures take them south to St. Petersburg, Missouri; past St. Louis, Missouri; and beyond Cairo, Illinois, where they intend to enter the Ohio River and travel northeast to Ohio, a free state where Jim can escape slavery. Fog foils their plans by separating them and thrusting Huck south to the Grangerford farm along the eastern shore of Arkansas. He concludes his adventures farther south at a farm 40 miles from Lafayette, Arkansas. Huck ultimately reunites with Tom Sawyer and Tom's aunts, Sally and Polly, and learns that Jim has been freed. With his appetite for freedom and adventure whetted, Huck decides to avoid the civilizing efforts of a new foster mother and flees west to Indian Territory, the fabled Wild West.

The locale of Twain's adventure story, which was the author's boyhood home, covers only a small segment of the second longest waterway in the United States (after the Missouri River). At 2,348 miles, the Mississippi River and its tributaries water 40 percent of the country and 31 states. In the area traversed by Huck and Jim, the river, wide and meandering, was marked by varying channels, heavy silt and floating trash, frequent flooding, and a treacherous, unpredictable current, all of which made (and still make) navigation difficult and, at times, dangerous, particularly for steamboats. These craft were frequently ruptured, scalding crew and passengers or sinking before rescue operations could get underway.

With a depth of 12 feet, the segment of the Mississippi River near Cairo, Illinois, is suitable for deep-water traffic, the profitable market that made the river a major artery of American transportation and commerce. The movement of cargo from factories in the north and plantations and farms to the south created a market for young men like Samuel Clemens, who longed to earn a living as riverboat pilots, an adventurous profession that appealed to the romantic minds of farm boys brought up in sight of churning sternwheelers. Although Clemens obtained his pilot's license, he saw his dream end after the Battle of Vicksburg in 1863, which halted river traffic for paddle-wheelers and barges until the end of the Civil War two years later. This disruption of Clemens's ambition sent him west to California with his brother Orion, a printer and editor who gave the budding young writer an opportunity to publish. Clemens adopted his famous pseudonym from "mark twain," the call of the leadsmen who threw weighted lines into the water to measure safe depths for riverboat passage.

Numerous stage, television, and film versions of Twain's novel have captured, with only limited success, the romance of *The Adventures of Huckleberry Finn*. A 1931 version, filmed in black and white by Paramount Pictures, starred Jackie Coogan as Huck and Junior Durkin as Jim. Eight years later, Joseph Mankiewicz made a longer picture for Metro-Goldwyn-Mayer (MGM) that had Mickey Rooney and Walter Connolly in the lead roles. Two color versions—a 1960 MGM remake starring Eddie Hodges and Archie Moore, and a lengthy 1974 United Artists version with Jeff East and Paul Winfield—received little box-office attention.

Further Reading

Bloom, Harold, intro. *Mark Twain's Adventures of Huckleberry Finn.* New York, Chelsea House, 1986.

Clemens, Samuel L. *Life on the Mississippi.* Irvine, CA: Reprint Services, 1988.

Ehrlich, Eugene, and Gorton Carruth. *The Oxford Illustrated Literary Guide to the United States.* New York: Oxford University Press, 1982.

Hart, James D. *The Oxford Companion to American Literature.* New York: Oxford University Press, 1983.

McCall, Edith. *Biography of a River: The Mississippi.* New York: Walker, 1990.

Parker, Weldon, and Dee Parker. *Down the Magical Mississippi.* Clear Lake, CA: Sun Seeker Books, 1985.

Wilson, Charles Reagan, and William Ferris, eds. *Encyclopedia of Southern Culture.* Chapel Hill, NC: University of North Carolina Press, 1989.

Detailed Itinerary

1. Pike County, Missouri

Identified by its dialect as Pike County, Huckleberry Finn's fictional hometown of St. Petersburg (probably Twain's hometown of Hannibal) lies above St. Louis on the west shore of the Mississippi River opposite Illinois. Reared by the Widow Douglas and her sister, Miss Watson, Hugh enjoys such sport as playing robbers and teasing Miss Watson's slave Jim, but chafes at the civilizing influences that require him to attend church and school, study the Bible, wear shoes, stop smoking and swearing, and sleep in his room rather than in the woods. Then Huck's absent and abusive father, Pap Finn, returns and tries to force Judge Thatcher to give him Huck's $12,000 trust fund and custody of his son. The judge refuses.

2. Illinois shore

In spring, Pap kidnaps Huck and takes him east across the river to the Illinois shore and a primitive cabin in the woods. Pap's alcoholic hallucinations and bouts of whippings force Huck to saw his way out of the locked cabin and hide a canoe so he can run away. Before leaving, he plants phony evidence that makes it appear that he has been murdered.

3. Jackson's Island on the Mississippi River

Across the river, two and a half miles downstream on Jackson's Island and a half mile from the bluffs of the Missouri shore, Huck finds a likely spot in which to lay low and avoid Pap. The next morning, he watches a ferry pass by, loaded with town residents, friends, Pap, and other searchers hunting for Huck's drowned corpse. After three days of camping, Huck hears voices and escapes in his canoe to the foot of the island, where he encounters Jim, who fears he will be sold for $800 "down to Orleans" by a slave trader. Huck decides to help Jim escape up North, where he will be free. The two recover useful items from a floating house; Jim finds a dead man in the house and conceals his identity from Huck.

4. St. Petersburg, Missouri

Opposite Jackson Island at St. Petersburg, 10 miles downriver from Goshen and 7 miles above Hookerville on the Missouri side, Huck, disguised as Sarah Mary Williams, elicits information from Judith Loftus, a woman living in a shanty. He learns that she suspects the runaway slave is hiding on Jackson's Island and plans to claim a reward offered for his return by sending a party to capture him. Quickly, Huck and Jim push on downriver.

5. Missouri shore

Huck and Jim tie their raft to a towhead on the Missouri shore 16 or 17 miles below St. Petersburg. Cliffs dot the Missouri side, and timber grows on the Illinois side.

6. St. Louis, Missouri

For five nights, the raft drifts with the current, eventually passing the bright lights of St. Louis, which lies halfway down the eastern border of Missouri. The raft continues south for five more nights.

7. Booth's Landing on the Mississippi River

During a storm, Jim and Huck are thrown from the raft and board the *Walter Scott*, a wrecked steamboat foundered near Booth's Landing. Aboard a skiff they cut loose from the wreck, they escape a gang of murderers and relocate the raft, which is still afloat. At dawn, Jim and Huck, laden with stolen articles from the steamboat, paddle to an island to sleep.

8. Cairo, Illinois, at the juncture of the Mississippi and Ohio rivers

Huck wants to continue down the Missouri shore and sell the raft at Cairo after three more nights' journey so that he and Jim can travel northeast up the Ohio to the free states. At Illinois' southern tip, they inadvertently pass Cairo in the fog and continue south on the Mississippi River.

9. Grangerford farm on the Arkansas shore

Separated from Jim after a steamboat swamps the raft, Huck arrives at the Grangerford farm and poses as George Jackson, a resident of southern Arkansas; he pretends to have fallen off a passing steamboat. The family treats him well and pairs him with their son Buck, who is about Huck's age, 13 or 14. A slave reunites Huck with Jim in a nearby swamp shortly before a long-standing feud between the Grangerfords and the nearby Shepherdson family breaks into violence. After Buck is shot, Huck, heartsick with the loss of his young friend, escapes to the raft with Jim.

10. South on the Mississippi River along the Arkansas shore

The raft drifts south two or three days. Then two con men, eluding pursuers, leap aboard with Jim and Huck. Three miles down the bend, the con men, who call themselves the Duke and the King, prepare to put on a Shakespearian revival. To explain why they are traveling south down the Arkansas shore with a black man, the con men print reward posters for Jim claiming that he ran away from the St. Jacques plantation 40 miles below New Orleans. The third night of the revival, the audience becomes wise to the tricks of the con men. The pair, along with Jim and Huck, race out of town and back to the raft, which they tie to a willow towhead in the middle of the Mississippi.

The King and Duke pose as William and Harvey Wilks and try to steal the inheritance money of Mary Jane, Joanna, and Susan, the daughters of Peter Wilks, whom they claim as nieces. Huck conceals the stolen money in Wilks's coffin and informs Mary Jane of his departure and the money's whereabouts. He tries to escape the con men, but they catch up with him at the raft.

11. Pikesville, Arkansas

The raft drifts for "days and days" and arrives further south, as is obvious by Spanish moss in the trees and a warmer climate. Two miles below Pikesville, Jim disappears. Huck, overcome with guilt, writes a note to Miss Watson divulging Jim's whereabouts, then tears up the note.

12. Phelps's Sawmill, 40 miles from Lafayette in Arkansas

Huck travels downriver to an island. Tipped off by the Duke, he heads inland to Phelps's Sawmill, 40 miles from Lafayette, to rescue Jim, who is locked in a shed. Huck, pretending to be Tom Sawyer, accepts the hospitality of Tom's Aunt Sally, who has never met Tom. Tom Sawyer arrives and poses as Tom's brother Sid, a ruse that further confuses the Phelps family. Meanwhile, local people capture the Duke and King and tar and feather them.

A lengthy, romanticized attempt to free Jim results in Tom getting shot. After Tom recovers, his Aunt Polly arrives and identifies both rascally boys. Huck learns that Miss Watson's will freed Jim. Now a free man, Jim discloses that the dead man on the floating house was Huck's Pap.

13. Indian Territory

Huck, unwilling to endure Aunt Sally's attempts to civilize him, plans to head for Indian Territory, the area west of Arkansas that, early in the twentieth century, became the state of Oklahoma.

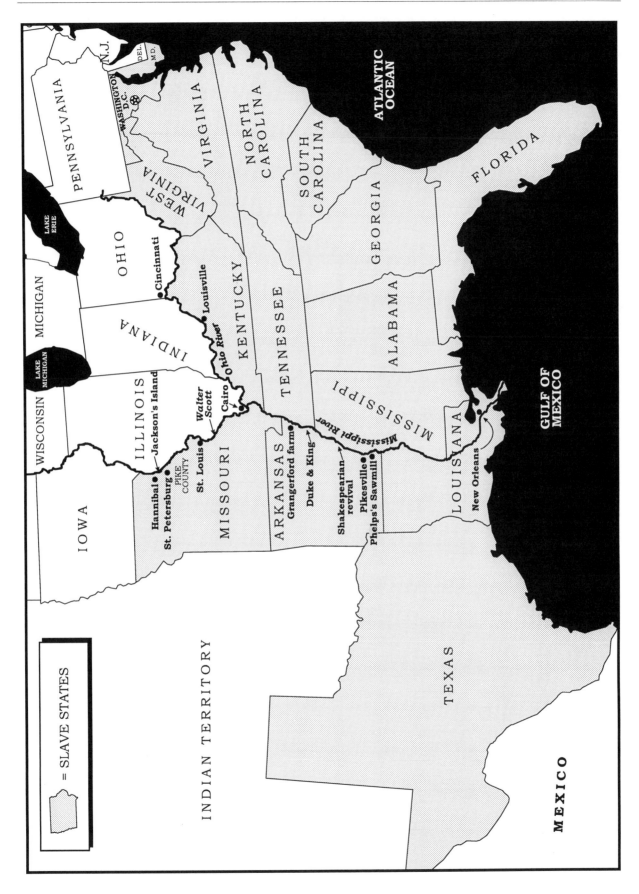

...And Now Miguel

BY JOSEPH KRUMGOLD

Young adult novel, 1953

Geographical Summary: On the Rio Pueblo, a river that winds down the western side of Taos in upper central New Mexico, 12-year-old Miguel Chavez is the young son of a large sheepherding family in Los Cordovas, eight miles southwest of Taos. Overwhelmed by family responsibilities and personal longings, he conceals his secret desire—to accompany the adult herders east to the Kit Carson National Forest in the Sangre de Cristo Mountains, where they pasture the flock for the summer. By demonstrating that he can accept responsibility, Miguel realizes his dream by traveling with the flocks to high-country pastures.

Re-created in a 1965 technicolor film version produced by Universal Pictures, ... *And Now Miguel* tells a story of coming-of-age and responsibility. The setting for the movie and for Krumgold's novel is a sparsely populated area; 37 percent of those who live there are Hispanic. Historically linked to cattle and sheep ranching, the steep terrain that Miguel's family inhabits encompasses the southern end of the Rocky Mountains—a rugged vista taking in the San Juan Mountains, the Sangre de Cristo Mountains, and the Rio Grande River, which flows south toward the Texas boundary with Mexico. Among the region's buttes, canyons, mesas, valleys, and sandstone outcroppings, herders have traditionally watched over flocks of sheep to protect them from predators, such as wolves and cougars; to search for strays and injured animals; and to assist ewes during lambing season. The herders are forced to move from place to place to find their flocks the best pasturage and water in this dry, sometimes inhospitable landscape.

Further Reading

Amholz, Jim. *New Mexico on My Mind*. Helena, MT: Falcon Press, 1990.

Davis, W. W. *El Gringo: New Mexico and Her People*. Lincoln, NE: University of Nebraska Press, 1982.

Line, Francis R. *Sheep, Stars, and Solitude: Adventure Saga of a Wilderness Trail*. Irvine, CA: Wide Horizons Press, 1986.

Roberts, Susan, and Calvin Roberts. *A History of New Mexico*. Albuquerque, NM: University of New Mexico Press, 1991.

Detailed Itinerary

1. Los Cordovas on the Rio Pueblo west of Taos, New Mexico

By means of a government permit, Miguel Chavez's grandfather Padre de Chavez established the family sheep business at Los Cordovas on the Rio Pueblo. He proudly narrates the family's Spanish ancestry. However, to Miguel's dismay, Grandfather and other family members ignore the boy when he tries to prove that he is grown up by taking part in the herding.

Miguel divulges to his young sister and brother, Faustina and Pedro, his plan to join the spring trip east to the Sangre de Cristo Mountains. He attempts to impress his father, Blas, and his older brothers, Blasito and Gabriel, by doing a good job of sheep keeping. During lambing season, he stamps the pairs—ewe and lamb—with numbers for easy identification. His family nicknames him "bookkeeper."

2. Navajo Reservation, Arizona

Part of Blasito's flock is lost in a storm, which blows east from the Navajo Reservation in Arizona.

3. Arroyo Hondo in New Mexico

Miguel overhears from his friend Juby that the dozen lost sheep are in Arroyo Hondo, northwest of Taos. That morning, Miguel leaves school and hunts on the mesa until late afternoon.

4. Los Cordovas, New Mexico

Miguel is about to give up the search when he finally smells the sheep and herds them across the river and back toward Los Cordovas. Blasito praises Miguel for recovering the sheep. Miguel again tries to air his ambitions, but the adults continue to ignore him. His only reward comes from Grandfather, who labels him a "real pastor."

Miguel, puffed up with overconfidence, interrupts Blas, who is helping Blasito repair the tractor, and requests a real summer job. His father refuses to include him on the trek to the summer pasture, instead assigning him to tend Jimmy, an orphan lamb. Miguel prays to San Ysidro, the patron saint of farmers and of the village of Los Cordovas. On festival day, May 15, Miguel visits the new statue of San Ysidro, which was carved by George Perez in Trampas, south of Taos. Miguel begs the saint to grant him a man-sized job.

After the fiesta, Blas asks Miguel's advice about collecting the flock and about designing a chute for the pens. Miguel tries hard to please his father, particularly when Juan and Johnny Marquez and the other shearers come south from Colorado to harvest the wool (later moving farther south to Texas to carry on their trade). Miguel earns the nickname "Twister" for sweeping the shearing floor, and he shares the noon meal with the rest of the crew.

That afternoon, Miguel stuffs bound fleece into a burlap bag. He accidentally falls in and sinks to the bottom of the sack. The packing goes on around him until the crew notices his absence. Blas halts and angrily pulls Miguel from the bag. Humiliated, Miguel and Jimmy wander off to the river.

Miguel's luck changes after Gabriel receives a draft notice. Miguel prays to San Ysidro to allow Gabriel to stay, and the next day he steals the induction notice. Gabriel catches him and explains that destroying the letter will not destroy the order to report to the army. Gabriel illustrates his point by tearing the letter into bits and tossing them into the Rio Pueblo.

Miguel confesses that he believes his prayer to San Ysidro caused Gabriel to be drafted. Gabriel eases the boy's conscience by admitting that he made a wish to see the ocean; by joining the army, he may achieve his wish. Gabriel concludes that a saint is not a fairy godmother: "For whatever you get, you got to give something." Miguel reconsiders his relationship with San Ysidro. The day before Miguel embarks on the journey to Sangre de Cristo, he promises Gabriel that he will finish carving the name "Carlotta" (Gabby's girlfriend in Taos) on a tree on the mountain.

5. Rancho de Taos, Espanola, Santa Fe, Arroyo Miranda, Springs of Ponce de Leon, Arroyo del Alamo, Kiowa Trail, and Picuris Peak in New Mexico

On the way from Los Cordovas, across the highway to Espanola and Santa Fe and east toward the mountains, Miguel becomes a full-fledged member of the herding Chavez family.

6. U.S. Hill, Sangre de Cristo Mountains in New Mexico

After five days on the trail, the men drive 1,800 sheep up the mountain.

7. Quien Sabe Creek, Cerro Vista Mountain, and La Cueva Peak in New Mexico

Over Quien Sabe Creek and up Cerro Vista Mountain southeast of Taos, Miguel finds trees with names carved in them by his grandfather and father. The herdsmen camp on the far side of La Cueva Peak.

8. Jicarito Peak, Carpio Canyon, Santa Barbara River, Middle Fork in New Mexico

Beyond Jicarito Peak and Carpio Canyon and up the Santa Barbara River to Middle Fork, Miguel adds T-T-A to Gabriel's unfinished spelling of "Carlotta." Knowing that he will return to the Sangre de Cristo Mountains, Miguel saves the task of carving his own name for a future trip.

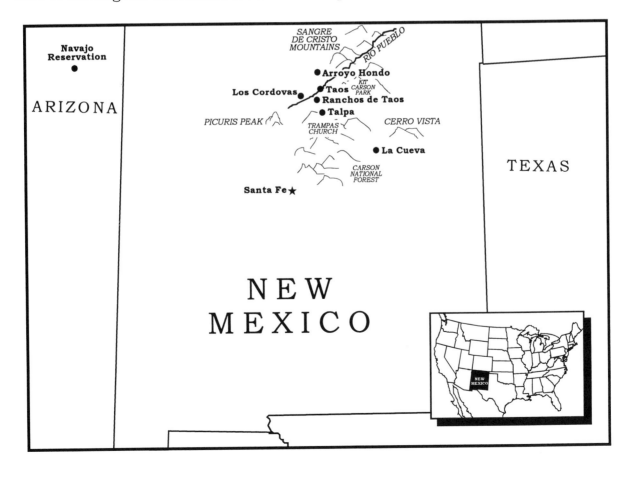

Around the World in Eighty Days

BY JULES VERNE

Adventure novel, 1872

Geographical Summary: One of the most engaging adventure tales of the nineteenth century, *Around the World in Eighty Days* follows a civil, self-contained gentleman on his 80-day circumnavigation of the globe in order to win a bet of £20,000. Setting out from London in a southeasterly direction, Phileas Fogg crosses the English Channel from Dover to Calais, France, traverses Europe to Turin, Italy, and embarks for Asia at Brindisi, above the heel of Italy's boot. Traveling by steamer through the Suez Canal around Yemen, Fogg and his valet, Jean Passepartout, reach Bombay, India, without much fuss. However, the overland route to Calcutta puts the men in the path of a savage marital custom—suttee, the ritual burning of Aouda, a rajah's young widow. Fogg rescues Aouda and continues southeast through the Bay of Bengal and the Indian Ocean, then north to Singapore, up the strait that separates Formosa from mainland China, and across the Tropic of Cancer. By some deft maneuvering, Fogg, who has been parted from Passepartout, reunites with him and arrives at San Francisco in the United States. The transcontinental rail takes them through Mormon territory at the Great Salt Lake and past hostile Indians as he journeys from Medicine Bow, Wyoming, to Julesburg, Colorado; Fort Kearney, Nebraska; and New York City.

The race seems doomed as the often-delayed Fogg and his party push from New York past the Hudson River and across the Atlantic Ocean to the British Isles. From Queenstown in southern Ireland, he crosses to Dublin and passes over the Irish Sea to Liverpool. After a minor disagreement with the law, he arrives in London in time to claim his bet and marry Aouda.

Jules Verne's delight in his hero's rapid transit demonstrates two central and interrelated attitudes of Victorian England—a fascination with inventions and an optimism that the world would be improved through technology. Fueled by innovations in steam locomotives beginning in 1830, the ease of transportation increased monumentally as plentiful coal and iron, extensive rail lines, and comfortable oceangoing steamers resulted in reliable, convenient service for travelers and commerce. At the same time, the United States revolutionized cross-country travel after the Union Pacific Railroad completed a transcontinental connection through Utah in 1869. Coinciding with the opening of the Suez Canal—an engineering feat that cut weeks off the journey from England to India—these improvements turned the 1870s into boom years for around-the-world trade and travel.

Among the customs and cultural oddities they encountered, the British found most repulsive the *suttee*, or *sati*, the practice of self-immolation by Hindu widows, who leaped onto their husbands' funeral pyres as demonstrations of wifely virtue and loyalty. Recorded in accounts of the Indian invasion of Alexander the Great, the ritual remained in use until the nineteenth century, when the British raj, at the insistance of progressive Hindus, outlawed it. A colorful, chillingly romanticized ceremony, the suttee included a procession, music, chanting, garlands, icons, and the placement on temple walls of a vermillion handprint from each widow who made her way to the site of cremation. This act of self-abnegation and sacrifice rendered the women sacred. The emotional impact of these ceremonies explains the danger to Fogg and his party when they rescue Aouda.

A 1956 United Artists/Michael Todd technicolor movie of the novel earned an Academy Award for best picture and nominations for best director, art direction, and editing. The lengthy film of the around-the-world chase starred David Niven, Ronald Colman, Cantinflas, Buster Keaton, John Gielgud, and Noel Coward. The most significant accomplishment of this complicated undertaking was the 44 cameo roles played by such unlikely participants as John Mills, Cesar Romero, Frank Sinatra, Ed Murrow, Beatrice Lillie, Jose Greco, George Raft, Trevor Howard, Glynis Johns, Evelyn Keyes, Charles Boyer, Shirley MacLaine, and Marlene Dietrich.

Further Reading

Freeman, Michael J., and Derek H. Aldcroft, eds. *Transport in Victorian Britain*. New York: St. Martin's Press, 1988.

Jhabvala, Ruth Prawer. *Heat and Dust*. New York: Simon & Schuster, 1975.

Kulke, Herrmann, and Dietmar Rothermund. *A History of India*. New York: Routledge, Chapman & Hall, 1990.

Link, O. Winston. *Steam, Steel and Stars: America's Last Steam Railroad*. New York: Harry Abrams, 1987.

Martin, Andrew. *The Mask of the Prophet: The Extraordinary Fiction of Jules Verne*. New York: Oxford University Press, 1990.

Padhi, Bibhu, and Minakshi Padhi. *Indian Philosophy and Religion: A Reader's Guide*. Jefferson, NC: McFarland, 1990.

Detailed Itinerary

1. London, England

Phileas Fogg, a wealthy, self-contained man who resembles the poet Byron, knows little of London, although he has lived there for many years. He visits the Reform Club each day and lives a discreet, conservative life bound up in tiny details, such as the exact temperature of his shaving water. Most of his time is spent in reading newspapers and playing whist. Having dismissed his former lackadaisical valet at exactly 11:29 A.M. on Wednesday, October 2, Fogg hires Jean Passepartout, an energetic, fortyish Frenchman who anticipates a quiet life serving "a domestic and regular gentleman."

At 7:00 P.M. that evening at the club, the whist players discuss a robbery of £55,000 three days earlier from the Bank of England. Fogg claims that, according to a tabulation in the *Daily Telegraph*, a traveler can circumnavigate the world in 80 days. Andrew Stuart, one of the players, rebuts that assertion with reminders of hazards of weather and accident. Stuart wagers £4,000 with Fogg that it can't be done. Fogg counters with a bet of half his wealth, £20,000 (the trip itself will devour the remainder of his money), and plans to depart by train that very evening for the southern English port of Dover at 8:45 P.M. with the promise to return to London on Saturday, December 21, at the same time in the evening. He extends his check in all seriousness and continues the card game, which he wins.

Summoning Passepartout to prepare to depart for Dover, Fogg sticks a copy of *Bradshaw's Continental Railway Steam Transit and General Guide* under his arm. With his valet's help, he departs from home with mackintosh, cloak, carpetbag, and £20,000 in cash, pausing to offer a beggar woman and her child the 20 guineas he won at whist, but charging Passepartout with the cost of the gas he accidentally left on at Saville Row.

Newspaper stories launch a frenzy of bets on the outcome of the adventure. The greatest doubts about Fogg's claims arise from his plan to cover India in three days and the United States in seven. The odds stand at 200 to 1. That same week, a police detective named Fix concludes that Fogg is the man who robbed the Bank of England; Fix follows his suspect as Fogg travels southeast toward India.

2. Overland from Calais, France, to Brindisi, Italy

Over six and a half days, Fogg journeys from London to Dover; crosses the English Channel to Calais, France; and continues east to Paris. Crossing Europe, he arrives at Turin in northern Italy, traverses the country, and embarks by steamer from Brindisi, a port city on the eastern coast near the heel of Italy's boot.

3. Across the Mediterranean to the Suez Canal in Egypt

Fogg calmly plays cards aboard the *Mongolia*, a steamer bound for Bombay, India, as it crosses the Mediterranean to the Suez Canal. Along the way, he proposes to buy enough clothing for the trip. Fix, in close pursuit, plans to apprehend Fogg in India, which is British territory, and charge him with bank theft.

4. Mocha, Yemen, to Aden, Yemen, on the southern end of the Red Sea

Fogg remains below deck playing whist as the steamer takes on coal at Mocha at the southeastern end of the Red Sea on October 13 and approaches Aden ahead of schedule. During this period, Fix, eager to test his theory that Fogg is a thief, pumps Passepartout for information, asking him about such things as the likelihood that Fogg is on a secret diplomatic mission. Fogg, who is unaware of Fix's obsession, goes ashore to obtain a visa to prove to the Reform Club that he has followed his proposed route. The *Mongolia* continues east toward India.

5. Bombay, India

As Fogg completes his thirty-third rubber of whist, he takes all 13 tricks in a grand slam shortly before arriving at Bombay on India's western coast on October 20, netting a gain of two days. He disembarks at 4:00 P.M. and has four hours to pass before boarding the train across India toward Calcutta on the eastern coast. Fix does not receive the warrant he needs to arrest Fogg and is disappointed, but continues trailing his man.

6. Burhampoor in the Sutpour Mountains of India

In the company of Sir Francis Cromarty, a fellow card player, Fogg departs Bombay at 8:00 P.M. Four and a half hours later, Passepartout, who had run afoul of Indic religious laws and lost his shoes while escaping angry Indians, purchases Indian slippers at a stop in Burhampoor northeast of Bombay in the Sutpour Mountains in India's central highlands.

7. Rothal to Allahabad, south of Benares, India

Passengers are forced to leave the train at Rothal, where the track ends; 50 miles of it are still to be laid to Allahabad. As insouciant as ever, Fogg buys an elephant named Kiouni for £2,000, hires a Parsee guide, and sets off with Cromarty into the forest for Allahabad, a town in northeastern India near Benares, Cromarty's destination. The little group encounters a funeral procession leading the drugged Aouda, a young widow, to a ritual funeral pyre for her husband, a rajah. Fogg is dismayed to learn that she will be burned on the pyre with her husband's remains, regardless of her wishes.

With 12 hours to spare, Fogg diverts from his around-the-world course and sets out to rescue Aouda. As the rajah's pyre is about to be lit, Passepartout, who has changed places with and disguised himself as the corpse, terrifies the mourners by arising and embracing Aouda. In the confusion that follows, he and Fogg seize the widow and flee. The rajah's people angrily pursue them, but they escape. At the end of the journey, Fogg pays the Parsee his wage and gives him Kiouni.

8. Calcutta, India

Departing from Cromarty, Fogg and his party board the train for Calcutta, which they reach at 7:00 A.M. the next day. Pleased with the company of the gentle Indian widow, Fogg has no regrets about the lost time. The train continues without incident to India's eastern shore. Meanwhile, Fix, anticipating that Fogg will run into difficulties for violating local customs, follows by rail.

To Fogg's surprise, he and Passepartout are arrested in Calcutta and tried for sacrilege. He posts bail of £2,000 and departs to complete his journey. Once more, Detective Fix is foiled before he can detain his suspect. Fogg, Passepartout, and Aouda board the *Rangoon* for Hong Kong.

9. Aboard the *Rangoon*, bound from Calcutta, India, through the Bay of Bengal and Indian Ocean to Hong Kong, China

Although shadowed by Fix, who plans to apprehend Fogg at the Singapore stopover, Fogg is oblivious to the detective. Nearby, the seasick Passepartout lies in his berth through the Bay of Bengal and Indian Ocean. While Fogg stays in his cabin playing whist with Aouda and learning her history, Passepartout concludes that Fix is a Reform Club spy. Delayed by storms out of Hong Kong, Fogg hopes to connect with the steamer *Carnatic* in order to travel northeast to the southern Japanese port of Yokohama.

In Hong Kong, Fogg sets out on a side mission—a search for Aouda's cousin Jeejeeh. Meanwhile, Fix tries to convince Passepartout that Fogg is the notorious Bank of England robber. Passepartout refuses to believe that a man who would risk losing a £20,000 bet to rescue Aouda would steal bank funds. Passepartout learns that the *Carnatic* will be sailing early, so, at an inn, the detective hands the servant a pipe of opium, which renders him unconscious. On arriving at the dock and finding neither Passepartout nor the *Carnatic*, Fogg remains unruffled and bribes John Bunsby, the captain of the *Tankadere*, £200 a day to reach Yokohama on time.

10. Shanghai, China

Bunsby transports Fogg, Aouda, and the tagalong Fix 800 miles up the Strait of Fo-Kien between the island of Formosa (Taiwan) and the Chinese mainland, across the Tropic of Cancer, and to Shanghai on China's east coast. In close contact with his suspect, Fix begins to doubt that Fogg is a thief. A typhoon arises, forcing the *Tankadere* rapidly across the waters, as it goes on to Yokohama, Japan.

11. Yokohama, Japan

At 6:30 A.M. on November 7, Passepartout staggers aboard the *Carnatic* as it puffs along the Shanghai quay. On the thirteenth, he arrives in Yokohama, Japan. Because he has no money, he sells his clothes for cash, dresses in used garments, and joins a troupe of acrobats. Fogg sees him during a performance. Reunited, the party boards the three-masted steamer *General Grant* bound for the United States. Fix follows them.

12. From Yokohama, Japan, to San Francisco, California

As the *General Grant* steams toward the United States, Fix realizes that his warrant is invalid off British soil and determines to let Fogg return to England so he can make the arrest. Fogg and his party cross the International Date Line and on November 23 enter the second half of their journey. The group docks at San Francisco, where Fogg buys them tickets on the Transcontinental Railway, and they set out for New York.

13. Across the American West to Salt Lake City, Utah

By December 5, Fogg's party is bound by train across the west toward the Great Salt Lake in Utah, where he hears a Mormon sermon and observes the peculiar institution of polygamy in Salt Lake City.

14. Salt Lake City, Utah, to Medicine Bow, Wyoming, and Julesburg, Colorado

Hindered by snow, the train races across a shaky suspension bridge at Medicine Bow near the center of Wyoming's southern border (it collapses behind them), then crosses the Platte River in the northwest corner of Colorado at Julesburg. En route, it is attacked by a band of Sioux, who kidnap Passepartout near Fort Kearney in south-central Nebraska.

15. Omaha, Nebraska, to Chicago, Illinois, to New York City

Fogg recovers his servant, travels by sledge and train to Omaha, and crosses Iowa and Illinois to Chicago. There is no problem obtaining passage across Indiana, Ohio, Pennsylvania, and New Jersey to New York. But on December 11, the group arrives at the Hudson River 45 minutes too late—the *China* has already departed. After a night at the St. Nichols Hotel on Broadway, Fogg offers Welsh captain Andrew Speedy £8,000 to divert his course from Bordeaux, France, and carry them across the Atlantic to England aboard the iron-hulled *Henrietta*, which is anchored at the Battery. Speedy declines to alter his course. Undaunted, Fogg's party books passage on the ship.

16. New York City, around Newfoundland, Canada, to Queenstown, Ireland

In a half hour, the *Henrietta* departs New York near the lighthouse at the mouth of the Hudson River, around Sandy Hook point, and into wintry seas. Shortly, Fogg wins over the crew and locks Speedy in his cabin as he changes the destination from Bordeaux to Liverpool, England. By December 13, the ship rounds Newfoundland. On the eighteenth, the coal supply is nearly depleted. Fogg frees Speedy and buys his ship for $60,000, burning the upper deck as fuel. With 24 hours left, the party reaches Queenstown (currently called Cork) on Ireland's south coast.

17. Queenstown to Dublin, Ireland, to Liverpool, England

From Queenstown, Fogg and company board the express train for Dublin and take the steamer halfway up England's eastern coast to Liverpool, arriving on Saturday, December 21, only six hours from London. At this point, Fix arrests Fogg and shuts him in the Liverpool Custom House. Passepartout blames himself for not telling his master about Fix's mission. After some hours pass, Fix returns with news: The real robber had been arrested on December 17 in Edinburgh, Scotland. Fix frees Fogg for the final dash to London aboard a special train and apologizes for the error. Fogg knocks him down.

18. London, England

Believing that he has arrived late and lost the bet, Fogg goes immediately to Saville Row. Passepartout rushes to turn off the gas he left burning and is then sent to fetch Reverend Wilson so that Fogg and Aouda can marry, even though Fogg is now penniless. But Wilson informs Passepartout that it is Sunday, not Monday—they gained a day when they crossed the International Date Line from west to east. Passepartout hurries home with the news, and he, Fogg, and Aouda rush to the Reform Club. They arrive with a second to spare, Fogg announcing, "Here I am, gentlemen!" He wins his £20,000, shares £1,000 with Fix and Passepartout, and marries Aouda.

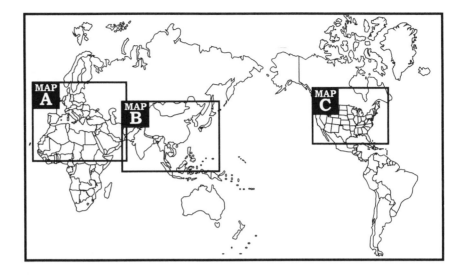

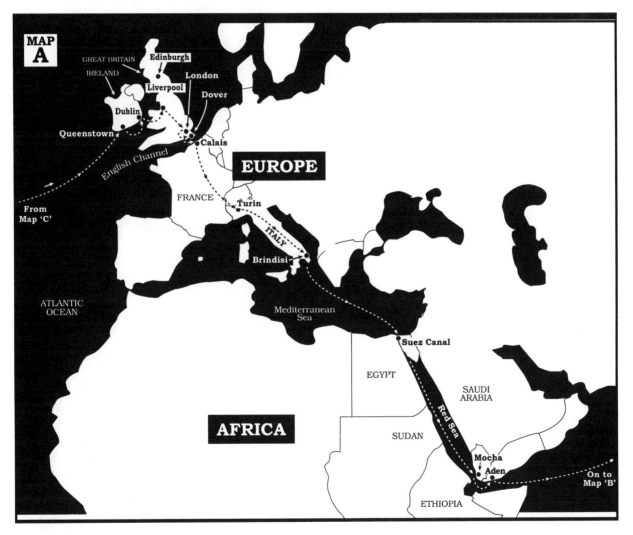

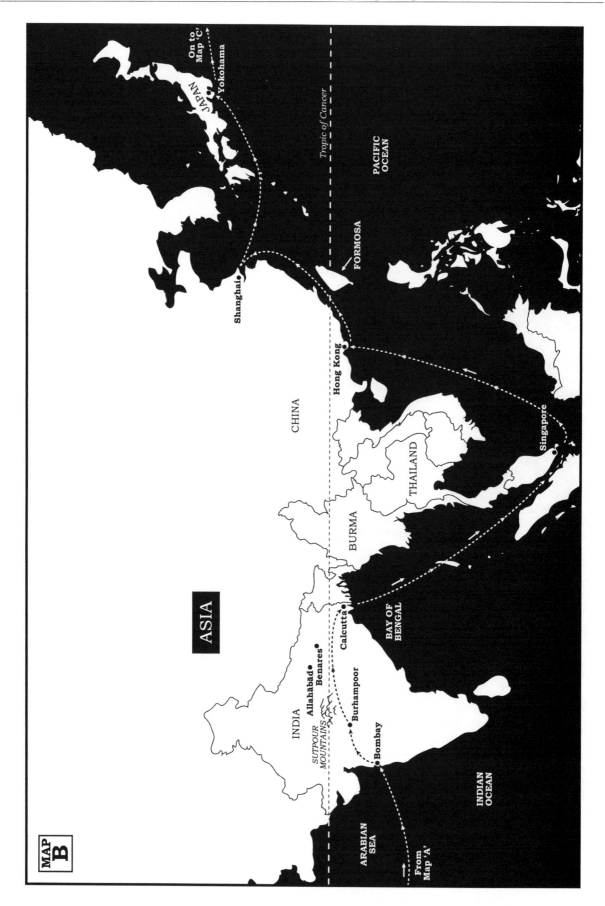

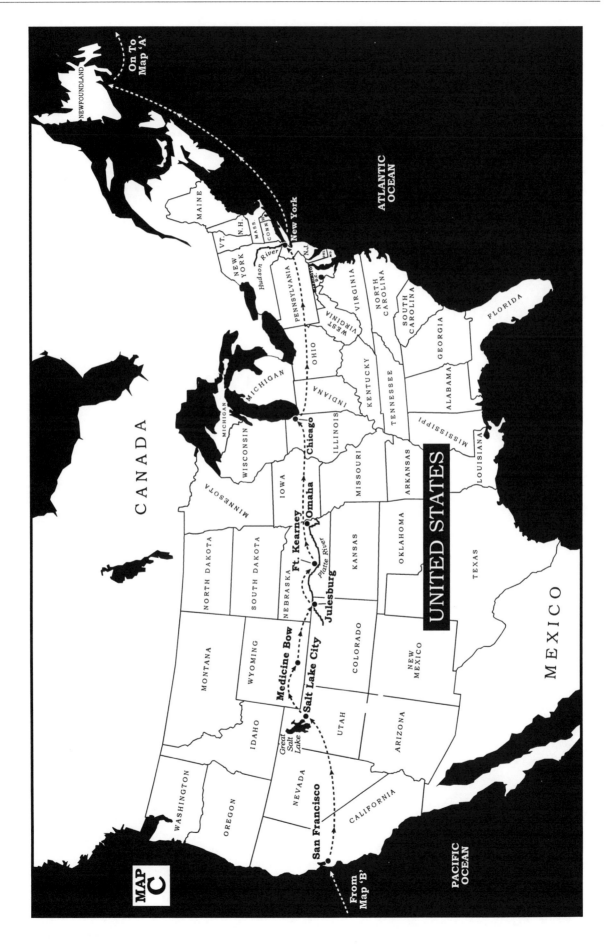

The Autobiography of Miss Jane Pittman

BY ERNEST J. GAINES

Historical fiction, 1971

Geographical Summary: *The Autobiography of Miss Jane Pittman* is a novel realistically composed as though it were derived from an editor's tape-recorded interviews with a former slave in Bayonne, Louisiana. It leads from Civil War times through Reconstruction and the Spanish-American War to Martin Luther King Jr.'s role in the civil rights movement of the 1960s. Miss Jane Pittman, the elderly protagonist, was born on Bryant Plantation, raised a friend's orphaned son during Reconstruction, and lived on a ranch on the Texas-Louisiana border with her husband Joe. She becomes a symbol of endurance and defiance against segregation, violence, and bigotry. The story is told through flashbacks; the author indicates that the meandering narratives initiated by Miss Jane find their way through the help of other narrators and end eight months prior to her death. As a whole, the novel delineates the African-American struggle to be free.

In an economic climate that blends the atmosphere of the plantation with the southwest livestock ranch, Gaines's settings reveal the reality of the slave era, its conclusion, and the civil rights movements that eventually brought black Americans legal equality. From unidentified agricultural roots in Louisiana, the main characters move to the Gulf Coastal plains, a region marked by heavy pine forestation and the vigorous ranching industry that formed the major portion of the Texas economy in the late nineteenth century. For Jane, the move east from Joe's horse-breaking job on the Sabine River to a residence in Creole country provides her a plentiful catch of fish and fertile soil for a garden. These factors stress a major theme: Miss Jane's desire for autonomy.

Historically, the 1930s demonstrate for Jane the rapid growth and change possible under Huey Pierce Long, the progressive, controversial U.S. senator who was assassinated in 1935. In the novel, the violent deaths of her son Ned, Albert Cluveau, Tee Bob, and Jimmy demonstrate the cost of change, which only slowly brings the acceptance of black citizenship to whites. By the end of this fictional autobiography, Jane has participated in a saga encompassing the worst of slavery, the Civil War, Reconstruction, and the dawn of the Civil Rights era. The 1974 film version, starring Cicely Tyson, Odetta, and Joseph Tremice, earned an appreciative television audience and an Emmy Award for Tyson's portrayal, which took her character from age 19 to 110.

Further Reading

Asante, Molefi K., and Mark T. Mattson. *The Historical and Cultural Atlas of African Americans.* New York: Macmillan, 1992.

Calvert, Robert, and Arnoldo DeLeon. *The History of Texas.* Arlington Heights, IL: Harlan Davidson, 1990.

Ploski, Harry A., and James Williams, eds. *The Negro Almanac: A Reference Work on the African American.* Detroit: Gale, 1989.

Post, Lauren C. *Cajun Sketches: From the Prairies of Southwest Louisiana.* Baton Rouge: Louisiana State University Press, 1990.

Ripley, C. Peter. *Slaves and Freedmen in Civil War Louisiana.* Baton Rouge: Louisiana State University Press, 1976.

Ross, David R., and others. *The Emergence of Modern America.* Arlington Heights, IL: Harlan Davidson, 1992.

Smith, Jessie Carney, ed. *Notable Black American Women.* Detroit: Gale, 1991.

Stephens, A. Ray, and William M. Holmes. *Historical Atlas of Texas.* Norman, OK: University of Oklahoma Press, 1990.

The Video Source Book. Syosset, NY: National Video Clearinghouse, 1987.

Detailed Itinerary

1. Bayonne, Louisiana

Through weekend visits to the home of Miss Jane Brown Pittman, an unnamed collector pieces together taped segments of her autobiography. At her death, he concludes that Jane has survived political and social changes spanning more than 110 years.

2. Bryant Plantation in Louisiana

On the Bryant Plantation in an undisclosed part of Louisiana, Ticey, an outspoken orphaned slave who was born around 1853, tends the mistress's children. Shortly before President Abraham Lincoln issues the Emancipation Proclamation, a passing Union Army soldier, Corporal Brown from Ohio, stops at the house for water and replaces her slave name with his daughter's name, Jane Brown. Despite the mistress's whip, Jane refuses to give up the new name.

In late spring 1865, the year that freedom comes, Jane joins Big Laura, her baby daughter, her son Ned, and other slaves to follow the North Star on a journey out of the South toward Corporal Brown in Ohio. After patrollers brutally kill Laura and the others, Jane, herself just a child, is left with Laura's fire-making stones and Ned, whom she leads with her and treats like a son.

3. Mr. Bone's Plantation in Louisiana

After an old man demonstrates on a map the impossibility of walking to Ohio, Jane gives up the quest and signs on to work for $6 a month for a white farmer named Mr. Bone. During 10 years of Reconstruction, Jane works in the fields while Ned, a natural scholar, attends school. Then secessionists take control of Bone's land. Jane remains to work for the new owner, Colonel Dye. After night riders threaten her because of Ned's pro-education activism, Ned leaves for Kansas.

4. Leavenworth and Atchison, Kansas

A year later, Ned's first letter arrives, explaining that he has moved from Leavenworth to Atchison in northeastern Kansas, is working for a white family, and is continuing his studies.

5. Cuba

Six years later, after Jane takes up with Joe Pittman, she learns that Ned has joined the army and gone to fight in the Spanish-American War in Cuba.

6. Sabine River, which forms the Louisiana-Texas border

Joe, a strong, active laborer, takes a job as chief horse breaker, pays his debt to Colonel Dye, and takes his family on a 10-day journey west to a ranch on the Sabine River. For 10 years, Jane works in Miss Clare's house. Near the eighth year of her stay, despite Jane's visit to a voodoo expert to save Joe from a death she foresees, he is killed by a renegade stallion.

7. St. Charles River in Louisiana

Jane moves to the St. Charles River area to live with a fisherman, Felton Burkes, who, after three years, abandons her. In 1899, at the end of the Spanish-American War, 40-year-old Ned, now known as Professor Douglass, and his wife and three children come to visit Jane. While Jane earns a living as a washwoman, Ned buys a house nearby and teaches local blacks to follow the philosophies of Negro leader Frederick Douglass and scientist and educator Booker T. Washington.

During a riverside lecture, Ned spies the LeCox brothers watching from the river. Ned realizes that Jane's premonitions are correct—he is doomed. Jane's fishing buddy, Albert Cluveau, a racist Creole, is plotting Ned's death, as he promised her. The attack happens as Ned returns with his wagon from buying lumber. Cluveau carries out his threats and shoots Ned three times.

Vivian returns to Kansas. Jane retaliates against Cluveau by convincing him that he will die when the Chariot of Hell comes for him. Ten years later, Cluveau dies raving. Ned's followers continue working on his school, which survives a flood in 1927.

8. Samson Plantation in Louisiana

In the spring of 1913, relocated seven or eight miles away on the Samson Plantation to be near Ned's grave, Jane works first in the field, then in the kitchen. She joins the church and becomes a Christian. Tragedy strikes the Samson family when Timmy, the master's half-breed son, departs and Tee Bob, his other son, locks himself in the library and kills himself with a letter opener over a fair-skinned black teacher.

During the 1930s, when Governor Huey Long runs Louisiana, Jane takes care of Miss Amma Dean. While attending the birth of Jimmy to Shirley Aaron in the quarters around 1935, Jane suspects that the boy is a potential leader in the civil rights movement. He is baptized and later begins preaching. But because he is a disciple of Reverend Martin Luther King, Jr., Jimmy is murdered before achieving his potential.

9. Bayonne, Louisiana

On the morning of Jimmy's death, Jane, who models her actions on those of Rosa Parks, joins other demonstrators at the courthouse in Bayonne to protest a segregated drinking fountain. Shaky and nearly blind, Jane makes her way to the bus and pays the children's fare with a borrowed $10 bill. Eight months later, she dies of old age.

Black Boy

BY RICHARD WRIGHT

Geographical Summary: Having suffered from poverty, religious fanaticism, racism, violence, and parental neglect, Richard Wright details in his autobiography, *Black Boy*, the struggle of his childhood from age four to his late teens. Shuttled between relatives in Mississippi and Arkansas and placed temporarily in an orphanage, he acquires the skills to earn his living near Beale Street in Memphis, Tennessee. Ultimately, dismay with racial violence and lack of opportunity drive him to Chicago, Illinois, where he intends to seek his fortune as a writer.

Opening in rural Mississippi in 1912, when Richard Wright was four years old, the autobiography carries him through numerous settings but centers on Jackson, Mississippi, and Memphis, Tennessee, before the conclusion 13 years later, when he leaves by train for Chicago, a city reputed to abound in opportunities for blacks. In the South, the social and economic climate of this era offered little in the way of education, health care, social acceptance, or jobs for blacks. To survive in a world dominated by capricious and, at times, menacing whites, youngsters like Richard learned to play the game of accommodation, smiling and shuffling to ease racial tensions and deflect possibly lethal blows. The one bright spot in Richard's odyssey through a parade of racist southern towns is Memphis, Tennessee, where he studies the optical trade and accesses the public library, his inspiration for a career in writing.

Historically, the creation of cultural havens such as Beale Street, Memphis' Mississippi riverfront commercial center, offered an outlet to disenfranchised ethnic groups, including Italians, Greeks, Asians, Jews, and blacks. In 1909, W. C. Handy immortalized the area as the home of the Beale Street blues, yet the popular surge of folk energy bound up in musical expression was not enough to empower such families as the Wrights, who subsisted on meager wages and substandard housing, education, and medical care. Richard's decision to leave Memphis profited him and his family by ending his struggle against forces too insidious, too entrenched for him to overcome.

Further Reading

Asante, Molefi K., and Mark T. Mattson. *The Historical and Cultural Atlas of African Americans.* New York: Macmillan, 1992.

Ehrlich, Eugene, and Gorton Carruth. *The Oxford Illustrated Literary Guide to the United States.* New York: Oxford University Press, 1982.

Fabre, Michel. *Richard Wright: Books and Writers.* Jackson, MS: University Press of Mississippi, 1990.

Gayle, Addison. *Richard Wright: Ordeal of a Native Son.* Magnolia, MA: Peter Smith, 1983.

Ploski, Harry A., and James Williams, eds. *The Negro Almanac: A Reference Work on the African American.* Detroit: Gale, 1989.

Wilson, Charles Reagan, and William Ferris, eds. *Encyclopedia of Southern Culture.* Chapel Hill, NC: University of North Carolina Press, 1989.

Detailed Itinerary

1. Roxie, Mississippi, 20 miles east of Natchez, Mississippi

At age four, Richard Wright, drawn to hot coals on the hearth, ignores his younger brother (Leon Alan, who remains unnamed in the text) and sets fire to broom straws and the hems of curtains in his family's cabin. Fearful that he will be blamed if his ailing Granny Wilson burns to death, he cowers under the cabin floor near the brick chimney and watches the feet of Ella Wright, his mother, as she dashes about in search of him, wailing. Then his father yanks him out of his hiding place, and his mother punishes him so stringently that he loses consciousness. He lies packed in ice, his mind beset by delusions of destruction, as he struggles to live.

2. Up the Mississippi River to Memphis, Tennessee

Aboard the *Kate Adams*, Richard and his brother and parents travel upriver to Memphis, in southwestern Tennessee, where they move into two rooms of a one-story apartment. His father works as a night porter in a Beale Street drugstore and requires quiet during the day so that he can sleep. The city seems bleak and lifeless to a child brought up in the country. Richard, punished for the least infraction, feels neglected and unwanted.

After Richard's father deserts the family and takes up with another woman, Ella struggles to feed herself and the two boys. She cooks for a white family and sends Richard to buy groceries. Because big boys attack him and snatch the grocery money, Ella insists that he learn to defend himself with a stick. On the next attack, Richard rids himself of fear by striking out at his aggressors.

Alone most of the day, six-year-old Richard entertains himself by peeking into a privy, learning to count, scribbling obscenities, and begging pennies at a saloon, where patrons entertain themselves by giving him liquor. He learns to like alcohol. Ella sues his father for child support, but the judge takes no action to force payment. Although Granny Wilson intervenes as the family sinks deeper into poverty, Ella grows desperate and places her sons at an orphanage directed by Miss Simon, who makes the children pull grass. Simon selects Richard for special treatment and allows him to seal envelopes in the office. He runs away; a white police officer brings him back to the orphanage.

Richard recalls vaguely why he depises his father, who once laughed at Ella's pleas for money. In front of the fireplace in his home, his father flaunted his kept woman, declared that he had no money to spend on the boys, and offered to keep Richard. The boy refused to stay with his father and turned aside from the offer of a nickel. Twenty-five years later, Richard sees his father as an aged, disabled Mississippi sharecropper and has little feeling for the parent whom he never loved.

3. Jackson, Mississippi

Ella claims Richard and his brother from the orphanage. During a brief visit to Granny Wilson at her two-story frame house in Jackson in south-central Mississippi, Richard discovers her to be a mean-tempered, light-skinned, ex-slave. The color of his grandmother's skin confuses him into thinking that she is white.

A local teacher who rents a room from Granny reads to Richard from *Bluebeard and His Seven Wives*. Granny denounces fiction, which she considers a devilish form of lying. Her religious fanaticism forbids pleasure; she beats Richard for innocent forms of boyish high spirits.

4. Elaine, Arkansas

Richard leaves Grandmother's house and moves west to Arkansas. In Elaine, at the fenced-in bungalow of Aunt Maggie and Uncle Hoskins, Richard is well fed and valued for the first time in his life. He admires Hoskins, who holds the prestigious job of local barkeep. However, because of his success, Hoskins is shot by white competitors. Maggie claims none of his assets.

5. Jackson, Mississippi

Fearful of violence, Maggie and Richard's family escape to Granny's house in Jackson.

6. West Helena, Arkansas

From Granny's crowded home, Ella and Maggie take the boys to West Helena, halfway down the eastern border of Arkansas. They share a duplex with prostitutes and cook for white families. Maggie lives with Professor Matthews, a secretive man who confesses to arson, theft, and murder.

7. Detroit, Michigan

Professor Matthews flees pursuers and takes Maggie north to Detroit, then deserts her.

8. West Helena, Arkansas

Struggling to support herself and the two boys, Ella finds work in a doctor's office for $5 a week. At the end of World War I, Richard enters first grade, learns to write his name, and treasures a single Christmas present—an orange.

Ella gets sick; the family moves to cheaper quarters near the center of West Helena, where Richard delivers clothes for a dry cleaner and sweeps floors. One morning, a stroke paralyzes Ella's side. Richard, unable to think of any other resource, writes a letter begging Granny for help.

9. Jackson, Mississippi

Ella, lying on a stretcher, is transported by train to Jackson. There, Maggie nurses her and helps Granny keep house. Richard, fearful for his mother, walks in his sleep.

10. Detroit, Michigan

Ella's seven siblings assume control and send Richard's brother to Detroit to live with Maggie.

11. Greenwood, Mississippi

Given a choice of homes, 12-year-old Richard opts for the four-room house of Uncle Clark, a contracting carpenter, and Aunt Jody in Greenwood in north-central Mississippi. But a neighbor tells Richard that his own son died in Richard's room. Richard, terrified of ghosts, begs to return to Jackson. Reluctantly, Clark returns him to Jackson.

12. Clarksdale, Mississippi

Ella is taken to Clarksdale for an operation, but her health does not improve.

13. Jackson, Mississippi

Feeble and dependent, Ella returns to Granny's house, where the meager vegetarian diet consists of peanut roast, greens, flour gravy, and mush. Richard swallows water from a hydrant to prevent his stomach from growling during school. Life with Granny is filled with false accusations and exaggerated discipline. None of Richard's relatives empathizes with his ambition to become a writer.

Aunt Addie, a parochial school teacher from Huntsville, Alabama, comes to teach in a one-room school. For a year, Richard is not allowed to play team sports and must attend strict Seventh Day Adventist classes and worship services. Addie, who insists that he call her Miss Wilson during class, threatens to beat him for refusing to inform on a boy who drops walnuts on the schoolroom floor. At home, the persecution continues. In protest, he reaches for a kitchen knife, but Ella stops him from committing greater violence.

Richard attends fifth grade at the Jim Hill school and is moved to sixth grade. He sells newspapers so he can obtain Zane Grey's *Riders of the Purple Sage*, but a customer who buys a paper divulges that it is actually Ku Klux Klan propaganda, so Richard stops selling the papers.

The summer before seventh grade, Richard computes policy collections for Brother Mance, an illiterate insurance agent. The money Richard earns helps build his esteem at home, where every dollar is a blessing.

Grandpa is a deranged veteran of the Civil War who complains that the Union Army denies him a pension because his name was recorded as Vinson instead of Wilson. After Grandpa dies, Richard stops going to church and scandalizes Granny by working on Saturday, a day she considers sacred. Ella gives him what encouragement she can. He does chores for a white woman who feeds him moldy food. Disgusted, he leaves her employ and takes a job with another white family, where he stuffs himself with eggs and milk while they are away. The behavior of white people alarms him, especially their family feuds and cursing.

When Richard reaches his teens, his mother shames him into joining the church. However, he gains no religious conviction from baptism or church membership. When his Uncle Tom threatens to whip him for being impudent, Richard brandishes a razor.

In the summer of 1924, Richard works as water carrier at a brickyard. At age 15, he enrolls for eighth grade and submits "The Voodoo of Hell's Half-Acre" to the *Southern Register*. The editor accepts the story and publishes it in three installments. He cannot pay Richard but offers to teach him to write, despite Granny's condemnation of stories. Richard plans to move north and become a writer.

Because he needs money for clothes, Richard applies at a sawmill, but the murder of a friend's brother by white men scares him away from the job. Home is still unpleasant, so he returns to work for Mrs. Bibbs and enrolls in the ninth grade. Sad and discontent, he grows increasingly melancholy after his brother returns from Chicago and treats him as scornfully as does the rest of the family.

In 1925, 17-year-old Richard finishes ninth grade at the top of his class. The black principal, who wants to impress the school's white officials, hands him a prepared speech. Family and friends agree that he should give up his plan to write his own valedictory. However, Richard chooses to make an original speech, thus spoiling his chance for a scholarship.

After graduation, Richard delivers parcels for a clothier. A carful of white men offer him a lift on the running board, then assault him with an empty liquor bottle. As a result, Richard becomes more distrustful of whites. He loses his job because the boss's son complains that he doesn't act as subservient as other blacks.

Mr. Griggs, who works at the jewelry store and is more successful at pleasing whites, tries to help Richard cope with "Jim Crow" expectations. He helps Richard get a job in an optical lab above the Capitol Street jewelry store with Mr. Crane, a native of Illinois. Then two competing white employees force Richard out of his position. Crane interviews Richard and learns of the harassment, but Richard fears retaliation and declares he must move north to escape the South's prejudice.

An introduction to corruption and crime alters Richard's behavior. As hallboy at a Jackson hotel, he delivers bootleg liquor to white prostitutes and learns about venereal disease and illicit sex. He takes another job at a movie house that caters to blacks, where he helps skim the proceeds by joining the ticket seller in reusing stubs. Next, he breaks into a college storehouse and steals canned fruit preserves, then steals a gun from a neighbor's house. Although he regrets leaving Ella behind, he uses the money gained from selling the stolen goods to acquire clothes, shoes, a cardboard suitcase, and his ticket out of Mississippi.

14. Memphis, Tennessee

In November 1925, promising to send for Ella, Richard takes the train for Memphis. On the way, he wipes tears from his face. He rents a room from Mrs. Moss, who tries to lure Richard into marriage with her slow-witted daughter Bess. He earns $12 per week plus two meals by washing dishes at a cafe.

Autonomous for the first time in his life, Richard enjoys eating canned beans and putting his feet up while he smokes in privacy. But Moss, still hopeful that he will marry Bess, makes him leave his room to eat with the family. Bess offers her love, but Richard is wary of entrapment.

One morning before Richard arrives at work, he meets a black boy who pretends to locate a cache of bootleg whisky under a bush on the riverbank. Richard helps him sell the liquor to a white man. The boy disappears with the $5 they receive. Too late, Richard realizes that he has been cheated.

Giving Crane's name as reference, Richard applies at an optical company. The manager offers him $8 week but refuses to train him because he is black, so Richard ends up washing and delivering eyeglasses. Learning of his thrift, Moss mourns that he has no interest in marrying Bess. Richard is more interested in getting an education and buys magazines from secondhand bookstores.

Mr. Olin, a fellow employee, lies to Richard about Harrison, a man who reportedly wants to stab Richard. Richard investigates the charge and learns that Olin and the employees where Harrison works are trumping up an exhibition match. Richard refuses a knife fight but agrees to box Harrison for $5 each. He and Harrison make a half-hearted attempt at a fight, then leave with the money, which shames them.

Richard borrows the library card of Mr. Falk, an Irish Catholic worker, then forges notes and checks out H. L. Mencken's *A Book of Prefaces*, Sinclair Lewis's *Main Street*, and Theodore Dreiser's *Sister Carrie* and *Jennie Gerhardt*. He is well fed, warm, and hopeful of relocation to the north.

That winter, his mother and brother join him in Memphis. Maggie also comes to live with Richard's family.They decide that she and Richard should try their luck in Chicago so that they can send money for train fare to Ella and her other son.

15. Chicago, Illinois

In 1925, Richard boards a train bound north for Chicago. Filled with anticipation, he longs for a better life.

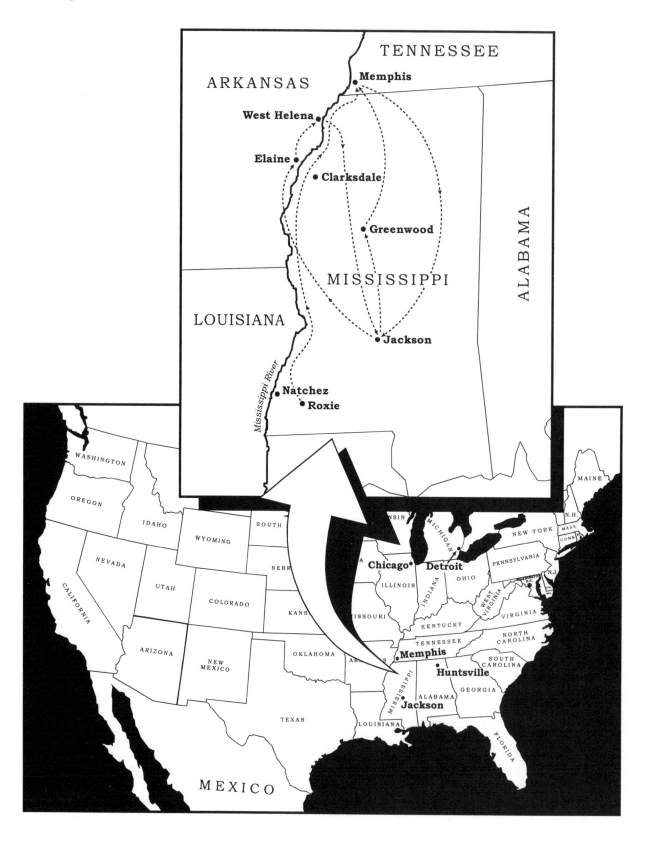

Born Free

BY JOY ADAMSON

Autobiography/animal lore, 1974

Geographical Summary: In retelling the life of Elsa the lioness, Joy Adamson narrates the period covering February 1, 1956, to December 20, 1959, in which she raises a cub as a pet in Kenya's Northern Frontier Province on the east coast of Africa. For nearly four years Elsa rules the family compound and follows Joy and her husband George on family vacations to the Somali border, on a seven-week safari around Kenya's mountains, and to the wilds of the Great Rift Valley. The Adamsons, who wish to return Elsa to the wild, hope she will acclimate herself to lion country and find a mate. The separation trauma the family faces in releasing Elsa is eased by her finding a mate and giving birth to cubs.

Over the varied terrain of Kenya—from the Indian Ocean on the eastern border, north to the Ethiopian border, and across the plateaus and uplands in the country's heartland to the Aberdare Range on the western border—Adamson carries her story to a variety of settings, climates, peoples, and landscapes. Encompassing savanna grasslands, craggy highlands, barren lakeshores, thick veldt vegetation, and the big cats and small fauna that populate the wild, the biography of Elsa introduces the reader to one of Africa's most-visited, most-filmed lands. The lions that form the focus of the story carry out the normal lifestyle of predatory cats, including mating, initiating their young, stalking and killing the quadrupeds that make up most of their diet, grooming shaggy ruffs and claws, and maintaining the prides or social units that protect them and their young from poachers and other predators. By depicting Elsa's response to a variety of scenes and stimuli, Adamson demonstrates the lioness's curiosity, flexibility, and loyalty to her family. In the successful 1966 film version, Columbia Pictures captures much of the animal lore, Kenyan landscape, and emotional effect of the book, which was followed by a television series, *Living Free*, as well as several documentaries. John Barry's popular title song for the movie earned him an Academy Award.

Further Reading

Adamson, George. *My Pride and Joy.* Guilford, CT: Ulverscroft, 1988.

Adamson, Joy. *The Searching Spirit.* Guilford, CT: Ulverscroft, 1982.

Amin, Mohamed, and others. *Kenya: The Magic Land.* North Pomfret, VT: Trafalgar Square, 1989.

Gess, Denise. *Kenya.* New York: Chelsea House, 1987.

Pease, Alfred E. *The Book of the Lion.* New York: St. Martin's Press, 1986.

Smuts, G. L. *Lion.* Portland, OR: International Specialized Book Services, 1983.

Walker, John, ed. *Halliwell's Film Guide.* New York: HarperCollins, 1991.

Born Free

Detailed Itinerary

1. Northern Frontier Province of Kenya, from Mount Kenya to the Abyssinian (Ethiopian) border

George Adamson, senior game protector for the East African Game Department, prevents the poaching and destruction of wild animals in the Northern Frontier Province of Kenya. On February 1, 1956, he finds three lost female lion cubs. The mother of the litter charges George. Realizing too late that she is protecting her young, he is forced to shoot her, thus orphaning the cubs.

2. Isiolo, Kenya

Returning to his residence near Isiolo in central Kenya, George remands the motherless cubs to his wife Joy, who feeds them every three hours. Her pet rock hyrax, Pati, helps entertain, train, and discipline the cubs, who learn to play tug-of-war, stalk, and climb. Elsa, the smallest, and her sisters Lustica and "Big One" become household pets.

3. Rotterdam-Blydorp Zoo, Holland

Because the three lionesses become too much for one family, the Adamsons send the larger two to the Rotterdam-Blydorp Zoo and keep Elsa. The big cat adopts Nuru, the Adamson's servant, as her keeper and becomes the center of attention.

4. Uaso Nyiro River in Kenya

The family introduces Elsa to camping during a safari along the Uaso Nyiro River in central Kenya.

5. Fishing village on the Kenya-Somali border along the Indian Ocean

In 1957, during the Adamsons' local leave, they take a three-day trip to a Barjun fishing village in eastern Kenya on the border of Somali and the Indian Ocean. Along the way, Pati dies. Elsa briefly meets a male lion and enjoys dips in the Indian Ocean, climbing mountains, and tasting new foods, including birds and fish that George provides. George suffers a bout of malaria shortly before the return to Isiolo.

6. Isiolo, Kenya

Back at her home, Elsa shows symptoms of hookworm, which she contracted on the coast. She languishes on a camp bed and enjoys being carted home like an invalid and photographed in her favorite haunts beside streams and rivers, on cliffs, and among wild herds. Treatment restores her to health.

7. Merti, north of the Uaso Nyiro River in Kenya

George takes Elsa in the Land Rover during a journey to kill a man-eating lion near Merti, north of the Uaso Nyiro River in central Kenya. The difficulty of the job keeps the Adamson family in the bush for 25 days. Elsa enjoys the trip.

8. Isiolo, Kenya

Back home, Elsa, at 18 months, shows signs of maturity and becomes more difficult to discipline.

9. Mount Marsabit, the Huri Hills, the Chalbi Desert, the North Horr oasis, Loyongalane, Lake Rudolf, Kenya

The Adamsons go on a seven-week safari 300 miles to the northwest over the Kaisut Desert to Mount Marsabit. They relocate farther north in the Huri Hills and move west to the Chalbi Desert and the North Horr oasis, then farther west along Lake Rudolf's south shore to the town of Loyongalane. During a 10-day trek, Elsa frolics in the water among the crocodiles and chases flamingos.

10. Mount Kulal, Kenya

After three days at Loyongalane to resupply the convoy, the group begins the second leg of the safari—climbing Mount Kulal, which lies to the southwest. Elsa, unaccustomed to high altitudes and still behaving like a house pet, shivers with cold and huddles in Joy's tent under a blanket.

11. Loyongalane, Kenya

The return trip down the lava to Loyongalane tires Elsa. Over the 300-mile walk, she refuses food and stays close to Joy.

12. Isiolo, Kenya

Back home early in 1958, Elsa, nearing her second birthday, grows restless and seems drawn to the wild. Every 10 weeks she goes into season and purrs to show her readiness for mating.

13. Great Rift Valley, Kenya

In May, 1958, as Elsa reaches 27 months, the Adamsons approach the time of their overseas leave and take Elsa on a 17-hour ride into the wild in the Great Rift Valley to introduce her to a pride of lions. They leave her over lengthening periods. Each time they return, she rushes to greet them, hungry and angry that her human family has abandoned her. The Adamsons stop feeding her so that she will learn to capture her own food.

14. Isiolo, Kenya

Returned to the Adamsons' home, Elsa becomes thin, shedding her golden coat. After her introduction to the wild, she seems more dependent than ever on her human family.

15. The wilds of Kenya

Successive attempts to teach Elsa proper lion behavior cause her to suspect the family's motives. In an ambivalent state, she returns briefly to camp, but acknowledges that the African bush is where she belongs. A five-week bout with hookworm and tapeworm is complicated by a tick-borne virus. The Adamsons continue to visit her at three-week intervals, each time leaving a gift of fresh-shot game for her to eat. She greets them with licks and rubs their legs with her head, purring, sucking Joy's thumb, acquainting herself with the new Land Rover, and sleeping on their camp beds. Yet, she becomes more restless and independent with each separation.

On a second release at a river 440 miles from Isiolo and 35 miles from her birthplace, Elsa breaks with the Adamsons and moves permanently to the wild, selecting a mate and bearing a litter of cubs. Before returning to England, Joy Adamson writes about raising Elsa as a pet. Joy notes the pain caused by a spiritual separation from Elsa on February 25, 1959, yet she rejoices that Elsa still loves them.

The Bridge of San Luis Rey

BY THORNTON WILDER

Didactic novel, 1927

Geographical Summary: In *The Bridge of San Luis Rey*, the movement of Thornton Wilder's eighteenth-century characters extends only 300 miles across the Andes Mountains, from Lima, the capital of Peru, to Cuzco and side journeys between Spain and America. In contrast to the physical locale, alterations in the interior landscape, which carry the characters great distances of the heart, bring peace to the survivors of five victims—Pepita, Esteban, Jaime, Uncle Pio, and Doña Maria—who die in the collapse of the willow bridge into the valley below.

At the time this novel takes place, the road west from Lima to Cuzco rose quickly from the coastal lowlands to cloudy elevations greater than 22,000 feet, crossing treacherous passes and drop-offs via flexible, hand-woven willow bridges, which saved travelers weeks of toil over twisting overland trails. Even more dangerous by eighteenth-century standards of transportation were the journeys of Doña Maria and her daughter Clara to Spain, which, in the era before the Panama Canal, could be completed only by lengthy sea journeys aboard vessels bound south along South America's west coast—through fiercely cold and churning waters around the deadly tip at Cape Horn, where Pacific waves pound against the rocks known as the Evangels, then north and east across the Atlantic Ocean to Spain. Wilder in no way exaggerates the perils of these travels or the consequences of freak mishaps. A black-and-white 1944 United Artists film version, starring Lynn Bari, Francis Lederer, Louis Calhern, Donald Woods, and Akim Tamiroff, won an Academy Award nomination for Dimitri Tiomkin's musical score.

Further Reading

Dobyns, Henry F., and Paul L. Doughty. *Peru: A Cultural History*. New York: Oxford University Press, 1976.

Goldstein, Malcolm. *The Art of Thornton Wilder*. Ann Arbor, MI: UMI Books on Demand, 1992.

Markham, Clements R. *Cuzco: A Journey to the Ancient Capital of Peru* and *Lima: A Visit to the Capital and Provinces of Modern Peru*. Millwood, NY: Kraus Reprints, 1992.

Wakefield, Celia. *High Cities of the Andes*. San Carlos, CA: Wide World Publishing/Tetra, 1988.

Detailed Itinerary

1. The highway from Lima to Cuzco, Peru

At noon on Friday, July 20, 1714, the collapse of a willow bridge hurls five wayfarers to the valley below.The bridge was the finest in Peru; it was woven by Incas around 1600 to connect a gap in the high road between Lima and Cuzco. Brother

Juniper, a Franciscan friar from Italy assigned to convert the Indians to Christianity, spends six years investigating the "Act of God." After filling scores of notebooks with data, Juniper publishes his book and is burned along with it in the Square for the crime of heresy—he questioned God's role in the catastrophe. Shortly before he dies, he calls twice to St. Francis and dies smiling. A secret copy of his skeptical chronicle is shelved in the library of the University of San Marco in Cuzco.

The unidentified narrator claims to know the true background of the accident victims. The first, Doña Maria, the Marquesa de Montemayor, lives in misery and alienation, and at her death leaves many letters, which become monuments of Spanish literature. At age 26, despite education, prestige, and wealth, she married a disdainful Liman nobleman who rejects her love. She compensated for his coldness by doting on their daughter, Clara. The girl, who immigrates to Spain after her marriage, proves as unloving as Doña Maria's husband.

2. Spain

Doña Maria attempts a friendly visit to Spain, where she and Clara, now the haughty Contessa d'Abuirre, quarrel. Doña Maria slips away aboard a ship to America.

3. Lima, Peru

On her return to Lima on the west coast of Peru near the Andes Mountains, Doña Maria composes charming, gossipy, monthly packets of letters to Clara, who shows no interest in her mother. Doña Maria longs to hear Clara ask forgiveness for neglecting her but waits in vain and grows old. Clara's husband, an important man in Spain, preserves the letters, which critics treasure for their wit, style, and grace.

4. The Convent of Santa Maria Rosa de las Rosas in Lima

Two years later, at the orphanage of the Convent of Santa Maria Rosa de las Rosas, Doña Maria, rich but unhappy and alcoholic, seeks a companion from the Abbess Madre Maria del Pilar, who is in charge of placing orphans with foster parents. The Abbess selects a little girl, Pepita.

5. Lima, Peru

Pepita dutifully follows Doña Maria on a daily jaunt through the streets and to the Comedia to see the actress Perichole play Doña Leonor. Because Pepita serves the Abbess, she endures the cruel jests of onlookers who ridicule Doña Maria.

6. The bridge of San Luis Rey

Borne in a sedan chair, Doña Maria makes a pilgrimage to the shrine of Santa Maria de Cluxambuqua at San Luis Rey to plead for an easy birth for her first grandchild, due that October. On her way, she crosses the bridge of San Luis Rey. Pepita, who never lets Doña Maria travel alone, grows weary of her task and composes a letter to the Abbess to request an end to her job as companion. After Doña Maria reads Pepita's words, she changes her self-pitying attitude and writes a strongly worded letter to Clara, causing Pepita to stop complaining about her overbearing mistress. Pepita and Doña Maria are returning to Lima when they recross the bridge on July 20, and it collapses.

7. The Convent of Santa Maria Rosa de las Rosas in Lima

Manuel and Esteban, identical twins who have been inseparable since infancy and are able to communicate via a secret language, grow up in the convent as favorites of the Abbess. The boys work as hired copyists until they grow weary of the work and become laborers. Alongside Indians, they load ships, drive teams, pick fruit, and pilot a ferry.

8. Lima, Peru

While carrying messages to the theater and copying for Camila, a dissolute actress nicknamed the Perichole, Manuel becomes enamored of her and distances himself from his brother. After Manuel's death three days after injuring his knee on metal, Esteban grows deranged from separation from his brother. Even the Abbess is unable to shake him from his depression. To ease his guilt and loneliness, Esteban changes his identity by adopting Manuel's name.

9. Cuzco, Peru

Esteban, still grieving, finds work copying for the university in Cuzco. A stranger, Captain Alvarado, offers passage on a voyage as a way to end the boy's grief. Esteban prepares to hang himself on an overhead timber, but Alvarado rescues him and convinces him that life is worth the effort, despite the hurt that comes from losing a loved one.

10. The bridge of San Luis Rey

Alvarado and Esteban set out for Lima and the Pacific coast. On the way west over the Andes Mountains from Cuzco to Lima, the captain, who oversees the transport of goods, descends to the stream. Esteban, following the high road, is on the bridge at the time of its fall.

11. Lima, Peru

Uncle Pio, a Castilian who grew up on the streets of Madrid, worships Camila Perichole, a cafe singer whose real name is Micaela Villegas. He takes her into his home and trains her to improve her acting style. With his help, she reaches the top. A pampered star, she becomes self-centered and rejects Uncle Pio. She basks in the adoration of rich admirers, including matadors, merchants, and actors. One of her suitors, Don Andrés de Ribera, the Viceroy of Peru, becomes her lover.

12. The hills near Santa Maria de Cluxambuqua

Perichole retires to her country estate and gives birth to three children, taking the most pleasure in the sickly Don Jaime. After smallpox and middle age ruin her looks, she becomes a recluse. Uncle Pio recedes farther from her interests. One day, he discovers her applying makeup to her pockmarked face. Enraged and embarrassed, she forces him to leave. By disguising his voice and adopting the alias of Estrella, he gains access to Perichole and forces her to reimburse him for years of acting lessons. Because she lacks the money to satisfy him, she lets Don Jaime become Uncle Pio's student.

13. The bridge of San Luis Rey

Uncle Pio and Don Jaime are crossing the bridge at the time of its collapse.

14. Lima, Peru

After the funeral at the Cathedral, the Abbess of the convent remembers Pepita and Esteban. She regrets that the children will be forgotten.

15. The Convent of Santa Maria Rosa de las Rosas in Lima

A year later, Perichole, who longs for the serenity found in serving God, enters the convent as assistant to the Abbess. Clara arrives from Spain and confesses that she had neglected and abused her mother. On the Abbess's advice, Clara discloses an answer to her own pining: "Love will have been enough; all those impulses of love return to the love that made them. Even memory is not necessary for love. There is a land of the living and a land of the dead and the bridge is love, the only survival, the only meaning."

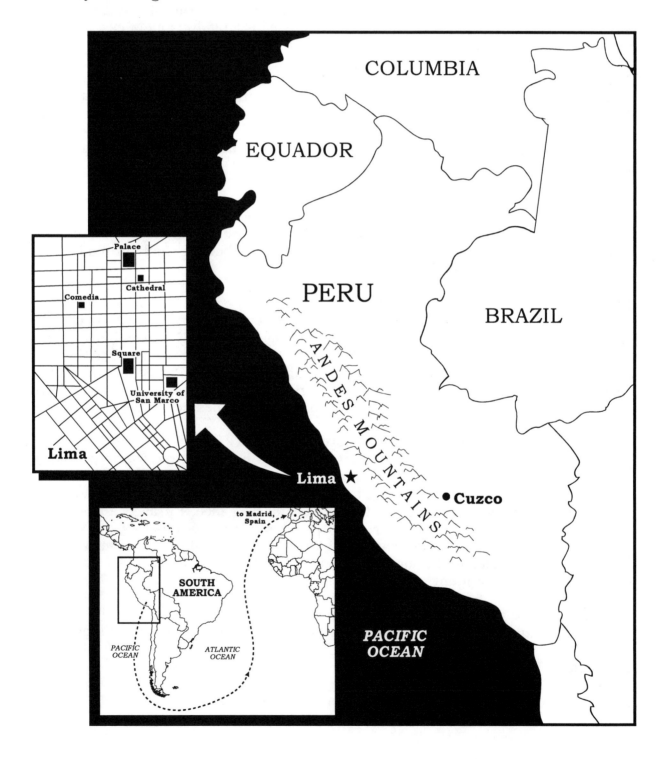

The Call of the Wild

BY JACK LONDON

Adventure novel, 1903

Geographical Summary: From a pampered life with Judge Miller in the Santa Clara Valley in California, the great-hearted dog Buck is kidnapped and transported by wagon, truck, and steamer up the U.S. coast to San Francisco and Seattle through Queen Charlotte Sound to Dyea on the southern Yukon coast in the far west of Canadian territory. Forced to cope with snow and ice, cold, deadly pack fights, and demanding masters who force him across the frozen terrain, Buck learns to survive and eventually leads the team.

In time, Buck develops a sense of belonging to the wild, which he perceives through dreams of the primitive past. A loving master rescues him from starvation and brutal beatings and reconditions him through patient care. Gradually, the lore of Buck's loyalty and strength spreads as far as Alaska. After Yeehat Indians kill his one human friend, Buck recedes into Yukon legend as a ghost dog that runs with wolves in answer to the call of the wild.

Jack London's knowledge of the Yukon plateau, derived from personal experience in the Klondike gained during the 1897 Gold Rush, supplied him with memories of trails, camps, way stations, hunting lodges, Indian territory, and the rugged coastline that formed the gateway to adventure and riches. Although places such as Sheep Camp and Five Fingers are no longer featured on Canadian maps, their historical significance figures prominently in the daily work of mail carriers, law officers, and supply trains that ferry parcels, food, clothing, gear, and weapons to isolated miners, hunters, and explorers. The greatest barriers to humans are the uncharted terrors of the subarctic forest—soft ice, howling winds, blinding blizzards, snow-banked streams and springs, predatory animals, and savage temperatures that can drop to -30 degrees during long winter months.

Further Reading

Brandenburg, Jim. *White Wolf: Living with an Arctic Legend.* Irvine, CA: Northwood, 1988.

Cellura, Dominique. *Travelers of the Cold: Sled Dogs of the Far North.* Bothell, WA: Alaska Northwest, 1990.

Gordon-Cooper, Harry. *Yukoners: True Tales of the Yukon.* Blaine, WA: Hancock House, 1990.

Lundquist, James. *Jack London: Adventures, Ideas and Fiction.* New York: Ungar Publishing, 1987.

Ogilvie, William. *Early Days on the Yukon and the Story of Its Gold Finds.* Salem, NH: Ayer, 1972.

Savage, Candace. *Wolves.* San Francisco, CA: Sierra Club Books, 1989.

Tjekema, Edith R. *Yukon Paradise.* Boon, MI: Northland Press, 1990.

Waldman, Carl. *Atlas of the North American Indian.* New York: Facts on File, 1985.

Detailed Itinerary

1. Santa Clara Valley south of San Francisco, California

In the fall of 1897, Buck, the pampered 140-pound offspring of a St. Bernard and a Scotch shepherd, lives on Judge Miller's estate in the Santa Clara Valley. He enjoys hunting, playing with children, and living well. One night, while the Judge is attending a Raisin Growers' Association meeting, the dog is kidnapped and sold by the gardener to cover gambling debts.

2. San Francisco, California

Taken from College Park, a little flag station, Buck rides in a baggage car as far north as San Francisco. His handlers, wary of his menace, choke him to the point of strangulation and transport him to a little shed behind a saloon on the waterfront, where his captor nets $50.

3. Seattle, Washington

Crated and moved by express clerks to a wagon, a truck, and a ferry steamer, Buck is deposited in an express car and shipped north up the West Coast to Seattle, Washington. A man in a red sweater clubs him into submission until a French-Canadian mail carrier named Perrault buys him and loads him and Curly, a Newfoundland, aboard the *Narwhal*.

4. North to Queen Charlotte Sound, Canada

The *Narwhal* crosses the Queen Charlotte Sound into Canadian waters. When fights break out after a large white dog steals Buck's food, François, Perrault's partner, lashes the animals. After many days of travel, Buck is brought on deck and experiences his first snowfall. His handlers laugh at his curious response.

5. Dyea beach near Skagway, Alaska

Buck arrives on Dyea beach near Skagway, a town in the far south of the Yukon, east of Alaska. The hierarchy of dogs is established with the death of Curly, torn to bits by her assailants. Buck learns the feel of harness and the bite of Dave, the wheeler. François is impressed with Buck's stamina and intelligence.

6. Sheep Camp, Scales, Chilkoot Divide, and Lake Bennett in the Yukon Territory

With nine dogs pulling their sled, the couriers move relentlessly north up the cañon through Sheep Camp, past Scales, and over Chilkoot Divide into the Yukon Territory. They arrive at Lake Bennett that night. Buck collapses with exhaustion and, emulating the other sled animals, digs into the snow to rest. As his inborn will to survive emerges, he learns to exist on scant rations of salmon and to fight for his portion.

7. Lake Le Barge to Thirty Mile River in the Yukon Territory

At Lake Le Barge (now Laberge), north of Skagway, the team is attacked by starving wild dogs from an Indian village. The bony, ravenous beasts steal half the team's food and leave them torn and bleeding. François fears his nine dogs may go mad on the remaining 400-mile trail to Dawson, halfway up the border between the Yukon and Alaska. The team pushes up Thirty Mile River, a passage that requires six days' toil over treacherous ice.

8. Houtalingua to the Big Salmon River, Little Salmon River, Five Fingers, and the Pelly River in the Yukon Territory

Bearing northeast, the team follows a grueling trail from Thirty Mile River to Houtalingua. The sled finishes 35 miles of travel at the Big Salmon River. Two more days' travel brings them to Little Salmon River and Five Fingers, where François makes moccasins out of his own boots to protect Buck's feet. When the team reaches the Pelly River, the dog Dolly goes mad. François smashes her skull. The dog Spitz lunges at Buck in a failed attempt to establish supremacy.

9. Dawson, Yukon Territory

Ending the drive at Dawson, on the west coast of the Yukon Territory, the team rests for a week. Before they move on, Buck responds instinctively to the Aurora Borealis.

10. Down the Yukon Trail over the Tahkeena River to Skagway, Alaska

Traveling south by way of the Barracks over packed snow to the Yukon Trail, the team travels quickly toward Dyea and Salt Water. Near the mouth of the Tahkeena River, Buck makes his move to unseat Spitz. Their clash brings Buck near defeat, but he gains supremacy over Spitz by breaking his forelegs.

François crows over the kill and tries to replace Spitz with Sol-leks. Buck refuses to give place and becomes unrivaled pack leader. From Thirty Mile River to Lake Le Barge, White Horse Rapids, Marsh, Tagish, and Bennett, the team pushes on to Skagway in 50-below temperatures, averaging a record 40 miles per day.

11. Skagway, Alaska, to Pelly River in the Yukon Territory and back

For three days, François and Perrault boast of their team in the bars of Skagway. With a week's rest, they repeat the run to Sixty Miles and Pelly. A change of drivers causes François to weep over Buck, his favorite. He sells the team to a Scotch half-breed, who guides them north toward the Yukon-Alaska border.

12. The trail northwest to Dawson, Yukon Territory

Pulling a heavy load, the team moves back over the trail to Dawson. Along the way, Buck looks into the past to a time when shaggy, half-savage men hunched over fires. The half-breed forces Buck to cease his daydreams and concentrate on pulling.

13. From the Barracks south to Cassiar Bar in the Yukon Territory

Along the return trip, the sled is loaded with mail. The dog Dave suffers from the hard drive, yet forces himself to the last of his strength. His owners realize that Dave cannot continue and replace him with Sol-leks. Dave bites through the traces to keep Sol-leks from replacing him. When Dave is reduced to dragging himself over the snow, the men shoot him. Buck is aware of the meaning of gunshots—the sorry end of a sled dog's life.

14. Skagway, Alaska

Thirty days after setting out, the Salt Water Mail returns from the 1,200-mile run to Skagway. The dogs are sore of foot and muscle. With only three days' rest, they are sold to neophyte mushers Hal, Charles, and Mercedes (Hal's sister and Charles's wife). Buck has by now become accustomed to the rapid changes in ownership.

The new owners overload the sled with luggage. Against the advice of more experienced drivers, the trio aims for White River, which crosses the border to the northwest between the Yukon and Alaska. Mercedes weeps when the men toss aside her personal belongings, and she pleads with Hal to stop whipping the dogs. The team breaks the sled out of its frozen tracks and bounds away, to the delight of Skagway onlookers. Hal and Charles increase the team to 14 dogs without realizing that the sled cannot carry enough food for all.

15. The trail to White River in the Yukon Territory

The new owners mismanage the supplies; they are half out of dog food after completing a quarter of the trip. Mercedes adds to the difficulty by riding on the sled. At Five Fingers, the men buy frozen horsehide for food. The combination of beatings, fatigue, and poor nutrition takes its toll on Buck.

At a logging camp on White River near the Alaskan border, John Thornton warns Hal and Charles that they should lay over because the trail is breaking up in the spring thaw. Hal ignores the warning and tries to force Buck to mush on. Buck, too weary to rise, endures a rain of blows. Thornton intervenes and rescues Buck. Hal and Charles push on over the dangerously thin surface and vanish—dogs, sled, and load—beneath a hole in the ice.

John, recovering from frozen feet, tends Buck's wounds. John's dogs, Skeet and Nig, display no jealousy as Buck revels in loving attention and learns to accept human friendship once more. But competing with the comforts of camp life is the call of the wild, which lures Buck repeatedly back to nature.

16. Dawson, Yukon Territory

John and his two partners guide their raft to a sawmill at Dawson. John thoughtlessly tests Buck's devotion by urging him to jump into a chasm, then he has to restrain the dog from obeying.

17. Circle City, Alaska

The trio travels into Alaskan territory past the headwaters of the Tanana River to Circle City in east-central Alaska. A bar fight prompts Buck to spring to John's defense. The authorities exonerate Buck for protecting his master, and the savagery of Buck's attack spreads his reputation among Alaskan camps.

18. Forty Mile Creek in the Yukon Territory

John and his partners return to the Yukon to Forty Mile Creek, northwest of Dawson. A boating accident hurls John into a torrent. Buck springs into roiling waters and rescues his master from the rapids. Towed to shore by rope, Buck is battered by rocks and breaks some ribs. John camps on the creek bank so his dog can recuperate.

19. Dawson, Yukon Territory

On their return to Dawson that same winter, a patron at the Eldorado bar bets John $1,000 that Buck cannot break out a 1,000-pound load. The wager rises to three to one. Buck astounds the group by pulling once to each side, then moving the load 100 yards. The Skookum Bench king offers to buy Buck for $1,200. John, overcome with love and admiration for his faithful dog, refuses the offer and uses his winnings to pay his debts.

20. Stewart River in the Yukon Territory

Lured by tales of a lost mine, John heads east to the Stewart River, Mayo, and McQueston—the backbone of the Yukon, which he traverses until the following spring. As he and his partners hunt for a fabled cabin, Buck grows more attuned to the call of the wild, sometimes staying away from camp for two days before returning and greeting John with affection. Buck learns to stalk moose and savor his prey. One day, three miles from camp, he trails Yeehat Indians and finds the corpses of dogs and John. In a vengeful spring, Buck rips the throat from a Yeehat chief. So virulent is his attack that the Yeehats, fearing an evil spirit, flee into the woods. Buck answers the call of the wolves and fades into Yeehat legends as the Ghost Dog.

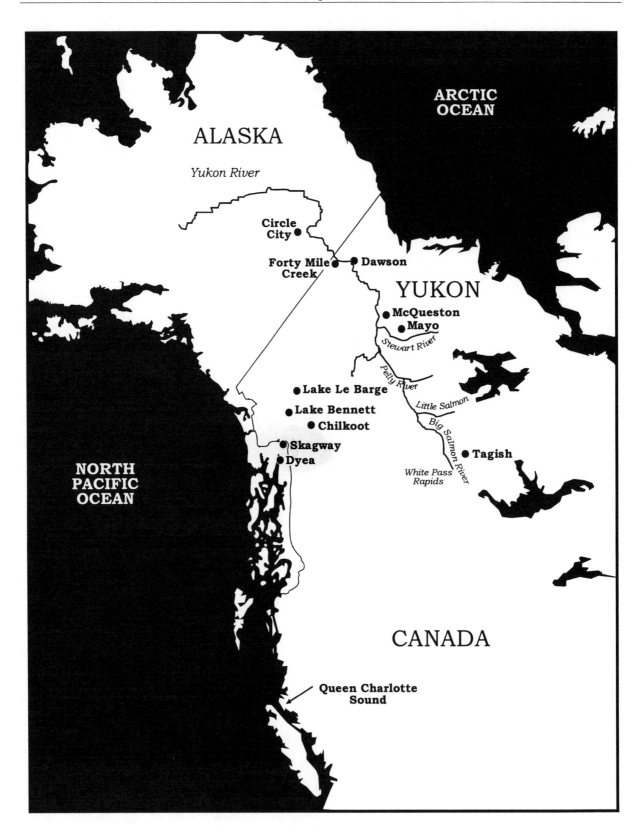

Catcher in the Rye

BY J. D. SALINGER

Young adult psychological novel, 1951

Geographical Summary: *Catcher in the Rye* begins in 1951 in a private mental institution outside Hollywood, California, following a disastrous Christmas holiday the previous year. Holden Caulfield remembers his miserable attempt to escape from failure and grief. His urban odyssey takes him from a private boys' school in the fictional town of Agerstown, Pennsylvania, to Manhattan, New York, and eventually to his parents' apartment, which he has been avoiding to keep from admitting that, for the fourth time, he has been expelled from high school. The narrative, set in such New York City landmarks as Radio City Music Hall, Central Park, the Museum of Natural History, the Museum of Art, Penn Station, and Grand Central Station, is also a personal journey into mental anguish, unresolved grief, and adolescent diffidence and despair.

J. D. Salinger once lived in the same Manhattan neighborhood in which the fictional Caulfields reside and is familiar not only with routes, museums, schools, shopping centers, and entertainment and transportation centers but also with the clothing, attitudes, and language patterns of native New Yorkers. Having attended private school at Valley Forge Military Academy in Wayne, Pennsylvania, he knew the pain of expulsion and the train ride that returned him, like Holden, in shame to his parents in New York. In adulthood, Salinger lived on Park Avenue and associated with artists, writers, and musicians in Greenwich Village; he therefore speaks knowledgeably of Holden's physical and emotional odyssey.

Further Reading

Appleberg, Marilyn J. *I Love New York Guide*. New York: Macmillan, 1989.

Bloom, Harold. *J. D. Salinger*. New York: Chelsea House, 1987.

Ehrlich, Eugene, and Gorton Carruth. *The Oxford Illustrated Literary Guide to the United States*. New York: Oxford University Press, 1982.

Larson, Kay. *New York New York*. Lawrence, KS: Spencer Museum of Art, 1988.

Detailed Itinerary

1. A rest home near Hollywood, California

The son of a prosperous corporation lawyer, 17-year-old Holden Caulfield suffers emotionally following the death of his brother Allie five years earlier, in 1946. Irresponsible and attention-seeking, Holden is bounced out of four private high schools and in his junior year ends up in a private psychiatric hospital on the West Coast. With frequent digressions, he narrates the story of his 48-hour odyssey of avoidance and subsequent nervous collapse the previous December. Lonely and self-defeating, Holden despairs of permanent friendships or the esteem of his parents and his remaining brother, D. B., a short-story writer in Hollywood, who may drive Holden home in his Jaguar in a month.

2. Pencey Prep, a fictional boys' school near Agerstown, Pennsylvania

After exams and before Christmas holidays, Dr. Thurmer, Pencey Prep's head-master, lectures Holden for two hours, then expels him for failing four courses and passing only English. Thurmer promises to write the Caulfields on Monday about their son's poor academic performance. On Saturday, Holden climbs Thomsen Hill to watch Pencey play Saxon Hall on the football field below. A failed fencing team manager, he chastises himself for losing the team's foils and equipment on the subway earlier that day and costing them a loss against McBurney School. In response to a note inviting him to stop by before leaving Pencey, Holden abandons the football game and crosses Route 204 in the cold so that he can say goodbye to Mr. Spencer, an elderly history teacher, who suffers from flu. A stern but under-standing teacher, Spencer berates Holden for his inept answer to a question on a history exam about the ancient Egyptians and for being expelled from Whooten School and Elkton Hills. Holden, his mind on the whereabouts of the ducks at the lagoon in New York's Central Park South, apologizes and worries about returning home on Wednesday. He refuses a cup of hot chocolate and departs.

Back at his dorm room, which he shares with Ward Stradlater, a football player, Holden puts on a red hunting hat he bought that morning at a sports store and reads *Out of Africa*. Robert Ackley, a round-shouldered senior from next door, interrupts and annoys Holden, who dislikes Ackley for his pimples and discourtesy. Ackley doesn't take the hint and annoys Holden further by asking about Stradlater's date.

At halftime, Stradlater returns to the room, asks to borrow Holden's hound's-tooth jacket, and requests that Holden write a descriptive composition for him. Holden tackles Stradlater, who reveals that his date is Jane Gallagher, Holden's friend. Holden, who met the girl while he worked as a caddy, recalls Jane's unhappy home life after her divorced mother remarried. He voices memories of the way she protected her back row while playing checkers.

3. Agerstown, Pennsylvania

After dinner, Holden, Mal Brossard, and Ackley take the bus into Agerstown to see a movie. They play pinball, eat hamburgers, and return at 8:45. Holden settles in to write a composition about the baseball mitt of his brother Allie, who died of leukemia four years earlier, on July 18, 1946. At 10:30, Holden finishes typing the assignment on Stradlater's typewriter. Stradlater returns, reads the composition, and ridicules the subject matter. Holden tears up the paper. Their conversation turns to Stradlater's date. Holden punches him for not respecting Jane; Stradlater bloodies Holden's nose. Holden decides to leave immediately, walk to the train station, take a train to New York City, and stay in a hotel until Wednesday so his parents can get used to the idea of his fourth expulsion from school.

4. Trenton and Newark, New Jersey

As the train moves northeast through New Jersey, Ernest Morrow's mother gets on at Trenton. Holden pretends to be Rudolf Schmidt and lies about how popular Ernie is. Before Ernie's mother gets off the train in Newark, Holden has pretended to have a brain tumor, which he claims will require an operation. She invites him to their summer home at Gloucester, Massachusetts.

5. Penn Station in New York City, New York

Holden is even lonelier by the time he reaches Penn Station in southwest New York City. He considers telephoning his 10-year-old sister Phoebe, who would be in bed. Instead, he hails a cab.

6. Midtown Manhattan, New York City

On the ride uptown, Holden accidentally gives his real address, then has the driver exit Central Park at 90th Street and return downtown to the Edmont Hotel, where Holden rents a room. From his hotel window, he watches the eccentric behavior of other people.

Holden goes downstairs to the Lavender Room, a hotel nightclub, and thinks about his sister Phoebe, a cheerful little girl who writes books about Hazle Weatherfield, girl detective. In the nightclub, Holden, pretending to be Jim Steele, flirts with three single women from Seattle and dances with each. The girls leave him so they can get up early Sunday morning to visit Radio City Music Hall in Rockefeller Center on 49th Street and the Avenue of the Americas.

Holden telephones Faith Cavendish, a friend of a friend who lives at the Stanford Arms at Broadway and 65th Street. She mispronounces his name and refuses a date because of the late hour.

7. Greenwich Village, New York City

Holden grows depressed thinking about his warm relationship with Jane Gallagher. He takes a cab to Ernie's, a night spot in Greenwich Village, west of Broadway near New York's southern tip. A poorly lit place where the underaged Holden has no difficulty ordering mixed drinks, Ernie's is filled with college students on holiday break. Holden worries that his father expects him to go to an Ivy League school. His evening is ruined by an encounter with Lillian Simmons, a gushy friend of his brother D. B.

8. Midtown Manhattan, New York City

Holden walks 41 blocks back to the Edmont. Maurice, the elevator operator, offers to bring a prostitute, Sunny, to Holden's room for $5, or $15 until noon. When Sunny arrives at his door, she offers sex, which Holden declines because he says he is recuperating from an operation on his "clavichord." He asks for conversation instead, but Sunny is obviously unaccustomed to talking with clients. Before exiting, Sunny raises the rate to $10; he gives her half the amount.

At daybreak, Maurice forces his way into the room and demands $5 more. He takes the money from Holden's wallet and hits him. Holden contemplates jumping out the window. Although he is hungry, he hesitates to order breakfast lest Maurice bring it to his room. Sometime after 10:00 A.M. Sunday morning, Holden calls Sally Hayes and arranges to meet her at the Biltmore Hotel at 2:00 P.M.

9. Grand Central Station in New York City

Holden transports his expensive Gladstone bags to Grand Central Station in mid-Manhattan, eats breakfast in a small sandwich bar, and converses with two nuns from Chicago. He talks about literature, presses them to accept a $10 contribution, and accidentally blows smoke on them, an act that he deeply regrets.

At noon, he begins walking west toward Broadway and buys a recording of "Little Shirley Beans" for Phoebe.

10. Central Park in New York City

Before his date, Holden buys tickets for a play called *I Know My Love*, starring Alfred Lunt and Lynne Fontanne, and, hoping to locate Phoebe, goes north toward the mall where she likes to skate.

11. Museum of Natural History in New York City

At the suggestion of a child in the park, Holden walks northwest to the Museum of Natural History, a favorite place where he used to enjoy Indian displays because they gave him a sense of permanence. At the museum door, he changes his mind about entering and takes a cab to the Biltmore instead.

12. Midtown Manhattan, New York City

Sally arrives at 2:10. Holden is delighted to see her. They take a cab to the show, which begins at 2:40. Holden is bored by the performance and the enthusiastic crowd in the lobby.

13. Radio City in New York City

At Sally's suggestion, they go to Radio City to ice skate. Holden, starting to lose control emotionally, asks Sally to run away to Vermont and Massachusetts to get married. She rejects his offer, argues with him, and leaves in anger. Holden eases his despair by watching the Rockettes' Christmas show at Radio City Music Hall and consults his address book, which contains only two numbers. He calls Carl Luce, a stuffy graduate of Whooten, to join him at the Wicker Bar for a drink.

14. Midtown Manhattan, New York City

North of Radio City on 54th Street, Holden meets Carl, annoys him with adolescent questions about sex and psychotherapy, and gets drunk. At 1:00 A.M. Monday morning, Holden calls Sally and drunkenly offers to help her trim her Christmas tree. He wets his head under the spigot in the men's room and sits on the radiator counting squares in the flooring.

15. Central Park in New York City

Because he is short of money, Holden walks out into the cold night air to Madison Avenue to wait for a bus, then changes his mind and walks north to Central Park to look for the ducks and skip his last few coins across the frozen lagoon. He inadvertently breaks the record he bought for Phoebe.

16. Midtown Manhattan, New York City

Not far from Central Park, Holden walks to his family's apartment and awakens Phoebe, who is glad to see him but scolds him for being expelled from Pencey. He telephones Mr. Antolini, his former English teacher at Whooten and hides when his mother arrives home. Before Holden leaves, Phoebe lends him her Christmas money—$8.65. The gesture touches him.

At Antolini's swanky apartment at Sutton Place, the teacher welcomes Holden and invites him to spend the night on the living-room sofa. Antolini tries to counsel Holden about his poor performance in school. Later, he awakens Holden by stroking his head. Repulsed by the gesture, Holden rushes out of the apartment.

17. Grand Central Station in New York City

From Lexington Avenue, Holden takes a subway to Grand Central Station. He tries to eat doughnuts and drink coffee at a restaurant but has difficulty swallowing.

18. Midtown Manhattan, New York City

By the time the stores open, Holden walks along Fifth Avenue, looking at the holiday decorations and hallucinating about disappearing. He longs to run away out West.

Holden continues north along Central Park to Phoebe's elementary school and leaves a note for her to meet him at the door of the Museum of Art at 12:15. An obscene word written on a wall dismays him; he tries to erase it so it won't influence young children.

19. The Museum of Art in New York City

Dragging a suitcase and wearing Holden's hunting hat, Phoebe arrives ready to run away with her brother. He realizes that he can't take her along and decides not to leave home.

20. Zoo in Manhattan, New York City

Phoebe bridles at the rejection and angrily walks south toward the zoo. With the money Holden returns to her, she buys a ticket for the carousel. Holden, admiring her in her blue coat, is happy in the rain as he watches her enjoy the ride.

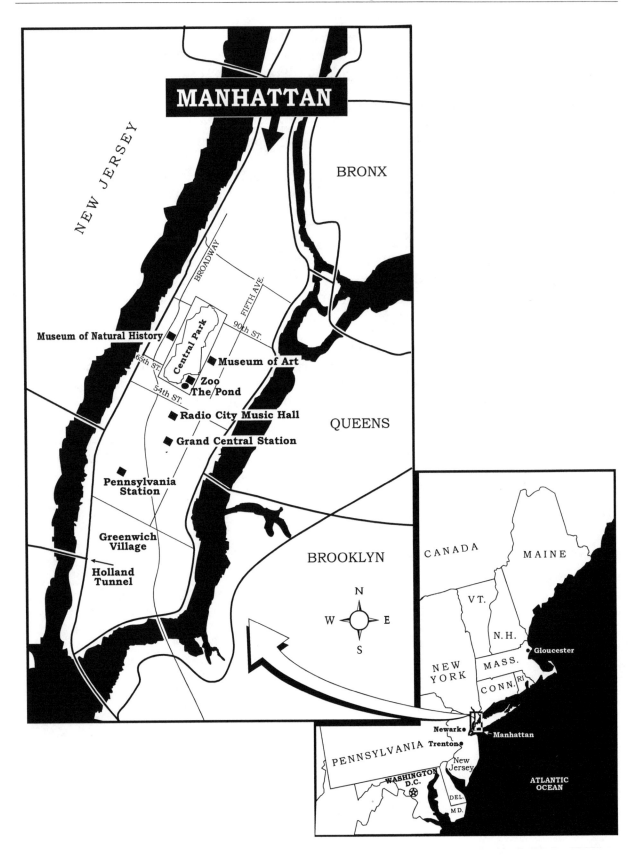

The Cay

BY THEODORE TAYLOR

Young adult adventure novel, 1969

Geographical Summary: The story of 11-year-old Phillip Enright is a physical journey as well as a quest of mind and spirit. It begins in 1942 in Willemstad, Curaçao, the largest Dutch island of the West Indies in the Caribbean Sea north of Venezuela. The island, which Phillip roams with a Dutch friend Henrik, is neatly bisected at the Punda and Otrabanda sections by St. Anna Channel. From the Enright home in Scharloo, the old Jewish district that once boasted fine homes, Phillip and Henrik explore Fort Amsterdam, Krup Bay, Seroe Male, and Koningin Emma Brug, the Queen Emma Pontoon Bridge—all landmarks within walking distance of the Enright residence.

After German submarines blow up oil tankers, Phillip's father decides to send his son and wife north to safety at her parents' home in Virginia until the end of the war. Their ship, traveling northeast, is torpedoed on its voyage northwest out of Colón, Panama, en route to Miami, Florida. The story moves northeast into the Caribbean Sea to an uncharted cay—a low sand and coral reef that is deserted and waterless—tucked into Devil's Mouth, where an elderly black islander named Timothy survives the sinking of the ship and cares for Phillip until the old man dies in a hurricane. After Phillip is rescued, he goes to Cristóbal, Panama, and receives medical care in New York; then he and his parents return to their adopted Caribbean home.

The route that Phillip follows on his odyssey from Willemstad to the cay and Panama covers the less-traveled Caribbean isles, many of which remain uncharted. As Taylor indicates, the late summer and early fall weather of these waters can be tricky when tornadoes form, especially for the small fishing boats that Timothy once worked. However, the author balances the threat of ravaging wind and high waters with the natural beauties of lagoons, palms, fragrant winds, temperate nights, and the easily obtainable fruit and seafood on Caribbean isles. During World War II, the value of petroleum refineries to the German navy and the outmoded Dutch harbor forts that once protected Curaçao made this location an easy mark for submarines, which disrupted the fuel supply to the Netherlands and other allies.

Further Reading

Ashdown, Peter. *Caribbean History in Maps.* White Plains, NY: Longman, 1979.

Churchill, James E. *Survival: The Basic Essentials.* Merrillville, IN: ICS Books, 1989.

Fermor, Patrick L. *The Traveller's Tree: A Journey Through the Caribbean Islands.* New York: Viking Penguin, 1991.

Heiligers-Halabi. *Curaçao.* Edison, NJ: Hunter Publishing, 1990.

Hemingway, Ernest. *Islands in the Stream*. New York: Macmillan, 1980.

Horder, Mervyn. *On Their Own: Shipwrecks and Survivals*. Dobbs Ferry, NY: Sheridan, 1988.

Detailed Itinerary

1. Aruba and Willemstad, Curaçao, north of Lake Maracaibo, Venezuela

In February 1942, German submarines fire on the Lago oil refinery at Sint Nicolaas, Aruba. Then they blow up tankers bringing crude oil from Lake Maracaibo, Venezuela, to Shell Oil Company reserves in Curaçao, an island north of South America in the Caribbean Sea. On February 21, the enemy torpedoes a Norwegian tanker off Curaçao. A day or two later, the enemy sinks the *Empire Tern*, a large British tanker, at Schottegat in Willemstad, the island's major city. The governor of the Netherlands West Indies requests military protection from the U.S. government.

As the situation grows more threatening to civilians, Phillip Enright, a U.S. fuel technician on loan to Royal Dutch Shell in Willemstad, prepares to send his wife Grace and son Phillip back to the United States. Boarding a small Dutch freighter, the S.S. *Hato*, in St. Anna Channel in early April, the pair set out due west for Colón, Panama, planning to sail northeast to Miami, Florida, where they will travel up the U.S. coast to Norfolk, Virginia, to visit Phillip's maternal grandparents.

2. Colón, Panama

On April 6 at 3:00 A.M., torpedoes strike the S.S. *Hato* shortly after it departs Colón. Phillip, dressed warmly in sweater and life jacket, abandons ship but loses consciousness and is separated from his mother. Four hours later, he regains consciousness on a raft and realizes that he is losing his vision. He receives care from an elderly black West Indian deckhand named Timothy, a native of Charlotte Amalie, St. Thomas (one of the Virgin Islands). A third survivor of the *Hato* is Timothy's large black and gray cat named Stew Cat. Phillip, who dislikes blacks, awaits rescue. Timothy scolds him for straying too near the edge of the raft, where a tumble into the shark-infested water could kill him. Chilled by sea winds, Phillip maximizes body temperature by cuddling near Timothy, hopes that his vision will return, and sleeps.

3. An unidentified cay in the Devil's Mouth, Caribbean Sea

Three days later, Timothy spies the cay, safely beaches the raft, and sets up a makeshift camp. On April 17, a welcome rain shower fills their keg with fresh water. Phillip helps the illiterate Timothy spell "HELP" with rocks so air searchers can spot their location.

A month later, Phillip, who has acclimated himself to blindness, nurses Timothy through a bout of malaria. In July, Timothy senses the approach of a pre-season hurricane and lashes Phillip and himself to a tree on the highest point of the cay. The storm rips their clothes and pelts them with sand and residue. Rising water threatens their location, then recedes when the winds subside. Timothy, who sheltered Phillip and sustained the most physical damage, dies from the buffeting of wind and water. Phillip, grieving at his loss, buries the old man on the cay.

Left with only Stew Cat for a companion, Phillip applies the knowledge he gained from Timothy by following his guide rope about the cay and fishing. In early August, Phillip lights a fire of sea grape vines to signal a passing plane, but fails to get the crew's attention. On August 20, however, he succeeds in creating enough black smoke to attract an American destroyer.

4. Cristóbal, Panama

The sailors, surprised to locate a boy on so deserted a stretch of islands, rescue Phillip and Stew Cat from the cay and transport them west to Cristóbal, Panama. Along the way, he tells the story of the sinking of the S.S. *Hato*. In Cristóbal, he reunites with his parents.

5. New York, United States

In December, Phillip journeys to an unspecified location in New York and undergoes three operations, which restore his vision.

6. Willemstad, Curaçao

In early April 1943, the Enright family returns to Willemstad. Phillip frequently visits St. Anna Bay and the Ruyterkade Market, a floating emporium composed of South American boats carrying fruit, fish, fabrics, and vegetables. The native dialects remind him of Timothy. He studies maps of the Caribbean, where he locates landmarks: Roncador, Rosalind, Quito Sueño, Serranilla Banks, Beacon Cay, North Cay, Providencia, San Andrés, and the Devil's Mouth. He hopes to find and return to the cay to visit Timothy's grave.

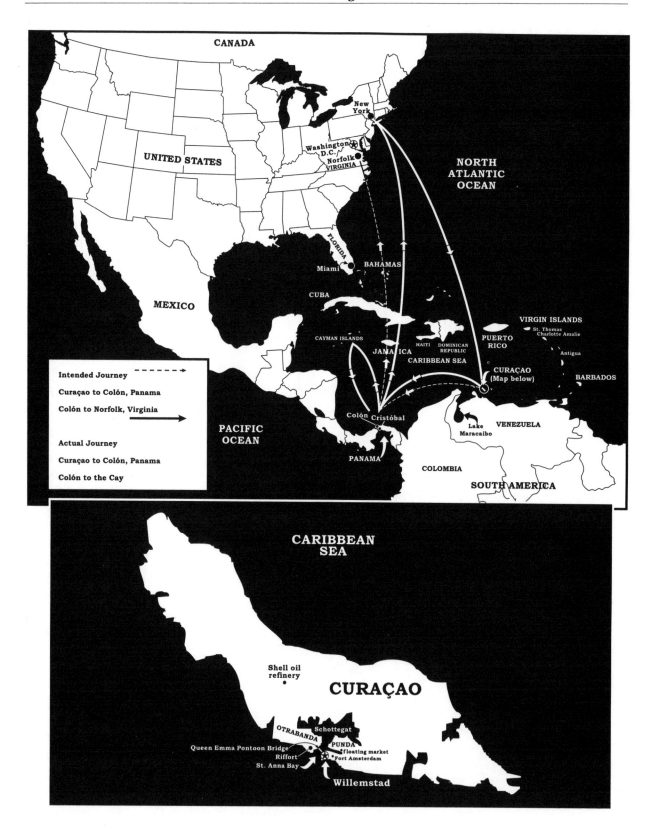

Cry, the Beloved Country

BY ALAN PATON

Sociological novel, 1948

Geographical Summary: Alan Paton's somber novel is set in post-World War II South Africa during a tense bus strike. There is strong anti-black feeling among the minority European residents. The book details the Reverend Stephen Kumalo's train trip from his rural home south of Durban, South Africa, northwest to Johannesburg, the capital city, to learn the fate of his son and sister. The journey answers his personal questions, at the same time reflecting the causes of urban crime, greed, squalor, and rootlessness in a violent city. After numerous investigatory trips into the suburbs of Johannesburg, Stephen visits the Johannesburg jail, where his son Absalom awaits transportation to Pretoria and execution for murder. Renewed by the promise of the next generation and an alliance with the father of the man Absalom helped murder, Stephen returns to his Zulu community in the plains near Ixopo along the Umzimkulu River.

The extreme contrast of life in the coastal plains near Durban with the racial and political ferment in and around Johannesburg predates the social climate of the later part of the twentieth century, as dispossessed and disenfranchised blacks press for democratic representation in government and an end to apartheid—the extreme separation of races on buses, park benches, swimming pools, and other public places, as well as a denunciation of interracial marriage. For Paton, a contributing factor in the degeneration of native morals is the rapid urbanization of immigrants, who leave the simplicity of rural life and plunge into the turmoil of Johannesburg's ghettos. With cash from readily available jobs in the diamond mines, unsophisticated youths such as Absalom and equally naive adults such as Gertrude, Stephen's sister, lose contact with country life and the institutional structure and support of school, church, tribe, and community. For Stephen, the contrast between locales is more than he can fathom and a far greater challenge than his simple faith can handle.

Further Reading

Christopher, A. J. *South Africa*. New York: John Wiley, 1982.

Comaroff, Jean. *Body of Power, Spirit of Resistance: The Culture and History of a South African People*. Chicago: University of Chicago Press, 1985.

Everett, Percival. *The Zulus*. Los Angeles, CA: Knightsbridge Publishing, 1991.

Schuettinger, Robert, ed. *South Africa*. McLean, VA: Council for Social and Economic Studies, 1977.

Detailed Itinerary

1. Ndotsheni, Natal
In the small village of Ndotsheni in the province of Natal, a 60-year-old Zulu priest, Reverend Stephen Kumalo, serves St. Paul's Anglican Church. The dry plain on which Stephen and his wife live lies south of Johannesburg, South Africa. Their family and the families of other locals have fallen prey to the lure of steady salaries and a reprieve from tribal traditions. Stephen's sister Gertrude, his brother John, and his son Absalom have migrated to Johannesburg and ceased communication with the family in Ndotsheni.

On Sepember 25, 1946, a fellow Anglican, Theophilus Msimangu, sends a message from Sophiatown, a poor suburb southwest of Johannesburg, that Gertrude is ill. Immediately, Stephen pulls together eight pounds, five shillings, and seven pence to buy train fare from Ixopo, to the south, to Johannesburg, leaving his wife only four pounds. She insists that he take the remaining money for incidental expenses.

2. Ixopo, South Africa
Traveling northwest from Ixopo on the Drakensberg highlands near the Umzimkulu River, through Carrisbrooke to Donnybrook, and over the Mooi River into Drakensberg, Stephen accepts the request of an unnamed parishioner to learn the whereabouts of Sibeko's daughter, who has also vanished from her family.

3. Johannesburg, South Africa
After the train reaches Johannesburg, Stephen is overwhelmed by city life. Naive and befuddled, he goes to the bus station, where he is quickly cheated by a con man who offers to take one pound to buy the minister's ticket, then departs with the money.

4. Sophiatown and Claremont, suburbs of Johannesburg
A fellow Anglican guides Stephen to Mission House in Sophiatown, where Theophilus explains that Gertrude's husband has abandoned her in Claremont, a disreputable suburb that lies north of Sophiatown outside Johannesburg.

5. Claremont, a suburb of Johannesburg
Stephen travels to Claremont and learns that Gertrude, a poorly educated woman who has been in prison, works as a prostitute, gambles, and sells bootleg liquor to support herself and her small son. Stephen visits her and scolds her for failing to write to her family, consorting with immoral people, and engaging in dishonest practices. Sick with despair, she collapses, weeping.

6. Sophiatown, a suburb of Johannesburg
Stephen engages a truck to move Gertrude's household to Mrs. Lithebe's residence in Sophiatown, where Stephen takes a room during his sojourn in Johannesburg. Ultimately, he plans to take Gertrude back to the village. He anticipates that his efforts will rescue other wayward Zulus and rebuild the tribe.

Next, Stephen visits the carpentry shop of his brother John, a politician who champions modern ways and rejects tribalism. John passes on important information: His wife Esther left him 10 years earlier; he is living with another woman; and Absalom and John's son Matthew have moved to Alexandra and are employed by Doornfontein Textiles.

Stephen does not find Absalom at Doornfontein and learns that his son, who left the factory a year before, once lived at End Street in Sophiatown.

7. Sophiatown, a suburb of Johannesburg
Weary and frustrated, Stephen returns with Theophilus to the mission for the night.

8. Alexandra, South Africa
The next morning, Stephen travels to Alexandra with Theophilus in search of Mrs. Mkize's residence. Dubula, a political agitator, warns the men that locals are boycotting the transit line. To support the black cause, Stephen and Msimangu do not ride the bus. They plan to walk the 11 miles through the white settlement in Orange Grove and north to Alexandra in search of Absalom, but they accept a ride from a white man.

Mrs. Mkize, a tight-lipped landlady, grudgingly reports that Absalom has been gone for nearly a year. She sends the men to a taxi driver for more information. Stephen deduces that Absalom has become a petty thief as a result of friendship with bad companions in Shanty Town in Orlando, southwest of Johannesburg.

9. Shanty Town in Orlando, a suburb of Johannesburg
Stephen grows homesick as the trail leads to more squalor. On Tuesday, a reformatory clerk tells Stephen that Absalom was once in jail, then gained release through rehabilitation. Stephen is not pleased by news that Absalom lives in Pimville with an unnamed girl who is pregnant with his child.

10. Pimville, a suburb of Johannesburg
The clerk drives Stephen and Theophilus to Pimville, where people live in half-tanks. Stephen learns from the pregnant girl that Absalom left her on Saturday and has not returned. The kindly minister sympathizes with the girl, a child herself.

11. Orlando, a suburb of Johannesburg
The reformatory clerk returns the two men to Orlando. Stephen vows not to give up looking for his son, who has deserted his job.

12. Sophiatown, a suburb of Johannesburg
The *Evening Star* reports the murder of Arthur Jarvis, a liberal living in Parkwold, who supported better conditions for South African natives. Stephen learns from Mrs. Mkize and the police that Absalom is the major suspect in the killing.

After a miserable evening at the Mission House, Stephen halts his search for a day to visit an institution for the blind at Ezenzeleni. His idealism, suppressed by fears for Absalom, is restored by Theophilus's lectures.

Stephen returns to John's shop to report the bad news that Absalom is in prison and that Matthew took part in the murder.

13. Johannesburg, South Africa
John and Stephen visit Absalom in prison. Absalom weeps over his bad behavior and blames evil companions for luring him into crime. Stephen asks Absalom not to write to his mother.

14. Sophiatown, a suburb of Johannesburg
With the help of Father Vincent of the Mission House, Stephen retains Mr. Carmichael, a lawyer who will defend Absalom without charge.

15. Pimville, a suburb of Johannesburg

Stephen returns to Absalom's girlfriend to tell her about the murder.

16. Sophiatown, a suburb of Johannesburg

With Mrs. Lithebe's permission, Stephen moves the girl to the boarding house, where she is grateful to sleep on the floor; she calls Mrs. Lithebe "mother."

17. Carrisbrooke, near Ixopo

Meanwhile, the authorities visit John Jarvis at High Place, his farm outside Carrisbrooke near the African coast, to report Arthur's death.

18. Johannesburg, South Africa

The Jarvises arrive at the Johannesburg Airport and join Mary, their daughter-in-law.

John Kumalo hires a lawyer to represent both Matthew and Johannes Pafuri, the third of the trio accused of breaking into Jarvis's home on October 8, striking the house servant with an iron bar, and shooting Jarvis. Absalom, who admits that he shot Jarvis and was arrested in Germiston, is condemned to hang at Pretoria. Matthew and Johannes are set free for lack of evidence.

Father Vincent agrees to marry Absalom and the girl at the prison so that their child will be legitimized. Absalom leaves money for the child, whom he requests to be named Peter. At the mention of Pretoria, Absalom falls on the floor, crying and praying. Stephen comforts him and embraces Absalom's new wife as a daughter.

19. Sophiatown, a suburb of Johannesburg

At John's carpentry shop, Stephen reminds his brother that Matthew and Johannes also took part in the crime for which Absalom will pay with his life. John orders Stephen out of his shop. Before returning to Ndotsheni, Stephen tries to locate Sibeko's daughter. On this errand, Stephen encounters James Jarvis, Arthur Jarvis's father, whom Stephen remembers from the courtroom. At the point of collapse, Stephen mourns that his son Absalom killed Jarvis's son. The two men comfort each other.

Stephen learns that Sibeko's daughter was jailed for selling liquor. He fails to locate her whereabouts.

Before Stephen leaves Johannesburg, he is treated to a small farewell party. Gertrude, whom Mrs. Lithebe has scolded for choosing unfit friends, hears a nun's lecture and suggests to Absalom's wife that she choose a religious life. Absalom's wife agrees to take charge of Gertrude's son if Gertrude leaves Johannesburg. At the dinner party Theophilus announces that he will enter a religious retreat. He leaves his money to Stephen. The next day, as Stephen packs to return to Ndotsheni, he discovers that his sister has abandoned her new clothes and left town during the night.

20. Ndotsheni, Natal

The train winds southeast through Transvaal to familiar territory, which Stephen points out to Absalom's wife. Back home in Natal, Stephen reveals that Absalom is condemned to be hanged. He presents to his wife Gertrude's son and Absalom's wife. Mrs. Kumalo accepts them lovingly. Stephen prays to recover from the wretched experiences, which have shamed him.

That night, James Jarvis's grandson knocks at Stephen's door and asks for a drink of milk. Because the parched village has no milk, Stephen offers the boy water.

Jarvis's grandson shows an interest in the Zulu language and learns a few simple words. The boy's friendship and Arthur's pro-black writings inspire James Jarvis to underwrite neighborhood projects, particularly milk for the children and the building of a new church. On the morning of the day that Absalom is hanged, Stephen prays for Africa and awaits the sunrise.

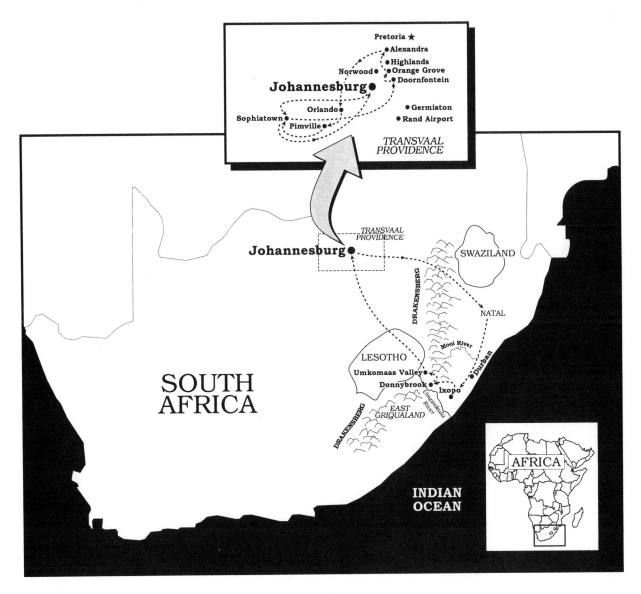

Dove

BY ROBIN LEE GRAHAM AND DEREK GILL

Travel and adventure, 1972

Geographical Summary: From 1965 to 1970, Robin Lee Graham, the youngest person to circumnavigate the globe alone, covers a meandering path as he travels in his sloop *Dove* west from California across the Pacific to Samoa, Fiji, and Australia, and through the Indian Ocean to the southern tip of Africa. After wooing Patti Ratterree, he marries her in an unofficial ceremony (and later does so legitimately), then takes an overland honeymoon across lush African savannahs. After parting with Patti as he initiates his Atlantic crossing, Robin fights loneliness and doubt before reaching Surinam, South America, where the couple reunites.

With the help of a *National Geographic* staff member, Robin resolves to complete his around-the-world journey and purchases a larger, sturdier sloop, which he names *Big Dove*. First pausing to rest with Patti in the Caribbean, he continues to Panama, south to the Galapagos Islands, and north to Los Angeles and home. At the end of his journey, Patti gives birth to a daughter on Catalina Island, where the couple had gone for a relaxing weekend. The Graham family sells the sloop and settles in a handmade cabin in Montana.

Details of Robin's physical journey around the globe parallel his emotional and cultural trek through hospitable Polynesian villages, tropical settings and toney harbor clubs in the New Hebrides and Solomon Islands, and native villages and English communities on South Africa's shores. Significant to his odyssey is the discovery of emotional strengths and a maturity that enables him to break with childhood and establish a family. The balance of sailing jargon, geographical data, weather information, and personal observations elevates his story from mere adventure to a universal act of initiation, a rite of manhood.

Further Reading

Chichester, Francis. *The Lonely Sky and the Sea.* New York: Paragon House, 1990.

Christopher, A. J. *South Africa.* New York: John Wiley, 1982.

Farnham, Moulton M. *Sailing for Beginners.* New York: Macmillan, 1986.

Fermor, Patrick L. *The Traveller's Tree: A Journey Through the Caribbean Islands.* New York: Viking Penguin, 1991.

Ferrell, Robert H., and Richard Natkiel. *Atlas of American History.* New York: Facts on File, 1987.

Schuettinger, Robert, ed. *South Africa.* McLean, VA: Council for Social and Economic Studies, 1977.

Tyler, Charles. *The Island World of the Pacific Ocean.* New York: Gordon Press, 1977.

Detailed Itinerary

1. Long Beach, California

Robin Lee Graham, near the end of his wife's pregnancy, re-creates the journey that brought him fame as the "youngest sailor to have circled the world single-handed." A lover of sailing since early childhood, Robin, an independent, free-spirited loner, inherited his passion from his father and uncle.

2. Nuku Hiva, Marquesas Islands

When Robin reaches age 13, his father Lyle sells his business and purchases the *Golden Hind*, a 36-foot ketch, and takes the family to Nuku Hiva in the Marquesas Islands.

3. Papeete, Tahiti, to Huahine, Tahaa, Bora Bora, Cook Islands, Pago Pago, and Hawaii

During the year Robin spends away from class, he undergoes an appendectomy in a hospital in Papeete, Tahiti's capital. The family enjoys a tour of the South Seas before arriving in Hawaii, then returning to California.

Robin rebels at the tight regimen of books and classes. To ease his son's chafing at school, Lyle allows him to sail on a 27-day journey aboard the *Valerie* to Hawaii.

4. Ala Wai, Hawaii

Enrolled at McKinley High School near Ala Wai, Hawaii, Robin makes friends with the brothers Jim and Arthur. They intend to sail the *HIC*, a 16-foot aluminum lifeboat, on a secret jaunt to Lanai.

5. Diamond Head, Hawaii

Departing January 29, 1965, the boys ignore gale warnings and head for the Molokai channel. As the boat nearly founders in high seas, the boys listen to news of their exploit on a transistor radio.

6. Lanai City, Hawaii

The *HIC*'s keel breaks away, endangering the boys more than they realize. Rescuers spend $25,000 looking for the trio.

7. Honolulu, Hawaii

A plane returns the boys to Honolulu, where a Coast Guard inquiry finds them guilty of reckless or negligent operation of a vessel endangering life.

8. San Pedro, California

Lyle is sensitive to his son's longing for sea adventures and helps him purchase the *Dove*, a 24-foot sloop. They work throughout July to ready it for a 30,000-mile circumnavigation of the globe. The five-year journey begins July 27, 1965, when Robin is 16. Well stocked with food, accompanied by two kittens, and listening to Los Angeles radio stations, Robin sets sail for Hawaii.

9. Ala Wai, Hawaii

On August 18, 1965, Robin enters the harbor, where reporters interview him about his adventures. Lyle flies into Ala Wai to help his son prepare for the next leg of the journey.

10. Fanning Island

Robin embarks for Fanning Island, 1,050 miles to the south, on September 14, 1965. Fifteen days later, he reaches English Harbor. Six days later he presses on for Pago Pago with a Royal Mail pouch on board. On October 7 he crosses the equator.

11. Apia, Upolu

On October 14, 1965, although aiming for Tutuila in American Samoa, Robin must settle for Apia on Upolu Island, 52 miles to the southwest, where for five months he waits out hurricane season, makes friends with locals, and hikes to Robert Louis Stevenson's burial mound, a famous tourist spot.

12. Pago Pago, American Samoa

By January 3, 1966, a 48-hour sail lands Robin in Pago Pago, east of Apia. On January 29, a hurricane threatens the island. Robin joins the natives in cleaning up the damaged villages.

13. Neiafu, Vavau

On May 1, 1966, Robin begins a four-day southwesterly sail to the Vavau cluster and harbors at Neiafu, where he makes friends with a Tongan chief.

14. Fulanga, Lau

Leaving the Tongans on June 21, 1966, Robin makes for Fulanga in the Lau group, due west of Vavau.

15. Suva, Fiji

Within two days, he is ready for another westerly passage to Suva, Fiji's capital, which he reaches on July 2, 1966. Two problems arise. An American consul helps him overcome the need of a $100 harbor bond, but no one can relieve the ache brought on by the death of Joliette, one of his kittens. The situation brightens considerably after he is introduced to Patti Ratterree, a pretty, adventurous Los Angeles native who needs a place to stay. Robin offers her a berth on the *Dove*.

16. Savala, Yasawa Islands

Patti and Robin sail northwest to Savala in the Yasawas to hunt for shells. Patti narrates her adventures hitchhiking in Mexico and Panama, from which she sailed to the Galapagos Islands, Tahiti, and the Fijis, where she jumped ship to escape a lecherous captain and met Dick Johnston, an old friend, in Lautoka.

17. Naviti, Vomo, Waialailai, Nalawauki, Nanuya Balava, Tavewa, Nalova Bay, and Lautoka in the Yasawas

Robin and Patti continue to Naviti, where their romance blossoms. On August 25, 1966, they sail from Vomo to Waialailai and by August 30 arrive at Nalawauki, where they find no shell life. The next day they sail back to Naviti and Nanuyu Balava. The first of September, they make a leisurely voyage to Tavewa (where *The Blue Lagoon* was filmed).

For several days there are warnings of strong winds at Nalova Bay, yet the *Dove* encounters only restful swells and island hospitality for its crew. From the northernmost archipelago, Patti and Robin move back to Lautoka. Lyle writes that he will join Robin in the New Hebrides to take photographs for the *National Geographic* article.

18. Vila, New Hebrides

Planning to journey to New Zealand, Patti embarks west for New Hebrides, an island cluster northeast of Australia. On the long trek to Vila, Robin composes letters to her to fight loneliness. His father arrives with news of Robin's brother Michael, an officer serving in Vietnam.

19. Malekula, Ambrim, Maewo, Santa Maria, the Torres Islands, San Cristóbal, Honiara, Guadalcanal, Florida, and Savo in the Solomon cluster

Robin is forced to chart a new route to bypass the Suez Canal. On November 8, 1966, he makes slow progress northwest toward Maewo Island, sleeps, then sails to Santa Maria. Twelve days later at Honiara, Guadalcanal, in the Solomons, Robin does not cross paths with Lyle, but he receives a letter from Patti. Robin learns about the Battle of Guadalcanal from his father, who departs before Christmas.

20. Port Moresby, New Guinea

Robin waits out hurricane season, then sails the *Dove* west toward Port Moresby, New Guinea, arriving March 24, 1967. He receives Patti's letter from Christchurch, New Zealand, far to the southeastern side of Australia.

21. Coral Sea, Dalrymple Island, and Darwin, Australia

On April 18, 1967, Robin sails west into the Coral Sea and Dalrymple Island. By May 4, he reaches Darwin, a port on Australia's northern shore, and locates Patti a few days later.

22. Arnhem Land, Australia

A *National Geographic* photographer plans pictures of Robin with Aborigines in the Arnhem Land reservation. Robin takes a construction job and receives an advance from the magazine. Lyle, fearful that Robin's romance will lessen his chances of completing the voyage, arrives from California to meet Patti.

23. Rodriguez, Cocos Islands

Robin departs on July 6, 1967, for Mauritius, off the east coast of the island of Malagasy (renamed Madagascar in 1975), and reaches the Cocos Islands 18 days later. After difficult sailing, he enters the port of Rodriguez.

24. Port Louis, Mauritius

Patti, who lacks passage from Melbourne, is unable to join Robin in Port Louis, Mauritius. They alter their plans and settle on a rendezvous in Durban, South Africa.

25. Réunion Island, Malagasy, Mozambique Channel

Robin arrives at Réunion Island on September 30, 1967, and makes a wobbly trek off the Malagasy coast and through the Mozambique Channel southwest toward Africa's southern tip.

26. Durban and Zululand, South Africa

The roughest sailing of Robin's expedition brings him at last to Patti on October 21, 1967. At Durban, they perform their own unofficial marriage and honeymoon by motorcycle at the Umfolosi Game Reserve in Zululand and the Kruger National Park.

27. South Africa: East London, Port Elizabeth, Plettenbergbaai, Knysna, Cape Town, Cape Agulhas, Stilbaai, Struisbaai

Robin reconditions the *Dove* and on March 8, 1968, embarks around the southeastern tip of Africa, with Patti following on land by motorcycle to East London. He completes the route by March 14; Patti arrives the next day. After smaller hops around the storm-battered coast, Robin leaves Knysna on April 25 in hopes of rounding Cape Agulhas. He settles for Stilbaai and Struisbaai while a search plane sent by *National Geographic* scours the coast.

28. Gordon's Bay, South Africa

At Gordon's Bay, Gilbert Grosvenor, the associate editor of *National Geographic*, assists Robin with plans for the transatlantic crossing.

29. Hermanus Bay, South Africa

Robin and Patti marry officially at Hermanus Bay, on Africa's southwestern tip. She books passage to Barcelona in hopes of catching up with Robin at Surinam (then called Dutch Guiana).

30. Clarence Bay, Ascension Island

Robin makes his major embarkation on July 13, 1968, from Cape Town. Twenty-three days later, he reaches Clarence Bay, Ascension Island, which is south of the equator on Africa's Atlantic side.

31. Paramaribo, Surinam

The hardest leg of the journey begins August 16, 1968, as Robin pushes on for Paramaribo, Surinam, which he nears by September 1. Letters from Patti detail her odyssey from Barcelona to Lake Geneva to London and back to Barcelona, where she booked passage for Trinidad. While in Surinam, Robin travels by plane to Paloemeu and by dugout up the Tapanahoni River, where Patti arrives by plane. Gil Grosvenor is dispatched from Washington to offer advance royalties to buy Robin a new boat so he will not give up his journey.

32. Barbados, Bimini, Nassau, Paradise Island, Spanish Wells, and Saint Thomas in the Caribbean

On October, 12, 1968, Robin sails to Barbados to complete negotiations to purchase a larger boat. They sell the smaller sloop and purchase *The Return of Dove*, which they call *Big Dove*. Robin and Patti spend over a year in the Caribbean on the *Big Dove*, enjoying the tourist havens of Barbados, Bimini, Nassau, Paradise Island, Spanish Wells, and Saint Thomas.

33. Porvenir, San Blas

On November 20, 1969, Patti boards the *Lurline* as Robin heads for the San Blas Islands off Panama's northern coast. At Porvenir, Patti announces her pregnancy.

34. Cristóbal, Canal Zone, Panama

The couple share Christmas at Cristóbal, Panama.

35. Balboa

On January 30, 1970, having completed passage through the Panama Canal, Robin departs from Balboa.

36. Hood Island, James Bay, San Salvador Island, Academy Bay, and Fernandina, all part of the Galapagos Islands

Patti flies out from Gauyaquil, Ecuador, to meet Robin for a charter cruise of the Galapagos Islands and a bit of rest. Patti returns to Baltra to fly to Ecuador and sail home to California.

37. Clipperton and Clarion islands; Cape San Lázaro, Baja California

On March 21, 1970, Robin embarks one last time and passes two tiny islands and the coast of Baja California, the Mexican peninsula south of California, on his way north to Long Beach.

38. San Clemente, California

Robin makes his historic arrival at the Long Beach Marina near San Clemente, California, on April 30, 1970.

39. Newport Beach, California

For six weeks Robin and Patti endure a barrage of news reporters and fan mail as they study the Lamaze method of natural childbirth.

40. Catalina Island, California

On a pleasure cruise, the couple sails off Catalina Island, west of San Pedro, California. On June 19, 1970, Patti goes into labor and gives birth to a girl, Quimby, at the island hospital.

41. San Francisco, California

Robin, who never graduated from high school, receives a scholarship to Stanford University, but has little in common with other students. He and Patti depart with Quimby.

42. Montana

Robin sells *Big Dove* to pay for a 160-acre home in Montana, where he builds a cabin and settles into the life of husband and father.

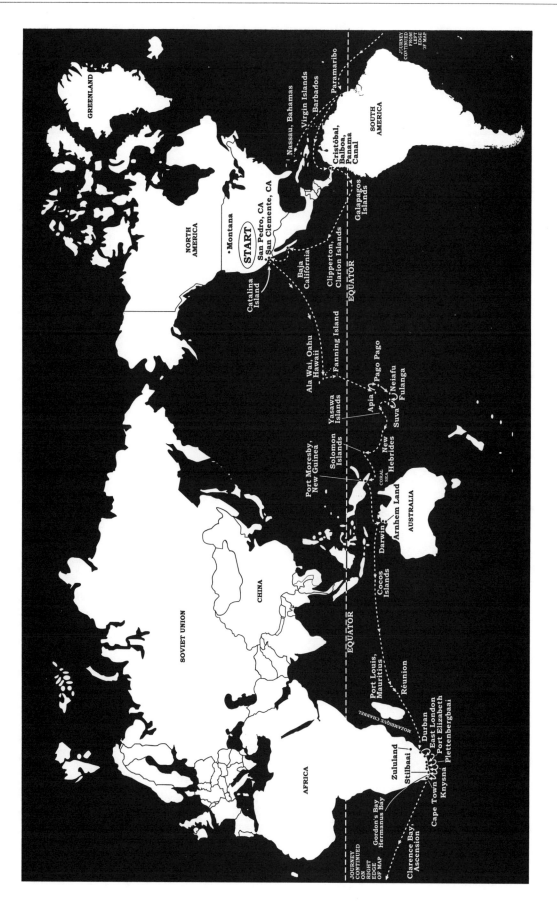

The Endless Steppe

BY ESTHER HAUTZIG

Autobiography, 1968

Geographical Summary: *The Endless Steppe,* an autobiographical account of Esther Rudomin Hautzig's childhood experiences during World War II, details the dissolution of a Jewish family during the Russian occupation of their homeland. Esther, a student at the Sophia Markovna Gurewitz Schools, learns Yiddish and enjoys the support of a close, extended family. Abruptly the Rudomins are arrested for being capitalists and are deported from the family compound in Vilna, Poland (a Jewish cultural center), in June 1941.

Crammed into tight cattle cars with other deportees, the Rudomin family journeys southeast by train to the Russian steppes (grasslands), a bitter, windy plain that extends across western Siberia from Ukrainian territory along the Azov and Black seas to the Altai Mountains. In the cheerless village of Rubtsovsk, Esther's life of poverty and rejection among hostile Russians characterizes her major strength—the ability to adapt to harsh circumstances, to make friends, and to grow and learn like a normal child. Ultimately, she reunites with her father in Lódz, Poland, in 1946 and travels by way of Stockholm, Sweden, to New York City.

The Rudomin family's abrupt uprooting from eastern Europe to the steppes required considerable adaptation. Following the Russian usurpation of Vilna along the Curzon Line in September 1939, trainloads of Jews suffered the same displacement as Esther's parents and grandparents. The political hostilities, the arid climate of Russia's grasslands, and its lack of trees contrasted with the close-knit family compound of Vilna and the social and cultural advantages of living among people who spoke the same language and came from similar religious and economic backgrounds. Among the tough Siberian people of central Russia, Esther and her family learned to exist on a potato-based diet; to occupy themselves with useful activities; to rise above fear, loneliness, and grief; and to confront the stark lesson of the steppes—that preparation for and survival of winter takes precedence over all other concerns.

Further Reading

Cole, J. P. *Geography of the Soviet Union.* Stoneham, MA: Butterworth-Heinemann, 1984.

Davies, Norman. *Heart of Europe: A Short History of Poland.* New York: Oxford University Press, 1986.

Friesel, Evyatar. *Atlas of Modern Jewish History.* New York: Oxford University Press, 1990.

Garlinski, Josef. *Poland in the Second World War.* New York: Hippocrene Books, 1987.

Jordan, Alexander. *Poland.* New York: Hippocrene Books, 1990.

Lange, Nicholas de. *Atlas of the Jewish World.* New York: Facts on File, 1984.

Symons, Leslie. *The Soviet Union: A Systematic Geography.* New York: Routledge, Chapman & Hall, 1990.

Detailed Itinerary

1. Vilna, Poland

In Vilna, Poland, 10-year-old Esther Rudomin enjoys the support and love of her parents and grandparents, who earn a good living and bring her up in comfort. Then, without warning, Russian soldiers arrest the Rudomins—Esther, her parents Samuel and Raya, and Grandmother Anna—at Esther's grandfather's house. Esther never sees her other grandmother, Sara, again.

2. Aboard the train to the Altai Territory in Siberia

Separated from Grandfather Solomon, who is assigned to a different compartment, the Rudomins travel with 40 other deportees for six weeks in a dim, foul-smelling cattle car through Byelorussia, Ukraine, and central Russia toward their unnamed destination, the Altai Territory.

3. Ural Mountains in Russia

To lighten Esther's terror over the discomfort, the unfamiliar country, and the unknown future, Samuel points out that they have crossed the Ural Mountains, the spine of central Russia, and are moving east into Asia. Along the way, a soldier confides that Germany has invaded Russia, dragging it into the war along with England.

4. Rubtsovsk in the Altai Territory, Siberia

Esther is numb with fatigue when they reach the rural depot and march a mile to the cobblestone square of Rubtsovsk, a frontier village in Russia's Altai Territory in the Russian Soviet Federated Socialist Republic.

5. Barracks outside Rubtsovsk, Siberia

Twelve miles from Rubtsovsk, the Rudomins lodge with 26 other deportees in one room of a wooden barrack that was once a school. They are fortunate to have gotten a corner of the building. The family members receive assignments for work at the gypsum mine—Grandmother shoveling gypsum, Esther in the potato fields, Raya as a dynamiter, and Samuel driving a horse cart.

At six o'clock the next morning, the whistle blows, summoning deportees to work. Esther and other children depart from their parents to weed the potato patch. At mealtime, the Rudomins line up at the overseer's office for scant rations of cheese and bread.

6. Rubtsovsk, Siberia

On Sunday, Grandmother and Esther walk 12 miles to the *baracholka,* or market square, to barter for food. They trade Raya's silk slip, Samuel's silk shirt, and Grandmother's black silk umbrella for a piece of meat, a bag of flour, and sunflower seeds. At sundown, they begin the long walk back.

7. Barracks outside Rubtsovsk, Siberia

The overseer announces that, as of July 30, 1941, Russia and Poland granted amnesty to Polish deportees. The Rudomins are free to leave the old school and move to the village.

A few kilometers from Rubtsovsk, the Rudomins share bleak barracks and sleep on plank beds topped with straw pads. Raya is assigned a bakery job; Samuel works as a bookkeeper on a construction project. Grandmother and Esther are excused from work.

8. Rubtsovsk, Siberia

On a Sunday, the Rudomins locate lodging in a log hut, which they share with Nina and Nikita Alexandrovich. In October, the first snow falls. Esther enrolls at the white clapboard school and is placed in the fifth grade. She is slow to progress because the teacher and students resent her more affluent background. She eventually masters the Russian language, which uses the Cyrillic alphabet.

The Rudomins, still recovering from the news of Grandfather Solomon's death in a labor camp, once again are forced to seek a new home. They locate a barren, dirt-floored hut. To make it liveable, they patch the walls with manure, dig a root cellar, and establish a vegetable garden. Officials force them to share their space with "Vanya the bum," a destitute Ukrainian shoemaker whose leg was amputated in a Siberian prison camp. Vanya turns out to be kind, but he stays only a short time.

Esther is devastated after Samuel is sent to a labor force on the front lines. Because of crop failure, the second winter is even more arduous than the first. To help out, Esther steals coal and wood shavings and knits sweaters out of thread raveled from discarded clothing.

In her spare time, Esther seeks warmth at the local library, where she loses herself in books. She prepares for the annual August declamation contest by memorizing a segment from Alexander Pushkin's *Eugene Onegin*. Because she arrives at the contest barefooted and dusty, the teacher forces her to run home for her mother's felt shoes; as a result of the delay, she loses the competition. The incident causes Esther to vow never to be humiliated again for being poor. To earn extra money, she trades goods at the market in Rubtsovsk.

The war ends. Esther asks for permission to remain for the next contest, but her mother insists on leaving on the first available train. On March 15, 1946, the family boards a cattle car on a train bound for Poland.

9. Ural Mountains in Russia

While admiring the view during a brief stop, Esther is nearly left behind at the platform. At the last minute a fellow passenger pulls her aboard.

10. Moscow, Russia

Esther anticipates sightseeing in Moscow, but after she bumps into a stove, the painful burn on her hand sidelines her plans.

11. Polish border

Anti-Semitic screams from onlookers mar Esther's excitement about returning home to Vilna. Still, her family rejoices at returning to their home, although it had been rifled by the secret police.

12. Lódz, Poland

In Lódz, Esther and her mother and grandmother rejoin Samuel.

13. Stockholm, Sweden

A year after her return, Esther and her parents move to Stockholm, Sweden.

14. New York City, New York

Esther immigrates to New York to live with her uncle. Later, her parents join her, but Grandmother Rudomin chooses to go to Israel. Esther graduates from high school, attends Hunter College, and marries a concert pianist. She ultimately becomes a successful author of children's and craft books.

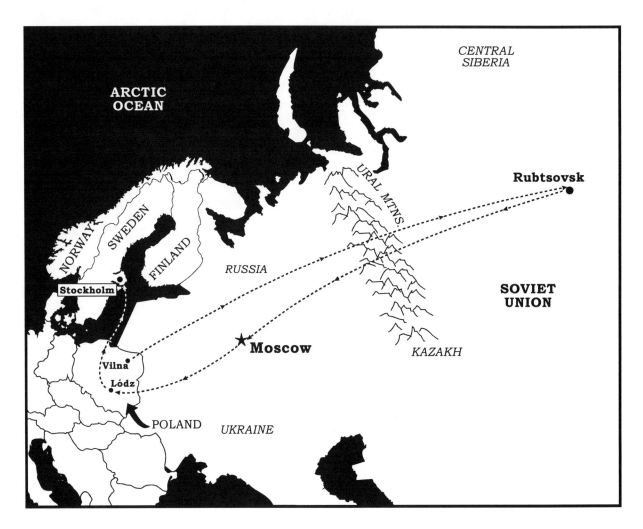

Farewell to Manzanar

BY JEANNE WAKATSUKI HOUSTON AND JAMES D. HOUSTON

Autobiographical memoir, 1973

Geographical Summary: *Farewell to Manzanar,* which opens with a timeline of historical background, details Jeanne Wakatsuki Houston's account of her family's incarceration during World War II. Her Japanese father is confined in North Dakota, leaving Woody, her older brother, with the task of helping the family move from Terminal Island to the Japanese internment camp at Manzanar, on the rim of the Mojave Desert and Mt. Whitney near Lone Pine, California. Their overland route takes them far from the ocean, where the Wakatsukis made their living on a fishing boat.

Beginning with her childhood view of privation and concluding with her return to Manzanar in adulthood, Jeanne and her husband James recall the misery and outrage of Asian-American citizens deprived of constitutional rights because of their race. Jeanne initiates the book by escorting her children from their home in Santa Cruz, California, in a southeastern loop that brings them back to Manzanar. On the completion of her pilgrimage, she exorcises the lingering suspicion that haunts 20 years of adulthood and rekindles her pride in her father's resilience.

The Houstons' vivid description of life in substandard housing in the Mojave Desert captures much of the hardship that so austere a landscape forces on its unwilling residents. Blasted with gritty gales and nighttime freezing temperatures, internees daily weathered physical and spiritual onslaughts. Their view of Mt. Whitney to the west broke the monotony of salt flats, creosote bushes, and burroweed that surrounded them. So desolate a setting, coupled with the blow to Japanese-American pride in U.S. citizenship and the worry over lost homes and businesses and sons fighting in the war, threatened many a patriarch besides Ko Wakatsuki and wearied a host of wives and children who hung on to the hope that the war would end soon and life would return to normal.

By the time that the Wakatsukis return west across the desert in their new car, they have traversed a world of difference between concentration camp and freedom. Jeanne's adolescent struggles with school and social challenge in Cabrillo Homes delineates the postwar readjustment for people with wartime experiences. Her decision to challenge her father's stereotyped notion of maidenly behavior, to pursue the American ideal of majorette and beauty queen, and to marry a Caucasian husband indicate that life at Manzanar taught her to value both experience and ambition and to heed inner wisdom.

Further Reading

Bosworth, Allan R. *America's Concentration Camps.* New York: W. W. Norton, 1967.

Cohen, Elie. *Human Behavior in the Concentration Camp.* Westport, CT: Greenwood Press, 1984.

Daniels, Roger. *The Decision to Relocate the Japanese Americans.* Melbourne, FL: Krieger, 1986.

Gesensway, Deborah, and Mindy Roseman. *Beyond Words: Images from America's Concentration Camps.* Ithaca, NY: Cornell University Press, 1987.

Humanaka, Sheila. *The Journey: Japanese Americans, Racism and Renewal.* New York: Orchard Books/Franklin Watts, 1990.

Knaefler, Tomi K. *Our House Divided: Seven Japanese American Families in World War Two.* Honolulu: University of Hawaii Press, 1991.

Robinson, Mei Li. *Farewell to Manzanar Notes.* Lincoln, NE: Cliffs Notes, 1994.

Tajiri, Vincent, ed. *Through Innocent Eyes: Teen-agers' Impressions of World War II Internment Camp Life.* Los Angeles, CA: Keiro Services, 1990.

Weglyn, Michi. *Years of Infamy: The Untold Story of America's Concentration Camps.* New York: William Morrow, 1978.

Detailed Itinerary

1. Long Beach, California
On Sunday, December 7, 1941, at the harbor in Long Beach in south-central California, the eight members of the Wakatsuki family are startled by the news that Japan has attacked Pearl Harbor, Hawaii. The war with Japan forces Asian-Americans from mainstrain American life and costs many of them their savings, homes, businesses, and self-esteem.

2. Terminal Island, California
While the Wakatsuki family stays at brother Woody's place on Terminal Island in San Pedro Bay, south of Los Angeles, California, Papa is arrested. On the basis of old spy photographs, he is accused of supplying oil to Japanese submarines and is incarcerated in a North Dakota prison. To be closer to her work, Mama, the family breadwinner, moves the children from Ocean Park to a rough Japanese neighborhood on Terminal Island near the Long Beach Naval Station.

3. Boyle Heights, Los Angeles, California
With the help of the American Friends Service (Quakers), the Wakatsukis move to a second Oriental ghetto in Los Angeles.

4. Fort Lincoln, Bismarck, North Dakota
The family receives a letter from Papa. He is imprisoned in an all-male camp for enemy aliens in Bismarck, North Dakota, near the U.S. northern border with Canada.

5. Manzanar, Owens Valley, California
President Franklin D. Roosevelt issues Executive Order 9066, which orders Japanese-Americans to abandon their homes and businesses and go to live in 10 internment camps, one of which, Manzanar, consists of makeshift barracks a few miles out of Lone Pine in Owens Valley, California. The Wakatsuki family stores their furniture and joins 10,000 other internees on an exodus to Manzanar. They are resettled in sight of Mt. Whitney on the edge of the Mojave Desert. Their crowded, poorly insulated rooms in Block 16 leak air and dust. The compound is guarded by armed sentries who aim inward at the inmates, and the family must deal with spoiled

food, biting wind, diarrhea, lack of privacy, and endless red tape. Woody continues as head of the family until Papa returns from North Dakota in September.

6. Miya-jima, Japan (now called Itsuku-shima)

In a flashback, the narrator recounts Papa's departure from the island of Miya-jima in southwestern Japan in 1904. A member of the prestigious samurai, or warrior, class, he had dropped out of school at age 17 to make a better life for himself rather than endure the genteel poverty suffered by his father, who ran a teahouse.

7. University of Idaho in Moscow, Idaho

Papa is a successful law student at the University of Idaho, where he meets Mama, a Hawaiian native born to Japanese settlers from Niigata, a city in north-central Japan.

8. Salem, Oregon

Without finishing law school, Papa elopes with Mama west to Salem, Oregon, near the Pacific coast.

9. Watsonville, California

A few years before Jeanne is born, Papa tends a 22-acre farm near Watsonville, a coastal town in central California.

10. Inglewood, California

The Depression ends Papa's hopes of prosperity. The family moves to Inglewood, outside Los Angeles.

11. Santa Monica, California

Giving up farming, Papa establishes a fishing business out of Santa Monica until his arrest.

12. Fort Lincoln, North Dakota

While imprisoned in North Dakota, Papa interviews other Japanese internees.

13. Manzanar, California

Returned to his family in a state of trauma, Papa drinks too much home-brewed wine and becomes an angry, bitter recluse and wife abuser. Jeanne avoids family disorder by hiding under the bed, attending Catholic catechism classes, playing hopscotch, and studying ballet.

In spring 1943, the Wakatsuki family moves to Block 28, where adjacent pear trees bring them hope. Papa takes up gardening. Jeanne enjoys a normal school experience, including glee club and yearbook. Mama does settlement work and also works as a dietician.

14. Hiroshima, Japan

On August 6, 1945, American planes drop an atomic bomb on Hiroshima, Japan. The war ends with the surrender of the Japanese emperor to American forces.

15. Ka-ke, Japan

In April 1946, Woody, bearing bags of sugar as a gift, visits his father's family in Ka-ke, west of Hiroshima.

16. Long Beach, California

Papa buys a car and transports his clan 225 miles across the Mojave Desert back to Long Beach. With additional help from the American Friends Service, the Wakatsukis move to Cabrillo Homes, a flimsy housing project in west Long Beach. Mama finds work in a fish cannery, but Papa's role shrinks as Woody increasingly becomes the leader of the family.

17. Santa Clara Valley, outside San Jose, California

In 1951, the family moves to a strawberry farm in the Santa Clara Valley in west-central California. Jeanne, who strives to live a normal American life, rebels against Papa's tyranny after she is elected homecoming queen. She refuses to conform to his notions of the ideal Japanese girl and eventually becomes the first of her familiy to finish college and marry a Caucasian.

18. Santa Cruz, California

In April 1972, some 30 years after her family's humiliating incarceration, Jeanne Houston feels compelled to return to Manzanar to expunge her bitter memories of internment.

19. Manzanar, California

Jeanne, her husband James, and their three children travel from their home in Santa Cruz to Lone Pine and on to the tumbledown remains of Manzanar, which include a flagpole base, tombstones, and a water spigot. Her memories return to her cocky, self-important father and his defiance of the forces that reduced the family to imprisonment.

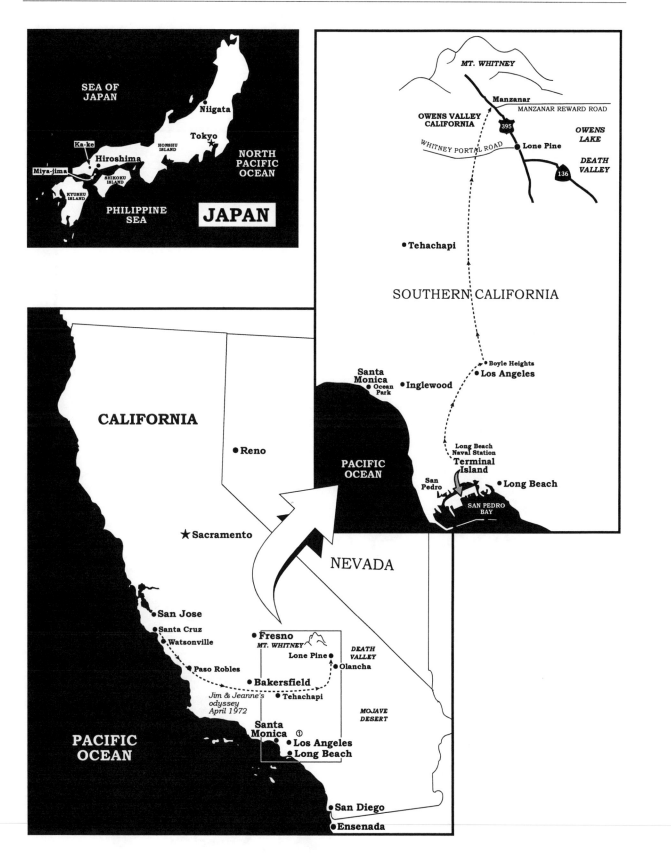

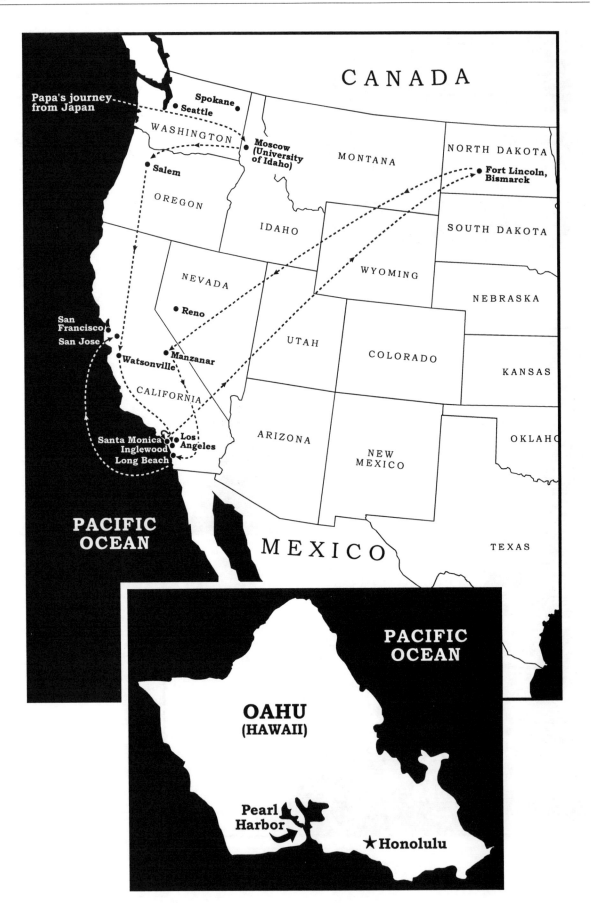

Hiroshima

BY JOHN HERSEY

Investigative nonfiction, 1985

Geographical Summary: Centering on six unrelated survivors of World War II, *Hiroshima* presents a journalist's meticulous account of the first use of the atomic bomb. It decribes in loose vignettes the devastation of total war—war against civilians as well as combatants. The central characters—a personnel clerk at the tin works, a physician, a surgeon, a widow, a German Jesuit priest, and a Methodist minister—figure in an hour-by-hour re-creation of what people were doing before and immediately after the blast, and how the cataclysm interwove their fates and affected their lives and those of their families in later years. Hersey's intense study reveals much about the organization and layout of Hiroshima over six tidal rivers, as well as the city's civil defense system. The heat, rain, radiation, and rising tide that result from the bomb's impact all add to the destruction. In its updated version, *Hiroshima* characterizes the fortunes of the same six civilians 40 years later and the social stigmas that have been attached to survivors, three of whom have traveled to the United States and Europe as testimony to their resilience.

Hersey does a thorough job of detailing the annihilation of Hiroshima, an industrial and trade center for the Chugoku region of Japan and the capital of Hiroshima prefecture. Founded in 1593, the city, whose name translates as "broad island," lies on the land and water routes joining the islands of Kyushu and Honshu. Prospering under the altruism and promotion of the Asano dynasty from 1603 to 1867, Hiroshima was Japan's seventh largest metropolis at the beginning of World War II. As a result of the atomic bomb (known as "Little Boy") that was launched from the B-29 bomber *Enola Gay* on August 6, 1945, all but 2 percent of Hiroshima's buildings were destroyed. More than 71,000 people died instantly, with 200,000 more succumbing by 1950 from injuries and radiation poisoning. Later decades brought more illness and death from pernicious anemia, leukemia, and atrophied organs. Today, Peace Memorial Park, dedicated to the victims of Hiroshima, draws visitors, historians, and foreign emissaries, who mourn the victims of the bomb and marvel at the resilience of a city that refused to die.

Further Reading

Barker, Rodney. *The Hiroshima Maidens.* New York: Penguin Books, 1985.

Hachiya, Michihiko. *Hiroshima Diary.* Chapel Hill, NC: University of North Carolina Press, 1969.

Harper, Stephen. *Miracle of Deliverance: The Case of the Bombings of Hiroshima and Nagasaki.* New York: Scarborough House, 1986.

Kurzman, D. *Day of the Bomb: Countdown to Hiroshima.* New York: McGraw-Hill, 1987.

MacDonald, Donald. *A Geography of Modern Japan.* New York: State Mutual Book and Periodical Service, 1987.

Nakazawa, Keiji. *Barefoot Gen.* Philadelphia: New Society Publications, 1988.

Thomas, Gord, and Max Morgan Witts. *Enola Gay.* New York: Scarborough House, 1977.

Detailed Itinerary

1. Hiroshima on the Kyo River, Honshu, Japan

On Monday, August 6, 1945, at 8:15 A.M., an atomic bomb explodes above the city of Hiroshima on the southwestern end of the island of Honshu, Japan. Six survivors cope with the aftermath, including the death and disfigurement of citizens and the destruction of buildings. Reverend Kiyoshi Tanimoto, American-trained pastor of the Hiroshima Methodist Church, organizes an air-raid defense. Dr. Masakazu Fujii and the private hospital he owns are catapulted into the Kyo River on the north end of the city. Father Wilhelm Kleinsorge is lying on his cot on the top floor of a mission house when the bomb explodes. At the Red Cross Hospital, south of the epicenter, Dr. Terufumi Sasaki begins treating the injured. Miss Toshiko Sasaki, an office worker, is engulfed in the rubble of falling shelves, her left leg twisted and fractured.

2. Asano Park, Hiroshima

Despite the intense heat, Mrs. Nakamura dresses her children in warm clothes and sets out for Asano Park, the nearest evacuation shelter, which is northeast of the epicenter, on the west bank of the Kyobashi River.

3. East Parade Ground, Hiroshima

Father Kleinsorge carries a victim toward the East Parade Ground, beyond the Kyobashi River's east bank. Moving against the flow of stunned refugees, Rev. Tanimoto progresses toward the city center.

4. Asano Park, Hiroshima

After swimming the Ota River, the main confluence that splits into six tributaries north of the heart of Hiroshima, Rev. Tanimoto begins aiding victims. Using a punt, he ferries the wounded away from the fire that the bomb ignited.

In the eastern tributary, Dr. Fujii clings to a stone to escape drowning, then wades toward Asano Park along with a host of survivors.

5. Hiroshima, Japan

Father Kleinsorge joins Rev. Tanimoto in returning to the center of town for supplies. A naval launch cruises Hiroshima's rivers to announce that a hospital ship is coming to aid the injured.

6. Asano Park, Hiroshima

Rev. Tanimoto continues rescuing people from the rising tide. By dawn, he discovers that many have drowned. Early on August 7, 1945, a radio broadcast by Japanese authorities announces that an American plane dropped a bomb more powerful than 20,000 tons of TNT on the city.

7. East Parade Ground, Hiroshima

Rev. Tanimoto goes to the East Parade Ground to get more medical aid.

8. Asano Park, Hiroshima

Failing to find a doctor, Rev. Tanimoto returns with food. Father Kleinsorge, lacking medicine and bandages, continues distributing water.

9. Hiroshima, Japan

On his way to the novitiate, Father Kleinsorge observes the extent of damage to the city. On Wednesday morning, men carry Miss Sasaki to an aid station at the tin works.

10. Ninoshima, Hiroshima

Miss Sasaki is transferred to a military hospital on the island of Ninoshima, northwest of the epicenter of the blast.

11. Mukaihara district 30 miles northeast of Hiroshima, Japan

On Wednesday, Dr. Sasaki, wearied by the stream of people seeking aid at the Red Cross Hospital and concerned about his mother, takes a train to her house in the Mukaihara district and sleeps 17 hours.

12. Nagasaki, Japan

On Thursday, August 9, 1945, radio reports indicate that American planes have dropped an atomic bomb on Nagasaki on the island of Kyushu, southwest of Hiroshima.

13. Fukawa, Japan

On Friday, Father Cieslik visits Dr. Fujii in the mountain village of Fukawa.

14. Hiroshima, Japan

Rev. Tanimoto returns to his church on Saturday to recover records and other items. He goes to a shelter to comfort a bomb victim, who dies while Rev. Tanimoto reads a psalm.

15. Hatsukaichi, Japan

Evacuated southwest from Hiroshima, Miss Sasaki is taken to the Goddess of Mercy Primary School in Hatsukaichi, where help arrives from Kobe, a sizeable seaport east of Hiroshima.

16. Red Cross Hospital, Hiroshima

As physicists arrive to study the bomb's effects, Dr. Sasaki returns to the Red Cross Hospital, where corpses are being cremated. On August 15, 1945, for the first time in history, the Emperor Hirohito addresses his subjects by radio to announce Japan's defeat. On September 9, Miss Sasaki is moved to the Red Cross Hospital, where Dr. Sasaki treats her.

17. Fukawa, Japan

On September 17, 1945, Dr. Fujii witnesses a typhoon, which drowns many medical investigators and patients. Survivors accuse Americans of dropping poison on them.

18. Epicenter, Hiroshima, Japan

Japanese physicists examine the epicenter, southwest of the juncture of the Honkawa and Motoyasu rivers, and decide that citizens may safely return to the city.

19. Tokyo, Japan

Father Kleinsorge, a victim of radiation poisoning, is transferred to Tokyo on the east end of the island of Honshu, where doctors debate his recurring anemia.

20. Kaitaichi, Hiroshima

Dr. Fujii purchases a private clinic in Kaitaichi, slightly north of the Red Cross Hospital.

21. Red Cross Hospital, Hiroshima

Throughout October and November, Dr. Sasaki treats Miss Sasaki's damaged leg. She is too ill to respond to visits from a young man and grows increasingly bitter and self-pitying as a result of her maimed leg.

22. Tokyo, Japan

In December, Father Kleinsorge is discharged from the hospital.

23. City Hall, Hiroshima

As Hiroshima rebounds from the multiple trauma of impact, fire, and radiation poisoning, the city receives a new municipal government. Refugees move into makeshift barracks and shanties. The total number of recovered corpses climbs to 100,000.

24. Red Cross Hospital, Hiroshima

On a visit to Miss Sasaki, Father Kleinsorge tries to explain to her why God allows suffering.

25. Koi, Japan

At the end of April, Miss Sasaki, still nervous and sore, leaves the hospital and returns home to Koi, a rural area northwest of Hiroshima.

26. Red Cross Hospital, Hiroshima

The Red Cross Hospital is repaired and restaffed. Dr. Sasaki, a widower, remarries.

27. Nobori-cho, Hiroshima

Mrs. Nakamura opens a street shop at her old hut in Nobori-cho, east of the epicenter on the Kyobashi River. In 1951, she moves into housing built by an American Quaker philanthropist and gets a job at Suyama Chemical wrapping mothballs. In 1966, she retires and takes up folk dancing.

28. University of Hiroshima, Hiroshima, Japan

Dr. Sasaki works 10 years to complete his doctorate.

29. Mukaihara district, Japan

In 1954, Dr. Sasaki builds a clinic in the Mukaihara district, one hour by train from Hiroshima. His diseased lung is removed in 1963. Following his second wife's death in 1972, he invests in a successful geriatric clinic and bathhouse.

30. Tokyo, Japan

Father Kleinsorge overextends his diminished energies and is again hospitalized and force-fed extra nutrients to combat anemia.

31. Misasa, Hiroshima

In 1948, Father Kleinsorge serves as priest of a church north of the city center in Misasa. Fully accustomed to living among Asians, he seeks Japanese citizenship and assumes the name Father Makoto Takakura. He organizes Bible study classes for the Hiroshima Maidens, a group of young victims disfigured by keloid scar tissue who are flown to New York City for reconstructive surgery. He presides over the funeral of one of the Maidens, who dies in surgery at Mount Sinai Hospital.

32. Red Cross Hospital, Hiroshima

Following a year's hospitalization at the Red Cross Hospital, in 1961, Father Takakura retires.

33. Mukaihara, Japan

After a lengthy illness, Father Takakura, lovingly cared for by his servant, dies on November 19, 1977.

34. Koi, Japan

In 1946, Miss Sasaki converts to Catholicism and takes a position at the Garden of Light orphanage.

35. Oita University and Beppu, Kyushu, Japan

Miss Sasaki earns a teaching degree from Oita University and teaches at the White Chrysanthemum Orphanage at Beppu, Kyushu, southwest of Hiroshima.

36. Misasa, Hiroshima

In 1954, Miss Sasaki enters a French convent; three years later, she is renamed Sister Dominique.

37. Kurosaki, Kyushu, Japan

Sister Dominique operates the Garden of St. Joseph, a retirement home, until she retires in 1977. The next year, she tours Europe.

38. Tokyo, Japan

In 1980, Sister Dominique is honored at the society's headquarters in Tokyo.

39. Kaitaichi, Hiroshima

Three years after the atomic blast, Dr. Fujii builds a new medical clinic south of the center of Hiroshima.

40. New York City, New York, United States

In 1956, Dr. Fujii accompanies the Hiroshima Maidens on a flight to Mount Sinai Hospital.

41. Hiroshima, Japan

To his wife's dismay, in 1963, Dr. Fujii, enthusiastically pro-Western, builds an American-style house. On New Year's Eve, he is permanently disabled by gas inhalation. He is bedridden for 10 years and dies on January 11, 1973. An autopsy reveals serious internal disorders, including brain atrophy, that relate directly to the effects of radiation on soft tissue.

42. San Francisco, California; Weehawken, New Jersey, United States

At the October 1948 invitation of Reverend Marvin Green, a classmate of Rev. Tanimoto who lives in Weehawken, New Jersey, Rev. Tanimoto sets out on the U.S.S. *Gordon* to visit 256 United States churches to solicit funds for peace. His first stop is San Francisco.

43. New York City, New York, United States

On March 5, 1949, Norman Cousins publishes Rev. Tanimoto's peacer-center memorandum in *Saturday Review*, and endorses the idea of creating an international peace consortium in Hiroshima.

44. Peace Memorial Park, Hiroshima

On August 6, 1949, the Japanese Diet establishes a commemorative park and a memorial to honor the dead. Despite rejection by President Harry S. Truman, General Douglas MacArthur, and Mayor Hamai, Rev. Tanimoto sets up a peace initiative in Hiroshima.

45. Senate, Washington, D.C., United States

On a United States tour in the summer of 1950, Rev. Tanimoto becomes the first Japanese minister to deliver the opening prayer for a session of the Senate.

46. Iwakuni Airport, Hiroshima

On May 5, 1955, Rev. Tanimoto departs from the Hiroshima airfield to accompany the Hiroshima Maidens to the United States for intense medical treatment arranged by Norman Cousins and other humanitarians.

47. Los Angeles, California, United States

On May 11, 1955, Rev. Tanimoto is featured on the television show *This Is Your Life*, where he meets the co-pilot of the *Enola Gay*, the plane that dropped the atomic bomb on Hiroshima.

48. Hiroshima, Japan

After many more trips to support peace, Rev. Tanimoto retires in 1982.

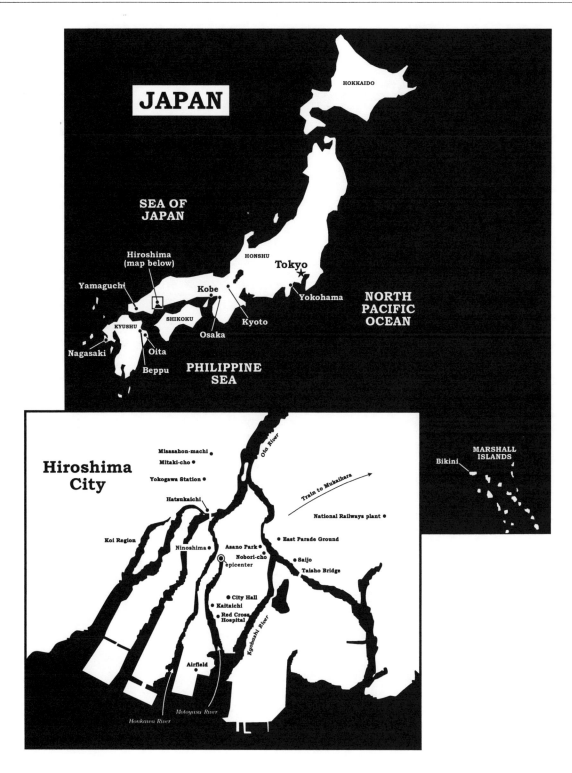

I Heard the Owl Call My Name

BY MARGARET CRAVEN

Young adult novel, 1973

Geographical Summary: In the mid-1960s, 27-year-old Mark Brian, an Anglican ordinand, serves an apprentice priesthood among the isolated band of Kwacutal of the Kwakiutl tribe at Kingcome, a small fishing village north of Vancouver Island on an inlet of the British Columbian mainland. On his initial voyage to Kwakiutl territory, he learns that Kingcome can be reached from Vancouver by a two-day journey northwest through the Georgia and Johnstone straits and east upriver into Kingcome Inlet in British Columbia. Through shared hardships and loving service to neighboring logging camps, float houses, and villages, the young priest earns the respect of his parishioners, who suffer from the erosion of Indian culture by white lifestyles, which influence natives to move to cities on Vancouver Island.

Realizing that he is dying of cancer and choosing to remain in Kingcome, Mark takes courage from local friendships. Ironically, he dies in an accident before the malignancy kills him. His friend Jim survives and, with Peter the wood-carver, honors Mark's role in Kingcome village life.

Craven's description of the waterway threading past Vancouver, British Columbia, and among Kwakiutl villages depicts the paradox of the beauty and the hardship of life on a remote Pacific coast. A rugged province of western Canada carved by glaciers during the Pleistocene age, British Columbia lies in the Coast Mountain chain and contains a segment of the Cascade Mountains north of the U.S. border. Especially during frequent fogs and rainstorms, the numerous inlets and islets present a challenge to the operators of small fishing, mail, and cargo vessels traveling north from Vancouver. For native residents, prosperity depends on the annual run of salmon, halibut, herring, pilchard, and cod and a plentiful supply of game animals, especially bear, moose, deer, mountain goat, and caribou. Trade items, such as the pelts of wolf, fox, mink, and wolverine, along with salt fish, lumber, and minerals, enrich this portion of Pacific coastline, the ancestral home of the Kwakiutl.

Further Reading

Bemister, Margaret. *Thirty Indian Legends of Canada.* Vancouver, BC: Douglas & McIntyre, 1973.

Crump, Donald J., ed. *Canada's Wilderness Lands.* Washington, DC: National Geographic Society, 1982.

Jonaitis, Aldona, ed. *Chiefly Feasts: The Enduring Kwakiutl Potlatch.* Seattle, WA: University of Washington Press, 1991.

Neering, Rosemary. *The Coast of British Columbia.* Bothell, WA: Alaska Northwest Books, 1990.

Rickman, David. *Northwest Coast Indians.* New York: Dover, 1984.

Robinson, J. Lewis, ed. *British Columbia*. Ann Arbor, MI: Books on Demand UMI, 1992.

Waldman, Carl. *Atlas of the North American Indian*. New York: Facts on File, 1985.

Detailed Itinerary

1. From the Powell River north up the Georgia and Johnstone straits to Kingcome, British Columbia

Unaware that he has fewer than two years to live, Mark Brian, an Anglican vicar, accepts the bishop's offer of a post in Kingcome, a remote coastal village that maintains a tenuous tie with the outside world through a temperamental diesel launch. Caleb, a retired minister living on Powell River, prepares him to live among the native Kwakiutl. Mark meets Jim Wallace, a shy Indian his own age, who is returning to Kingcome after a year's work in a mill town. Jim escorts Mark into the Georgia Strait, the tortuous waterway leading past Lund, Cortes, Redonda Island, Yuculta Rapids, Shoal Bay, Ghost Island, Gilford Island, Cramer Pass, and Pamphrey's Pass, and, at last, arriving in Kingcome.

2. Shoal Bay, British Columbia

At dark, Jim and Mark stop for the night at Shoal Bay and prepare supper.

3. Cramer Pass, British Columbia

After passing a school of porpoise, the launch makes its way to the last point of contact with the outside world, where Jim and Mark stop for oil and water, buy groceries, and meet the oil agent and his wife, who passes along a mud-stained cassock that Caleb left behind.

4. Kingcome, British Columbia

Maneuvering through Pamphrey's Pass into the 20-mile Kingcome Inlet, the launch glides by Calamity Bill's float house and a crag known as Whale Pass, and docks at the government float three and a half miles from Kingcome. The cliffs along the river are decorated with paintings marking the 1936 potlatch. Mark recalls what the bishop told him of the mythic foundations of the village, which lies across the river from Whoop-Szo, the Noisy Mountain, which looms from the north shore. The two men spend the night and awaken early to load a new pump organ on canoes and to launch a smaller boat to carry them past the 50-foot "Welcome" totem of the village.

At the Kwakiutl village, Mark finds the church and the vicarage in a wretched state of repair. He is immediately needed to bury a small boy who drowned 10 days earlier and whose body must remain above ground until Constable Pearson of the Royal Canadian Mounted Police (RCMP) can complete the investigation of his death. Outside the vicarage, an old Kwakiutl woman mourns loudly for the boy. After Mark conducts the service, he departs to let the natives complete the rite in their own style. He then receives a letter from the bishop promising a prefabricated home, which Mark must erect himself.

5. Clearwater, British Columbia

In September, at the height of salmon season, Mark and Jim go northeast upriver by canoe to Clearwater at the foot of Che-kwa-lá Falls, above which tribe members join in a traditional smoking of fish. Jim explains why he expects to marry Keetah.

6. Mount Quanade, British Columbia

In October, Mark joins a party of hunters, who trail a bear upriver on Mount Quanade. Mark recognizes how valuable Jim's friendship has become in light of the sometimes bewildering lifestyle, language, and customs of the Kwakiutl.

7. Alert Bay, British Columbia

One foggy November night, Mark and Jim take a boy ill with appendicitis by canoe west across Queen Charlotte Strait to Alert Bay on the east coast of Vancouver Island. They return to find soup and homemade bread left them by Marta, the village wise woman.

8. Kingcome, British Columbia

In December, Mark becomes exhausted from trying to maintain the boat and the balky generator that lights the church and from delivering donated Christmas gifts to distant logging camps and float houses. He takes comfort in a growing relationship with the villagers and acquiesces to God's call.

9. Gilford Island, British Columbia

In January, during clamming season, Mark counsels Keetah about her distress at her sister's unmarried state and the fact that if she marries the white man with whom she is in love, she will no longer belong in Kingcome. Mark goes to Gilford to conduct Evensong before a ceremonial dance and potlatch, a festive banquet and dance, and strains to catch sight of the man from the forestry boat who has promised to marry Keetah's sister.

10. Kingcome, British Columbia

Mark returns from taking a sick child from Turnour Island to the hospital in Alert Bay to find that the man Keetah's sister plans to marry has tricked a villager into selling him a valuable mask by getting him drunk. The older family members, shamed by the deception, leave Kingcome for a deserted village.

11. Alert Bay, British Columbia

To save the girl from abuse and promiscuity, Mark goes to the government school at Alert Bay to arrange for her education. He tells the RCMP officer about Keetah's sister's departure with the white man.

12. Kingcome, British Columbia

The RCMP officer comes to the village in March to report to Mark that Keetah's sister was abandoned in Vancouver by the man she was to marry. She prostituted herself for three months and died of a drug overdose, possibly a suicide. In June, Mark promises a woman dying in childbirth that he will help educate her oldest son, Gordon, who attends school in Alert Bay. The whole village joins in the burial service, sings hymns, and drops shovelfuls of dirt on the coffin.

To reward Mark for his kindnesses to the Kwakiutl village, village men help him erect a new vicarage. During the interim, he resides with Marta. In July, the bishop, Caleb, and six city rectors visit Kingcome. In August, an insensitive English anthropologist arrives for a short, unpleasant stay, among other insults blatantly mispronouncing *Kwakiutl*. She regrets that Christianity has spoiled the native culture.

13. Vancouver, British Columbia

Late in the summer, Mark and Jim journey southeast through the straits to Vancouver, capital of British Columbia, to obtain an annual boat overhaul. They escort Gordon and three other boys to school at Alert Bay. Mark's twin sister from Victoria, in the south end of Vancouver Island, meets him across the strait in Vancouver.

14. Kingcome, British Columbia

On his return north to Kingcome via Broken Island and Chatham Sound, Mark finds the village at peace, even though alcohol is now available to Indians. He meets with elders who are concerned about their traditional burial ground, which has fallen into decay. He supervises the gathering of bones and coffins and presides over a mass burial. At Christmas, Gordon returns to Kingcome in white shirt and tie, dismaying the tribe with his outsider's ways. When he departs, he takes Keetah with him. Mark insists that Gordon will be a good representative of the Kwakiutl.

15. Whale Pass, British Columbia

In February during clamming season, Mark finds Calamity Bill near death from a fall, which has broken his hip and left him too helpless to feed the fire or cook. Mark remains to comfort his last hours and to arrange for his cremation and dispersal at the point on Knight Inlet that Calamity marked on his map.

16. Kingcome, British Columbia

In March, Keetah, pregnant with Gordon's child, returns from Alert Bay to Gilford Island and Kingcome. She understands that she must live apart from Gordon, who belongs in the white world. Mark hopes that she will someday replace Marta as village wise woman. Jim indicates that he still plans to marry Keetah and raise the child as his own.

Late that month, Mark shows signs of approaching death, which the bishop acknowledges will come soon. After scattering Calamity Bill's ashes, Mark hears the owl call his name, an indication that he will die soon. The bishop promises to care for Mark at the end of his sojourn in Kingcome.

Keetah asks Mark to remain at Kingcome rather than return to the bishop. Mark encourages Jim to be a good husband to her and to treat her with respect. When Jim and Mark depart on an errand, a rockslide buries their boat. Jim survives and grieves for his dead friend. Marta pronounces the benediction on Mark's departing spirit.

I Know Why the Caged Bird Sings

BY MAYA ANGELOU

Autobiography, 1970

Geographical Summary: In this spirited autobiography, Maya Angelou contrasts her memories of the black section of rural Stamps on the Arkansas-Texas border with the fast and dangerous world of St. Louis, Missouri. In an exciting urban setting, she learns to love and admire her mother, Vivian Baxter Johnson, a cardsharp and occasional nurse whom Maya's brother calls "Mother Dear."

After Vivian's live-in lover is murdered for raping Maya, she and her unwilling brother are shipped by train back to Stamps to their grandmother's care. At the end of eighth grade, Maya and Grandmother "Mama" Henderson travel by train to join Vivian in Los Angeles. Grandmother departs, leaving Maya with her mother and stepfather through two more moves, from Los Angeles to Oakland to San Francisco. Maya goes to southern California to vacation with her father, Bailey Johnson, and his girlfriend, who live in a trailer park. Near the end of her high school years, Maya travels southeast with Bailey on a brief jaunt to Ensenada, Mexico, where the prostitutes and good timers in Mexico admires her savvy, flamboyant father. Maya drives him to Calexico on the U.S. side after he gets drunk in a cantina. For a month, Maya hides out in a junkyard in an unnamed town in southern California before flying back home to Vivian. In San Francisco, Maya reaches for self-esteem by forcing city transit officials to give her a job as streetcar conductor. In mid-adolescence, she gives birth to a son, embraces womanhood, and makes peace with herself.

The contrast of settings in this autobiography delineate important trends in the American black experience. In Stamps, Maya and her brother live in a repressive southern atmosphere that reflects plantation conditions, with its limited educational opportunities and cruelties toward blacks. The children's sojourn in St. Louis takes them out of this severe segregation to a controlled political precinct where Grandmother Baxter—her skin more white than black—rules the community and where the Baxter uncles exact a brutal revenge against the man who rapes Maya. After the children's return to Stamps, the move to California introduces a new set of racial values—the denigration of Japanese-Americans, who suffer the ill will of racists who blame them for the bombing of Pearl Harbor.

The 1979 CBS television version, filmed in Vicksburg, Mississippi, stars Esther Rolle as Mama Henderson, Diahann Carroll as Vivian Baxter Johnson, Ruby Dee as Grandmother Baxter, and Constance Good as Maya. Critics lauded the film's warmth and humanity and its willingness to portray unpleasant truths, particularly child abuse. However, the film covers only the early portion of the novel and ends with Maya's graduation from eighth grade, thus omitting the car trip to Mexico, the idyll with the teenage gang, and the birth of Maya's baby boy.

Further Reading

Angelou, Maya. Interview by Bill Moyers for Learning, Inc. *Creativity*, WNET-Public Broadcasting System, 1982.

————. "Why I Moved Back to the South." *Ebony*, February 1982, 130-34.

Elliott, Jeffrey M. *Conversations with Maya Angelou*. Fairfax, CA: Virago Press, 1989.

Shuker, Nancy. *Maya Angelou*. Englewood Cliffs, NJ: Silver-Burdett, 1990.

Wilson, Charles Reagan, and William Ferris, eds. *Encyclopedia of Southern Culture*. Chapel Hill, NC: University of North Carolina Press, 1989.

Detailed Itinerary

1. Stamps, Arkansas

At the beginning of the Depression, three-year-old Marguerite "Maya" Johnson and her brother Bailey Junior, or "Ju," who is four, arrive by train in Stamps, Arkansas, just east of the Texas border near Texarkana, Texas, to live with their father's mother, Annie Henderson, and Willie, her crippled son. Under their grandmother's firm hand, the children perform store and house chores, attend lengthy services at the Colored Methodist Episcopal Church, and enroll in elementary school, where Maya escapes racism and poverty through reading.

The Johnson children, who are close, wonder about their absent parents and also ponder the racial gap that separates whites and blacks in Stamps. To weather the financial unpredictability of the Depression, their long-suffering grandmother maintains a rapport with lower-class white workers, to whom she serves lunch, but she must hide Willie in the onion bin while vigilantes search for a black suspect who "messed with a white lady."

2. Stamps, Arkansas, to St. Louis, Missouri

After four years in Arkansas, Daddy Bailey, who works as a hotel doorman and professional cook, drives south in a big De Soto and reunites with Maya and Ju. Daddy Bailey takes the children north to St. Louis, Missouri, to live with their mother, Vivian Baxter Johnson, and her parents in a big house on Caroline Street. After completing his mission, Daddy Bailey departs.

In contrast to the political maneuverings of her mother, Vivian concentrates on dancing, card playing, and partying. Her lover, Mr. Freeman, rapes Maya and warns that he will kill her brother if she tells anyone. Vivian discovers Maya in physical and emotional distress and learns the truth, and Mr. Freeman is tried in court. After Maya testifies against him, he is found guilty, but his lawyer gains his release. An informant tells Grandmother Baxter that Vivian's brothers kicked Mr. Freeman to death in the lot behind the slaughterhouse. Maya, overcome by guilt that her testimony helped convict Mr. Freeman, refuses to speak to anyone but Ju. Vivian grows discouraged with efforts to rehabilitate her daughter, and, to restore Maya's emotional health and voice, she sends the children back to their grandmother.

3. Stamps, Arkansas

Mrs. Bertha Flowers, a local aristocrat, raises Maya's self-esteem by assigning her poetic passages to memorize. No longer mute, Maya takes a job as a maid; after a temper tantrum, she is fired for breaking dishes and defying her employer.

In 1940, 12-year-old Maya graduates from the eighth grade at Lafayette County Training School with honors for high marks and perfect attendance. The commencement ceremony showcases a white politician, who dismays his black audience with condescending racist rhetoric. At the end of the humiliating speech, the class valedictorian stands and leads the singing of the Negro national anthem, "Lift Every Voice and Sing," a unifying song that restores the class's spirits.

4. Texarkana, Texas

Because Stamps' white dentist refuses to treat Maya's toothache, Grandmother Henderson reminds him that she loaned him money and gets $10 from him. Maya is proud of her feisty grandmother. They then go across the state line to a negro dentist in Texarkana.

5. Los Angeles, California

Grandmother Henderson sews new clothes for Maya's train trip to the West Coast, where she will live with her mother. Maya moves into her mother's home in Los Angeles, California. After a month, Ju joins them. Their grandmother stays with them for several months, then returns to Willie in Stamps.

6. Oakland, California

At the beginning of World War II, Vivian remarries. Her second husband, businessman Clidell Jackson, becomes a real father to the children. The family moves north to an apartment in Oakland on the California coast.

7. San Francisco, California

Settling in the Fillmore section of San Francisco, Maya learns about racial prejudice toward the Japanese. She attends George Washington High School, where she blossoms in Miss Kirwin's civics class because of her interest in current events. Because of her talent and scholarship, Maya receives a scholarship to the California Labor School to study drama and dance.

8. Southern California

Fifteen-year-old Maya takes a vacation to visit her father at the trailer park where he lives. She immediately dislikes Daddy Bailey's pretentious girlfriend Dolores, who makes life miserable with her incessant carping. The atmosphere of the trailer grows tense as the two women compete for Bailey's attention.

9. Ensenada, Mexico

Maya accompanies Daddy Bailey in his Hudson on a shopping trip southeast over the Mexican border to Ensenada. They drive to a backwater community and stop at a cantina where Bailey is well liked for his rollicking humor and generosity. He departs with a willing woman, leaving Maya to fend for herself among strangers. During their visit, he drinks too much tequila and is unable to handle the car on the return trip to southern California.

10. Calexico, California

Maya, who is too young to have a license, manages to steer the Hudson down the mountain and north to the border town of Calexico, where she causes a minor car accident. Bailey, who is fluent in Spanish, sobers up enough to settle the resulting squabble.

11. Southern California

Returned to Daddy Bailey's trailer, Maya slaps Dolores for maligning Vivian. In return, Dolores stabs Maya in the side. Maya hides in the car until Bailey comes. Angered by the flow of blood from the wound, Bailey takes Maya to friends for first aid and a bed for the night.

The next day, Maya awakens in a strange house and runs away to an unspecified town. She reads science fiction at the public library and takes refuge at a junkyard in an abandoned car, joining a band of runaways who live communally and earn money by competing in dance contests. After a month of freedom, Maya telephones her mother for plane fare back to San Francisco.

12. San Francisco, California

Because of arguments with Vivian, Ju moves to a rooming house, then makes up with his mother, who agrees that he is old enough to be on his own. Later, he joins the Merchant Marines and stays in touch with his sister through letters.

For three weeks Maya seeks a job by petitioning the transit office and making up references. She becomes San Francisco's first black streetcar conductor and distances herself from school, which no longer interests her.

Insecure with her femininity, Maya asks a neighborhood boy for sex and, after a single encounter, conceives a child. Because Vivian goes to Alaska to open a night club, Maya is able to hide her pregnancy from her family until three weeks from delivery. Two days after V-J Day, she graduates from Mission High School and confesses her plight. She gives birth to a son and, with Vivian's help, learns to enjoy motherhood.

Ishi: Last of His Tribe

BY THEODORA KROEBER

Young adult biography, 1964

Geographical Summary: *Ishi: Last of His Tribe* relates the poignant story of Ishi, a young Yahi tribesman from northern California, who survives the extinction of his culture. Following the death of six of the remaining seven Yahi (Fire People), including his mother, only Ishi remains alive to preserve their habits, language, and religion. He roams Yuna Canyon near Mount Lassen, and in 1911, after a severe clawing from a bear, he collapses near a slaughter pen in Oroville in north-central California.

The Oroville sheriff puts Ishi in jail under protective custody and locates an anthropologist who can communicate in the Yahi language. Willingly Ishi departs east to San Francisco on the northern California coast. His last five years, spent in private quarters at the Anthropological Museum of the University of California, serve as a living exhibit of Native American skills and lore and help preserve for all time the lifestyle of a tribe gone forever after the coming of gold prospectors to the Sacramento Valley. In 1916, after one brief visit to his home territory with white friends, Ishi dies of tuberculosis at the museum. The anthropologists release Ishi's spirit Yahi-style at the Pacific shore.

The setting of this story lies adjacent to gold-rush country, the ore-rich valleys and meadows of the Sacramento River basin and the peaks of the Sierra Nevada mountain range. In the two years following the discovery of gold at Sutter's mill in January 1848, an influx of settlers tripled the immigrant population. While mining peaked within four years of the first strike, the settlers spread grain fields, orchards, and vineyards over land that had once been the hunting grounds of many different tribes of Native Americans. The story of Ishi captures the despair of a single remnant of a culture supplanted by newcomers. Ishi's ability to survive in a new environment vastly different from Yahi lifestyle is a tribute to his adaptability and to the museum curators who facilitated his transition from forest Indian to city dweller.

Two films center on Ishi's experience. A 15-minute 1983 documentary from Centre Productions, titled *Ishi, the Ending People*, narrates the outlines of the Yahi's story. The second screen version, a 1992 romanticized made-for-cable television movie, is not true to the biography. However, the portrayals of the gentle, sensitive central character (played by Graham Greene, a Canadian Cree) and his anthropologist friend, Alfred Kroeber (played by Jon Voight), capture the unique friendship that eased Ishi into a technologically advanced culture while preserving his dignity and value to society.

Further Reading

Cullen, David J. *Historical Northern California: Mother Lode.* Tarzana, CA: Heritage Map Company, 1986.

Heizer, Robert F. *The Indians of California.* Berkeley, CA: University of California Press, 1962.

Heizer, Robert F., and Albert B. Elsasser. *The Natural World of the California Indians.* Berkeley, CA: University of California Press, 1980.

Kroeber, Alfred. *Native Tribes Map.* Berkeley, CA: University of California Press, 1966.

Patterson, Lotsee, and Mary Ellen Snodgrass. *Indian Terms of the Americas.* Englewood, CO: Libraries Unlimited, 1994.

Vallejo, Mariano Guadalupe. *Great Indians of California.* Santa Barbara, CA: Bellerophon Books, 1991.

Waldman, Carl. *Atlas of the North American Indian.* New York: Facts on File, 1985.

———. *Who Was Who in North American History.* New York: Facts on File, 1990.

Wolfson, Evelyn. *From Abenaki to Zuni.* New York: Walker, 1988.

Detailed Itinerary

1. Tuliyani in Yuna Canyon near Mount Lassen in California

Around 1875, seven members survive from the gradual demise of the Yahi tribe, a branch of the Yana nation that once inhabited the meadows, caves, and creek banks of the Sacramento Valley in north-central California. At their home at Tuliyani in Yuna Canyon near Waganupa (Mount Lassen), the elder uncle of 13-year-old Tehna-Ishi ("Bear Cub Boy") serves as *majapa* (spokesman). The small band of Fire People includes Ishi's widowed mother; his paternal grandparents; Tushi, his female cousin on his mother's side; and Timawi, an unrelated man from the village of Bushki at the eastern extreme of Banya Creek and south of Waganupa.

2. Black Rock in the Sacramento Valley, California

Avoiding white settlers, Ishi often creeps up Banya Creek northeast of his village to his secret overlook at Black Rock above the ridge trail, from which he observes gold seekers and waits to hear the train whistle, far below in Yuna Canyon. He allows his mind to explore dreams in hopes of spiritual guidance.

3. Tuliyani in the Sacramento Valley, California

Ishi enjoys playing with the sweet-natured Tushi and anticipates initiation rites, which will require him to construct his own sinew-strung bow and arrows. To mark the occasion, he prays at Three Knolls to the northeast and collects juniper wood for a sacred lodge fire.

4. Round Meadow in the Sacramento Valley, California

Northwest of the village across Yuna Creek at Round Meadow, Tushi and Ishi cut sedgegrass for Grandmother and play the Meadow Game.

5. Tuliyani in the Sacramento Valley, California

In fall, Ishi's tribe prepares for harvest and winter. Grandfather tells traditional tales. Uncle takes Ishi to sleep with the men in their separate dwelling, where the boy undergoes a ritual sweat bath. Grandfather narrates how gold prospectors came to Yahi country and scalped a tribe member. Winter depletes their food stock, but spring relieves their hunger with the return of the salmon.

6. Ancestor Cave in the Sacramento Valley, California

At age 16, Ishi follows his dreams by reliving memories of his father, who was killed while fighting 20 white invaders. Ishi goes alone to visit the burial site of his ancestors at a cave on Banya Creek, southeast of the village.

7. Gahma in the Sacramento Valley, California

From the cave he walks southwest down Banya Creek to Gahma, the old village where he was born and where his family saved Tushi from an attack by white settlers. Despite requests from a party of Yahi ambassadors, the white men departed with three female captives. From that time on, the Yahi concealed themselves in the brush of Yuna Canyon, where no one suspects their presence.

8. Dry Cave in the Sacramento Valley, California

Avoiding white settlers, Ishi roves northwest to Dry Cave on Yuna Creek, where 18 Yahi hunters were scalped. Nearby, a Yahi was hanged in an old oak.

9. Green Cave in the Sacramento Valley, California

Farther to the northeast, Ishi enters Green Cave, where many Yahi are buried. He offers sacred tobacco as a gesture of respect and dreams of the Outer Ocean and the Edge of the World.

10. Yuna Creek in the Sacramento Valley, California

Ishi completes his quest with a ritual sweat bath, a swim, and ritual prayers. He sets out across Round Meadow and over the creek to his village.

11. Tuliyani in the Sacramento Valley, California

The initiation ritual complete, Ishi returns to his family as an adult tribesman. The elders respect his passage and ask no questions. As his grandfather and mother smile at his accomplishment, Ishi takes his first nourishment in days—acorn mush and venison stew.

That spring, while he and Tushi are gathering bulbs and counting the beavers in the marshes, they discuss Tushi's rejection of Timawi's gift of a sweetgrass bracelet. Then a mounted white man tries to lasso Tushi. Ishi shoots the man and his horse with arrows and flees toward home. He returns to the spot to reclaim his arrows, but fails to find the one that penetrated the white man's wrist.

12. Mount Waganupa; Bushki, California

The event threatens to reveal the Indians' presence in the canyon, which they have occupied safely for seven months. To save the Yahi from white invaders, Ishi and Timawi seek new quarters for the tribe far to the northeast above Upper Meadow on Mount Waganupa among free-standing boulders. While Ishi sleeps, Timawi burns a settlement storehouse at the white village of Bushki at the north end of the ridge trail. Attacked by dogs, he is shot and killed. Ishi awakens to the smell of smoke, locates Timawi's firedrill, and retrieves the man's corpse, which lies under an oak.

13. Ancestor Cave; Tuliyani in the Sacramento Valley, California

For six days Ishi goes without food while he transports Timawi's remains south to Ancestor Cave. There Ishi performs burial rites by burning sacred tobacco and juniper wood and purifying the corpse, which he seals in the cave with a rock slab. With hair burned to the scalp and face painted with stripes of mourning, he rejoins his tribe at Tuliyani and tells them the obvious news that Timawi will not return. Elder Uncle blesses Ishi with a puff of dried tobacco and weeps for Timawi, now named "Our Friend" and "The Restless One" out of respect to the dead, whom the tribe refrains from calling by name. Tushi rejects the sweetgrass bracelet a second time and describes a dream that takes her far from home to an ice house.

14. Wowunupo Mountain in the Sacramento Valley, California

Traveling south and making certain they are not followed, the six remaining Yahi migrate to a rock ledge and abandoned bear den on Wowunupo Mountain, south of Gahma on the opposite shore of Banya Creek. They construct an earthen storage house, drying and smoking shelter, and lodge. In the center, Ishi clears a circle for village functions. His mother and Tushi build a women's shelter.

Three years later, Ishi's grandfather and grandmother die, leaving the four survivors to contemplate their tribe's extinction. At age 20, Tushi is pleased that they are able to hide from whites, who are rapidly populating the area.

The work crew of a power company discovers the tribe's new residence in 1908. Elder Uncle escapes the eight white men with Tushi; Ishi climbs a tree to guard his ailing mother, whose legs are bandaged. After the invaders depart, Ishi carries his mother to safety in his work hollow. Ishi returns to the cave to find his tools and personal belongings gone.

15. Banya and Beaver creeks in the Sacramento Valley, California

Ishi searches the banks of Banya Creek and Beaver Creek for Elder Uncle and Tushi but finds only Tushi's necklace and his uncle's walking sticks. The two appear to have slid down an embankment and drowned in the creek.

16. Fishing shelter in the Sacramento Valley, California

Ishi and his mother resettle down the mountain at the fishing shelter. They live as best they can on fish and acorns. A month later, they cling together and weep for their departed family. That winter, five days before Ishi's mother dies, she compliments him on his manly appearance, which reminds her of her husband.

17. Ancestor Cave in the Sacramento Valley, California

Now the last of his people, Ishi performs his mother's funeral rites at Ancestor Cave and remains in mourning until the new year. He sustains himself on porcupine meat and fish.

18. Mount Waganupa in the Sacramento Valley, California

Dazed and lonely, Ishi takes shelter in a cave far to the north on Mount Waganupa, where a bear lacerates his arm and shoulder with its claws. He binds the wound with herb poultices and sleeps through much of the winter in the flint cave.

19. Yuna Canyon in the Sacramento Valley, California

In spring, Ishi rouses and searches for clover and fresh bulbs along Yuna Canyon. He discovers that the spirit presences have gone, leaving him behind. He examines his reflection in the water, finds his face thin and lined, and anticipates death.

20. Oroville, California

In 1911, Ishi collapses near a slaughtering pen far south in the town of Oroville. He lies inert, waiting to die, but the Oroville sheriff rescues him from white tormentors, covers him with an apron, and handcuffs him. Ishi fears that he will be hanged.

The sheriff takes Ishi to jail by wagon and provides him with coffee, soup, and bread; clean clothes; and water to bathe in. The passing of a train nearby terrifies Ishi. The next day, a stranger visits his cell and speaks a few Yahi words. Eager for conversation, Ishi talks until he is exhausted. He rejects a return to the canyon and refuses to go to a reservation.

21. Museum of Anthropology, San Francisco, California

By train, ferryboat, and trolley, Ishi travels west to a new home at a museum next to the medical school on Parnassus Heights at the University of California, San Francisco. He receives clothes and a room of his own and, as his dreams predicted, swims in the Pacific Ocean and climbs a bluff overlooking the Golden Gate Bridge. Ishi flakes arrowheads for the curator, who tells him about World War I and promises to write a book about him. In the Sutro Forest, below the hill on which he lives, Ishi befriends a blond girl and enjoys nature walks in the arroyo.

Among the museum's collection, Ishi finds two baskets that Tushi made shortly before her death. Also, he reclaims his quiver and rock-glass knife in a squirrelskin case, which arrived at the museum with an anonymous letter signed "A friend." After the curator departs, Ishi sits clutching his treasures.

22. Ancestor Cave in the Sacramento Valley, California

In 1914, at the beginning of the new year, Ishi leads the curator and a young white boy he calls Maliwal ("Young Wolf") to the Yahi world. For two months he eats native meals, enters a sweat lodge, sings, tells stories, plays the Meadow Game, smokes, and journeys to Ancestor Cave.

23. Museum of Anthropology, San Francisco, California

A month and a half later, Ishi, at peace with his fate, returns to his room in the museum. In 1915, he is stricken with tuberculosis. Surrounded by friends, he dies in March 1916 at the age of 55 and is honored with a traditional five-day funeral.

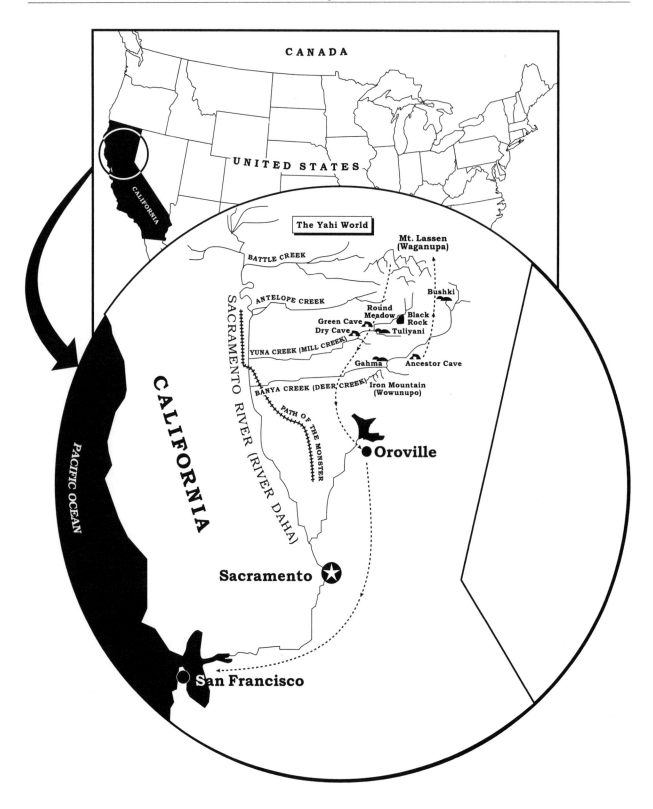

The Island of the Blue Dolphins

BY SCOTT O'DELL

Historical fiction, 1960

Geographical Summary: A fictional biography based on a singular figure in California history, Scott O'Dell's *Island of the Blue Dolphins* details the daily struggle of a 14-year-old native girl marooned on a craggy Pacific island west of Los Angeles, California. After the death of her father, Karana, the chief's daughter, prepares to emigrate aboard a schooner bound for the California mainland. But she loses sight of her little brother as the boat pulls away from shore, and she leaps into the ocean in search of him.

Alone on the island, the two anticipate the return of a boat to reunite them with the tribe. Then Karana's brother is killed, leaving her to coexist with the animals, birds, and sea creatures. Later, she explains her success in surviving alone until her rescue to a mission in Santa Barbara on California's west coast. Once established in a home, she continues to live apart from her tribe with a white family. At her death, Karana's exile and language remain a mystery.

Described in an article for *Scribner's Monthly* in 1880, the "Lone Woman of San Nicolas Island" piqued interest in the Santa Barbara Islands, mere dots in the Pacific off the California coast. Lying southwest from the shore 25 miles off Santa Barbara, these channel islands—Anacapa, San Clemente, San Miguel, San Nicolas, Santa Barbara, Santa Catalina, Santa Cruz, and Santa Rosa—are small, San Nicolas being about eight miles long and four miles wide. The cluster was for decades used by itinerant shepherds, who established herds, then returned for annual shearing. Even earlier, the island group provided seal and otter beds for trappers, who came from as far away as Russia and Japan. As does Karana, island inhabitants of the sixteenth century collected abalone, dried the meat, and carved the shells into jewelry, buttons, and ornaments.

Archaeological studies of Native American islanders have created a picture of life similar to that of O'Dell's historical fiction. Villagers, whom Spanish seamen described as fair-skinned and comely, dressed in the skins of sea lions and embellished their garments with bracelets, pendants, and carved earrings. Like California Indian tribes, the islanders used soapstone dishes and cooked meals of seaweed and fish in waterproof baskets, into which they dropped hot stones. Among the remnants of this extinct civilization are basketry, stone ollas, awls and needles, bone and shell fishhooks and spear points, and seaworthy canoes.

From the logbooks of a Boston sea captain, historians know that the rapid decline in the San Nicolas populace occurred about 1830. Following a massacre of male islanders by invading Kodiak otter hunters, fewer than 40 people remained behind after the victorious Kodiaks killed the warriors and abducted boatloads of women. Coinciding with island history was the arrival of Father Junipero Serra and a team of Franciscan missionaries, who established missions east of the channel islands with the aid of Indian slaves. To supply burgeoning orchards and flocks with laborers, the priests recruited island natives and introduced them to Christianity as well as to the advances of European civilization.

In April 1835, Isaac Sparks and Lewis L. Burton, a team of American entrepreneurs, sailed the *Peor es Nada* from Santa Barbara to San Nicolas, loaded it with sea otter pelts, and prepared to evacuate the remaining 20 islanders. During a fierce gale, the expedition departed, leaving behind a child. In a rescue attempt, the mother, a 23-year-old widow, plunged into the waters and swam to shore as the ship labored on toward the San Pedro Channel. The remaining islanders were distributed to work sites in Los Angeles and San Gabriel.

Because the *Peor es Nada* was in constant demand, the captain was unable to return for the marooned pair. A few weeks later, the ship sank. Interest in the widow waned until 1850, when Father Gonzales paid Thomas Jeffries to locate the lost woman and child. Jeffries discovered stone vessels, a wigwam, and a fence made of whale ribs, but, because he failed to locate inhabitants or signs of life, he assumed that the widow drowned or died on the island. In 1851, hunters returned and reported a human shape in the distance, but no proof of habitation. From his discovery sprang numerous ghost stories about the lost woman.

In July 1853, the hunters beached their boat on the northeast side of San Nicolas, where Captain Nidiver (called "Nidever" by O'Dell) found a human footprint. He discovered a basket containing needles, thread, fishhooks, jewelry, and a robe fashioned of bird feathers. The crew mounted a search and located a marooned woman in her mid-forties. No one could translate her dialect, but the men understood that she invited them to share her food. When the crew indicated in sign language that she could board their ship, the woman packed her belongings and joined the crew, who provided her with a dress they stitched from ticking. She pantomimed that her child had disappeared and that she had survived on fish, blubber, roots, and shellfish. Upon landing at Santa Barbara on September 8, 1853, the native woman saw her first oxen and horses.

Accepted into the home of Captain Nidiver and his wife, who refused to allow their guest to be exhibited like a wild beast, she spent much time with the Nidiver children. None of her kin or tribe members were ever found. Still nameless at the time of her death, the woman was christened Juana Maria and buried in the walled cemetery of Santa Barbara Mission. Her needles and basket remained with the people who befriended her. Mission officials sent her green cormorant feather robe to the Vatican in Rome.

Further Reading

Bleeker, Sonia. *Mission Indians of California.* New York: Morrow Junior Books, 1956.

Heizer, Robert F. *The Indians of California.* Berkeley, CA: University of California Press, 1962.

Heizer, Robert F., and Albert B. Elsasser. *The Natural World of the California Indians.* Berkeley, CA: University of California Press, 1980.

Patterson, Lotsee, and Mary Ellen Snodgrass. *Indian Terms of the Americas.* Englewood, CO: Libraries Unlimited, 1994.

Sturtevant, William C., ed. *Handbook of North American Indians.* Washington, DC: Smithsonian Institution Press, 1984.

Vallejo, Mariano Guadalupe. *Great Indians of California.* Santa Barbara, CA: Bellerophon Books, 1991.

Waldman, Carl. *Atlas of the North American Indian.* New York: Facts on File, 1985.

———. *Who Was Who in North American History.* New York: Facts on File, 1990.

Wolfson, Evelyn. *From Abenaki to Zuni.* New York: Walker, 1988.

Detailed Itinerary

1. Island of the Blue Dolphins (San Nicolas Island, California)

On an island less than 10 miles long and 75 miles west of Los Angeles, California, 12-year-old Karana ("The Girl with the Long Black Hair"), her older sister Ulape, and little brother Ramo live at Ghalas-at with their widower father, Chief Chowig, decision-maker for their tribe. When Russian and Aleut hunters arrive, Chowig realizes that they want to cheat him of valuable pelts and tries to negotiate with them. In view of the assembled women, the hostile Aleuts kill 28 of the 43 native males, including the chief.

2. Captain Hubbard's schooner

Kimki, the new chief, sets out alone by canoe to a distant land, leaving Matasaip, the interim chief, in charge. In Kimki's absence, tribe members board Captain Hubbard's schooner to sail to a new home on the mainland. Karana collects her belongings and joins them. Before the ship sails, she discovers that her brother has returned to the village for his fishing spear. She dives overboard and swims ashore to find him.

3. Ghalas-at, the village on San Nicolas Island

Near the deserted village, Karana rejoins her brother as the ships sails away without them. On the second day of their marooning, she searches for food. She returns to their shelter and finds that wild dogs have killed Ramo, leaving her alone on the island. Days later, Karana shakes off her deep depression and burns the village.

4. Headland of San Nicolas Island

Karana moves a mile west of Coral Cove to the island headland and makes her home near a spring until the ship can return for her. She learns to fish, hunt, and paddle a six-passenger canoe. She weaves whale ribs and kelp into a fence, builds a shelter, and selects a cave as an alternate dwelling, which she stocks with dried meat, baskets, water, and handmade weapons. For companions she tames a wild dog named Rontu and feeds Tainor and Lurai, a pair of red-winged blackbirds.

5. Cave on San Nicolas Island

Two years later, Aleut hunters return. Karana hides from them in the cave and occupies herself by sewing a cormorant skin skirt. Unexpectedly, she encounters Tutok, an Aleut girl, who gives her a black stone necklace. They become friends. Karana makes a shell circlet as a gift.

After Tutok leaves, Karana's dog Rontu dies, leaving her once more companionless and lonely. She tames a red fox and a pup she names Rontu-Aru ("Son of Rontu"). After a tidal wave and earthquake destroy her canoe, she locates materials to build another one.

6. Bay on San Nicolas Island

Eighteen years after Karana is marooned, a ship anchors in the bay. Karana remains out of sight until the men depart. In two years, the ship returns. Karana, her face marked with the ritual blue and white clay designs of an unmarried woman, greets three men, one of whom is a priest, Father Gonzales. The men make her a dress from two pairs of blue pants and teach her to thread a needle.

7. Santa Barbara Mission, California

Captain Nidever transports Karana and her birds and dog eastward to the Santa Barbara Mission on the California mainland. Father Gonzales indicates by hand signals that the ship that carried her tribe capsized in a storm. Without the ship, there was no way for mainlanders to rescue her. Thus, for 18 years she was forced to remain alone on the island.

For the rest of her life, Karana lives at the mission. She never learns to speak Spanish, instead communicating by hand signs. Called the Lost Woman of San Nicolas, at her death she is buried near the mission. Her robe is sent to Rome.

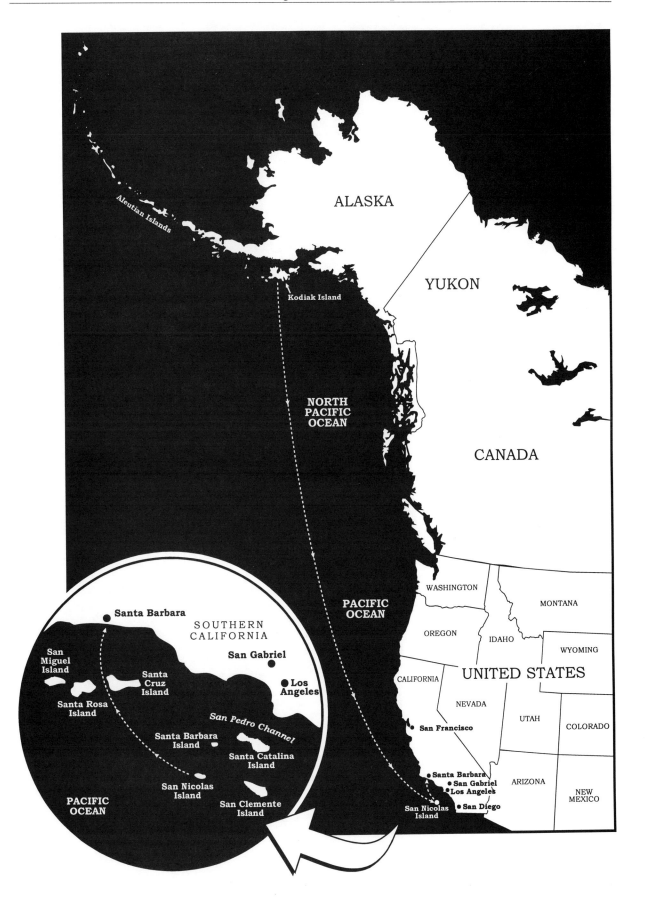

Jubilee

by Margaret Walker

Historical fiction, 1966

Geographical Summary: In Margaret Walker's famous Civil War novel, Elvira "Vyry" Dutton Innis, common-law wife of Randall Ware in Terrell County in the southwest corner of Georgia, finds her life turned upside down after President Lincoln frees the slaves. She copes with hardship, illness, and hunger for seven years before marrying Innis Brown and moving west to Abbeville, Alabama. From there, Vyry, Innis, and Randall's children Jim and Minna move around Alabama in search of a prosperous piece of farmland and a peaceful life for their family. After they settle in Greenville in south-central Alabama, Vyry, who serves as the local midwife, reveals, to both Innis and Randall, who comes for his wife and Jim, what slavery has done to her. Vyry chooses to remain with Innis; Randall departs to reestablish himself with his son Jim. He leaves money for Minna's education.

Historical study of the Civil War and Reconstruction eras corroborates the emotional and economic stresses outlined in Walker's story. Black men and women like Randall Ware contributed to the labor force that backed up the Union advance. From Georgia came 3,486 black laborers; from Alabama, 2,969. Of the 169,038 former slaves who formally entered the service, 68,178 died. Women performed such nonmilitary tasks as foraging for food, supplying shelter and clothing for the homeless, and staffing literacy schools; men fought, cooked, dug trenches, assisted at field hospitals, buried the dead, and hauled heavy equipment and artillery.

From slave narratives of the post war years come myriad stories of ambitious families like Vyry's, who eagerly grasped freedom, education, and advancement. Because most emancipated slaves were illiterate and could not trust strangers to give them directions or answer questions about their families and friends, many blacks wandered among way stations and safe houses in search of news. Their lack of map skills and money for transportation defeated efforts to reunite families. Communities sprang up where wayfarers ministered to each other with the tenderness of parent to child.

The arrival of freedom to this era—a significant segment in the black diaspora—carried a debilitating burden of poverty and violence, particularly from vigilantes and hate groups, such as the White Camellia and the Ku Klux Klan. For three years after Lee's surrender at Appomattox, the white citizens of Alabama refused to ratify the Fourteenth Amendment to the Constitution, which granted citizenship to former slaves. The state maintained peace by means of military control; it was readmitted to the Union in June 1868. The Freedman Aid Society opened offices in Decatur, Birmingham, and Montgomery to help refugees find work, feed hungry families, locate medical care, and avoid disgruntled white troublemakers. Still, by the last quarter of the nineteenth century, Alabama, Georgia, Mississippi, Louisiana, and Texas led the nation in lynchings. Against the uncertainty of this political background, newly freed blacks farmed the coastal plains (known as Alabama's Black

—111—

Belt); harvested yellow pine, hickory, and red cedar; worked the sawmills of the Cumberland Plateau; and helped to rebuild a state that had lost 25 percent of the 100,000 men it sent to fight for the Confederacy.

Further Reading

Asante, Molefi K., and Mark T. Mattson. *Historical and Cultural Atlas of African Americans.* New York: Macmillan, 1992.

Ferrell, Robert H., and Richard Natkiel. *Atlas of American History.* New York: Facts on File, 1987.

Morris, Robert C. *Reading, Riting, and Reconstruction: The Education of Freedmen in the South, 1861-1870.* Chicago: University of Chicago Press, 1981.

Muskat, Beth T., and Mary A. Neeley. *The Way It Was: 1850-1930 Photographs of Montgomery and Her Central Alabama Neighbors.* Montgomery, AL: Landmarks Found, 1985.

Wilson, Charles Reagan, and William Ferris, eds. *Encyclopedia of Southern Culture.* Chapel Hill, NC: University of North Carolina Press, 1989.

Detailed Itinerary

1. Dutton Plantation near Dawson, Georgia
The story opens on a plantation near the Flint River, east of the Chattahoochee River and south of Kinchafoonee Creek in Terrell County, Georgia. Elvira, or "Vyry," is the mulatto daughter of John Morris Dutton, an aristocratic plantation owner who possesses much of southwestern Georgia, and his black slave, Sis Hetta. Vyry could pass as a twin of Lillian, the white daughter of Dutton and his wife Salina. After Hetta's death, two-year-old Vyry comes under the slave Aunt Sally's care; at age seven, she enters the big house kitchen, where Salina torments her to avenge John's adultery.

2. Lee County, Georgia
Outside the plantation, tension grows between slaves and owners. In the spring of 1851, a revolt brews to the east in adjacent Lee County and is quelled by a tough sheriff. During free time, Vyry and Lillian play together like sisters until Lillian enrolls in school.

3. New Orleans, Louisiana
Vyry takes the responsibility of master cook after Sally is sold to a new owner in New Orleans, Louisiana. About the time that the runaway Lucy is branded with an R, Lillian marries West Point graduate Kevin MacDougall and parts with Vyry.

4. Lee County, Georgia
On the Fourth of July, Vyry travels east to the county seat, where two black women are hanged. When Vyry returns to the plantation, Lucy has run away. Vyry secretly wishes Lucy well.

5. Dutton Plantation near Dawson, Georgia
At age 15, Vyry selects a husband, Randall Ware, a strong and intelligent free black blacksmith and miller. She bears three children: Jim, Minna, and a stillborn

infant. To keep Vyry enslaved, John Dutton refuses to sanction legal marriage to a free black, but he promises to manumit her in his will. However, local hostilities against free blacks force Randall to abandon his family. He urges Vyry to run away with him on the Underground Railroad northeast to Maryland and farther north to Canada.

Vyry agrees to flee the plantation but insists on taking the children. Patrollers and Grimes, the overseer, capture the runaways and lash Vyry's back. She remains with the Duttons and loses contact with her husband. Hard times come after the Civil War depletes the plantation and the master breaks a leg.

6. Montgomery, Alabama

On March 4, 1861, Abraham Lincoln is elected president, the same day that Montgomery, west of the Dutton plantation in Alabama, is proclaimed the Confederacy's capital.

7. Dutton Plantation near Dawson, Georgia

Later that spring, John Dutton develops gangrene and dies. Grimes and Salina Dutton manage the few field hands who remain.

8. Fort Sumter, Charleston, South Carolina

War breaks out following the firing on Fort Sumter on the coast east of Charleston, South Carolina.

9. Dutton Plantation near Dawson, Georgia

Vyry receives a note from Randall saying that he will come for her when the war ends.

10. Richmond, Virginia

In July 1861, the capital of the Confederacy is moved northeast to Richmond, Virginia.

11. Dutton Plantation near Dawson, Georgia

Dutton's son, Johnny, takes over management of the plantation and promises to free all the slaves who remain faithful during the war.

12. Chickamauga, Georgia

Following the Battle of Antietam, Johnny joins the cavalry and on September 19, 1863, fights at the Battle of Chickamauga in southwest Georgia, where he receives a chest wound. Jim, one of Dutton's slaves, finds a wagon and transports Johnny home to die.

13. Cincinnati, Ohio; Cairo, Illinois

Meanwhile, Randall Ware wanders from Cincinnati, Ohio, southwest toward Union headquarters at Cairo, Illinois, to offer his services as a blacksmith for railroad construction.

14. Lookout Mountain and Missionary Ridge, Tennessee

By November 1863, Randall finds himself back in the South in service to the Union army. He encounters Jim, who brings news from Lee County.

15. Atlanta, Georgia

In late fall of 1863, as General Sherman takes control of Atlanta, Georgia, north of the Dutton plantation, Randall lies ill with fever and is left behind as Union forces move east.

16. Ocean Pond, Florida

On February 20, 1864, Kevin is wounded shortly before he is to be discharged from service.

17. Dutton Plantation near Dawson, Georgia

Kevin dies soon after returning home.

18. Andersonville, Georgia

To keep up the farm, Salina travels to Andersonville, a notorious, concentration-camp-like prison for captured Union soldiers, to acquire prisoners to serve as laborers.

19. Dutton Plantation near Dawson, Georgia

Salina dies from a stroke. Lillian, now a frail widow with two children, manages the plantation. Jim reports to Vyry that Randall Ware probably died in Atlanta. Vyry continues to wait for his return. Meanwhile, Innis Brown, a homeless field hand, helps her plant and harvest crops. Vyry learns to spin and weave for the family and stretches food supplies to feed the family.

The Northern army invades the property and announces to the assembled slaves that President Lincoln has set them free. The news of the end of the war is eclipsed by sadness over Lincoln's assassination.

Lillian is wounded in the head. Vyry contacts Lucy Porter, John's cousin, who transports the befuddled Lillian and her children to Alabama. At Christmas 1865, Vyry despairs of reuniting with Randall Ware and marries Innis Brown.

20. Abbeville, Henry County, Alabama, near the Chattahoochee River

In January 1866, Vyry and Innis load a farm wagon and travel west across the Chattahoochee River to Abbeville in Henry County, Alabama. Their new home seems prosperous until a flood indicates that they have built in the flood plain.

21. Dutton Plantation near Dawson, Georgia

After attending a Freedman's Convention in Augusta, Georgia, Randall returns to the plantation and finds the place deserted and a for-sale sign posted. He learns that Vyry has remarried and moved away.

22. Montgomery, Alabama

The Innises travel northwest toward Montgomery and take over a vacant tenant farm. Vyry gives birth to a son, Harry. When Vyry and Innis realize that Pippins, the owner, intends to cheat them, they abandon the farm.

23. Troy, Pike County, Alabama

In 1868, Vyry and Innis move southeast to Troy in Pike County. There they work with the Jacobsons and build a home. That winter, they anticipate the birth of another child. But their contentment is short-lived after masked white riders burn them out, leaving Vyry immobilized with despair.

24. Luverne, Crenshaw County, Alabama

With Innis's help, Vyry recovers and moves the family west to Luverne, Alabama. Three weeks after the move, their infant dies at birth.

25. Greenville, Butler County, Alabama

Before Vyry agrees to build another home, she travels west to Butler County to Porter's Store, where Lillian and her children live with Lucy Porter's family. Porter is impressed with Vyry's devotion to Lillian and promises to assist Innis in securing legal claim to the new farm.

The Innises live in substandard housing in a poor neighborhood until the Freedman Aid Society locates a suitable piece of farmland for them near Greenville, in south-central Alabama, in the spring of 1870. While selling eggs and vegetables door to door, Vyry stops to help a woman in childbirth. That summer, the neighbors, who believe Vyry is white, offer to build her a new house if she will accept the role of midwife. On August 29, Innis whips Jim for allowing a sow to drown in the mud. Vyry becomes hysterical at the sight of a whip.

In September, Randall arrives at the Browns' new house. He listens to the family's history and relates his struggles since he left to join the army. He describes how he hid underwater in a grist mill from the Ku Klux Klan. Both Randall and Innis are horrified to learn the story of the scars on Vyry's back. Determined to leave Vyry in peace with Innis and find another wife for himself, Randall leaves with Jim, whom he plans to enroll in school. Vyry, anticipating the birth of another child and schooling in Montgomery for Minna, remains with Innis.

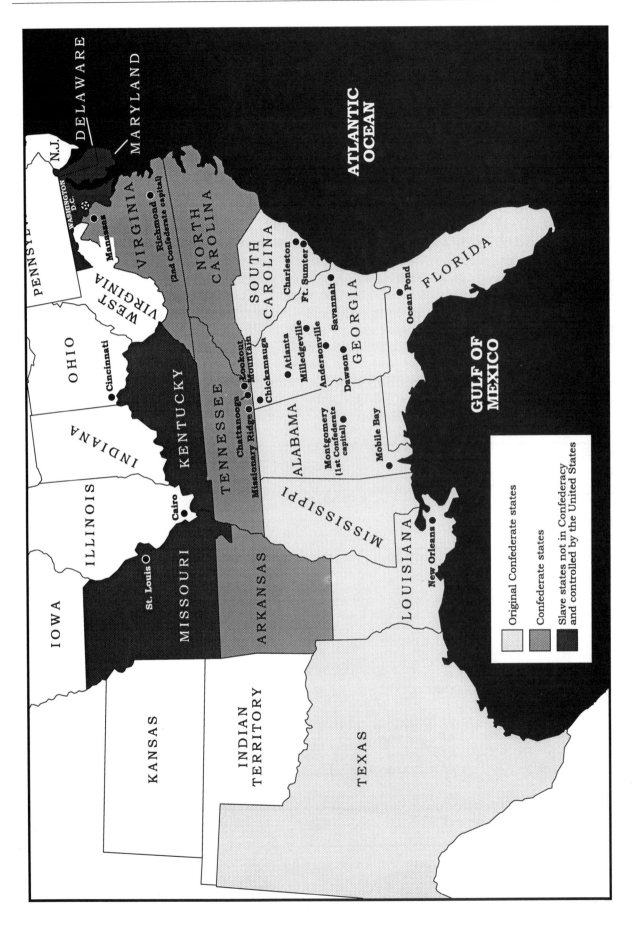

ATLANTIC OCEAN

GULF OF MEXICO

DELAWARE

MARYLAND

N.J.

PENNSYL.

WASHINGTON D.C.

Manassas

WEST VIRGINIA

VIRGINIA

Richmond (2nd Confederate capital)

NORTH CAROLINA

SOUTH CAROLINA

Charleston

Ft. Sumter

FLORIDA

GEORGIA

Savannah

Ocean Pond

OHIO

Cincinnati

KENTUCKY

TENNESSEE

Lookout Mountain

Chattanooga

Missionary Ridge

Chickamauga

Atlanta

Milledgeville

Andersonville

Dawson

ALABAMA

Montgomery (1st Confederate capital)

Mobile Bay

INDIANA

ILLINOIS

Cairo

St. Louis

MISSOURI

IOWA

ARKANSAS

MISSISSIPPI

LOUISIANA

New Orleans

KANSAS

INDIAN TERRITORY

TEXAS

Original Confederate states

Confederate states

Slave states not in Confederacy and controlled by the United States

Julie of the Wolves

BY JEAN CRAIGHEAD GEORGE

Young adult fiction, 1972

Geographical Summary: Nine-year-old Julie Miyax Edwards, a motherless girl living in Mekoryuk on Nunivak Island off the southwest coast of Alaska, lives until adolescence with her Aunt Martha and attends school in Barrow in the far north off the Arctic Ocean. The disappearance of her father and the failure of her marriage to a retarded boy sends Julie fleeing west over the Brooks Range on the North Slope toward Point Hope in hopes of joining her pen pal in San Francisco, far to the south on the California coast.

An Eskimo couple discovers Julie living alongside a pack of wolves, Eskimo-style, and surprise her with the news that her father, Kapugen, lives in the village of Kangik near Wainwright in northern Alaska. She resolves to join him. Her reunion with Kapugen and his new wife Ellen is not without its problems, but after the death of her pet plover, Julie decides that she belongs with her father.

In terms of terrain, Julie undergoes a vast change in climate and landscape when she moves northeast from Nunivak on the Alaskan panhandle to the Arctic coastal plain, which extends from the Brooks Range north to the Arctic Ocean. Not only does permafrost underfoot and severe windchill rob her body of heat, but she also encounters the lengthy Arctic winter, where the darkness can last 24 hours a day. However, tundra conditions favor the Arctic wolf, as well as caribou, foxes, and polar bears. Weighing up to 175 pounds and growing as long as six and a half feet, the Arctic wolf lives a predatory life. Packs ranging in number from 8 to 36 members depend on strong leadership from the alpha (lead) male. Nomadic by nature, packs mark their territory with urine and evict or kill interlopers that threaten their pups. Although the wolves depend on moose, elk, caribou, musk-oxen, bison, and mountain sheep for food, they seldom attack human beings.

Further Reading

Brandenburg, Jim. *White Wolf: Living with an Arctic Legend.* Irvine, CA: Northwood, 1988.

Hartman, Charles W., and Philip R. Johnson. *Environmental Atlas of Alaska.* Seattle, WA: University of Washington Press, 1984.

Hughes, Jill. *Eskimos.* New York: Gloucester, 1984.

Mowat, Farley. *Never Cry Wolf.* New York: Bantam Books, 1963.

Patterson, Lotsee, and Mary Ellen Snodgrass. *Indian Terms of the Americas.* Englewood, CO: Libraries Unlimited, 1994.

Newman, Gerald. *The Changing Eskimos.* New York: Franklin Watts, 1979.

Savage, Candace. *Wolves.* San Francisco, CA: Sierra Club Books, 1989.

Smith, J. H. Greg. *Eskimos: The Inuit of the Arctic.* Vero Beach, FL: Rourke, 1987.

Sturtevant, William C., ed. *Handbook of North American Indians.* Washington, DC: Smithsonian Institution Press, 1984.

Waldman, Carl. *Atlas of the North American Indian.* New York: Facts on File, 1985.

Wolfson, Evelyn. *From Abenaki to Zuni.* New York: Walker, 1988.

Yue, Charlotte, and David Yue. *The Igloo.* Boston: Houghton Mifflin, 1988.

Detailed Itinerary

1. North Slope of Alaska

In mid-August on a barren stretch 300 miles from Brooks Range and 800 miles from the Chukchi Sea, Miyax, a 13-year-old Eskimo girl, attempts to make her way from Barrow, Alaska, to Point Hope. Following the example of her father, she observes a black wolf, a member of a pack, and waits patiently for it to respond. Educated in the ways of the wild by her father, Kapugen, she calls in Eskimo and English, "Amaroq, ilaya, wolf, my friend."

As a storm brews, Miyax thinks of her adoptive mother, Martha; her attendance at the Bureau of Indian Affairs School in Barrow; and her husband Daniel, whom she had left a week earlier. With no North Star for guidance in the long, nightless summer, she ponders the tundra, where she could easily die before completing a walk west to Point Hope to meet the *North Star*, a ship bringing supplies to villagers on the Arctic Ocean.

2. San Francisco, California

Far to the south in San Francisco lives her pen pal Amy. A week earlier, Miyax had headed toward Amy, the Golden Gate Bridge, and freedom from Daniel, whom she hated.

3. North Slope of Alaska

To protect herself, Miyax uses her *ulo* to cut out a sod house to protect her from the wind. She lines the floor with a caribou ground cloth and settles into her moosehair sleeping skin. She hopes for anything, even a lemming, to stave off hunger, which she keeps at bay with bites of moss. She befriends a wolf pup, who she names Silver, and observes two other adult wolves, which she calls Nails and Jello. By imitating wolf behavior and roughhousing with the pups, she receives an anointment of wolf scent, which signals her acceptance by the pack.

While Miyax sleeps, the wolves make a kill. Miyax races toward the food before realizing how easily she can lose sight of her sod house. She returns and collects a serving of Arctic peas. By coaxing Kapu, the lead wolf, she wins his confidence and gains a portion of meat to cook in her pot, which she heats with a fire kindled from moss and caribou droppings. In a heavy fog, a plane circles overhead, indicating the pilot's need for a landing place.

Miyax's wolf friends gallop away toward a caribou herd. After the kill, Miyax uses her knife to remove strips of meat, which she dries over the fire. To protect her food cache, she digs a cellar into the permafrost and covers the hole with sod. When Jello digs into her stocks, she smacks him smartly on the nose with her knife. Jello backs away.

4. Mekoryuk on Nunivak Island, Alaska

Memories of her mother, who died nine years earlier, leave Miyax with a sense of emptiness and a longing for her father, who lived in Mekoryuk on Nunivak Island, west of Alaska. Grieving for his wife, he abandoned his possessions and job as manager of a reindeer herd and ceased to care about his old interests. Filled with enthusiasm for the wild, he taught Miyax wolf lore as well as respect for all animals and skills that could save her life if she ever needed food or shelter from a storm. Kapugen immersed himself in paddling his kayak and hunting for whales and seals while Miyax played on the beach with the other children. During this period of her childhood, her father was called Charlie Edwards. Miyax's English name was Julie.

One day when Miyax was nine, while Kapugen sewed her a coat out of a silver-gold sealskin, a boat brought Aunt Martha and a legal paper saying that Miyax must attend school while Kapugen serves in the military. Miyax clings to her father, who promises that if she is unhappy with Aunt Martha, she can marry Daniel, the son of his friend Naka in Barrow. He leaves her in Aunt Martha's care.

At first, Miyax longs to reunite with her father. Then she learns that he left in his kayak and disappeared. A month later, bits of his kayak wash up on shore. Miyax realizes that she now has no choice but to live with Aunt Martha. She attends school, works at the hospital, and makes friends with girls who laugh at Eskimo ways. One day, Mr. Pollock of the Reindeer Corporation in Mekoryuk stops his jeep to ask if Miyax would like to be a pen pal to his daughter Amy in San Francisco. Miyax accepts and falls in love with an imaginary picture of life in California.

Life with Aunt Martha grows more difficult, between weekend chores and complaints about disrespect toward elders. Miyax tolerates the mistreatment and waits for two spots of cheer—letters from Amy and an invitation to come to Barrow to marry Daniel. When Miyax reaches marriageable age, an agent for the Bureau of Indian Affairs presents the agreement signed between Kapugen and Naka. Leaving Aunt Martha to whine about old age, Miyax climbs into the plane bound northeast for Barrow.

5. Barrow, Alaska

At the airport, Miyax meets Nusan, Naka's wife, and Daniel, a retarded boy who cleans animal cages for the Arctic Research Laboratory of the University of Alaska. The next day, a minister performs the wedding of Julie and Daniel. For the occasion she wears a white sealskin suit made by her mother-in-law. The wedding does not change their lives; Miyax lives as a daughter of Naka and Nusan, who teaches her to sew. Pearl, an Inuit girl who also married young, befriends Miyax and tells her that dissolving a marriage is easy—she only has to run away.

The summer and fall pass. Winter keeps Naka indoors. He drinks too much and beats Nusan. Miyax flees to the Quonset hut to meet Pearl. After the midwinter festival, Naka goes to jail. While Nusan attends to bail, Miyax sews. Daniel, whom the boys ridicule for his unconsummated marriage, enters and tries to kiss Miyax. She packs; says goodbye to Pearl; and, carrying Pearl's sleeping skin and hide, sets out on foot for Point Hope to board the ship *North Star* for San Francisco.

6. North Slope of Alaska

While Miyax lives on the frozen North Slope, memories of Daniel and Barrow fade from her memory as she turns to a more important matter—Jello has emptied her food cache. Following her compass, she moves westward as winter grows colder and more frightening. Jello follows and steals her pack, containing food, *ulo*, needles, and boots. Miyax fears that she will die on the tundra. The next day, she discovers

Jello's body and her pack. Amaroq had rescued her belongings and killed the thief. Kapu brings her a leg of caribou. She rescues a plover and names it Tornait.

Overhead, the sound of a plane means that hunters circle her shelter. To the armed passengers above, she looks like a bear. They fire on her and miss, but hit Amaroq. Miyax hides Kapu as the plane banks to return, then changes direction and follows the river away from the wolf pack. She tries to heal her friend, who dies and is mourned by the howling pack.

Winter grows more threatening. To pass the time in constant darkness, Miyax snuggles Tornait and carves a totem to honor Amaroq. The pack grows disorganized from lack of leadership but continues to provide food for Miyax. When snow falls, she cuts an ice house.

Then Roland and Alice, a Upik couple from Kangik, a small village near Wainwright, arrive. Miyax encourages them to speak Upik, so they introduce themselves as Atik and Uma and their baby as Sorqaq. Miyax, hungry for conversation with humans, talks with her new friends late into the night. Uma tells of her home in Anchorage on Alaska's southern coast and reveals that Kapugen lives in Kangik and taught Atik how to hunt. Miyax prepares to leave with the couple. Before departing her ice home, she glares at the wolves to keep them from following her.

7. Kangik on Kuk Bay at the mouth of the Avalik River

On arriving at the 50 huts that make up Kangik, Miyax is tense. She stops at her father's door and offers him Tornait. Indoors, she introduces herself as Julie Miyax Edwards Kapugen and meets Kapugen's new wife, Ellen. Mention of Kapugen's job as a pilot and guide for hunters saddens her with thoughts of Amaroq's death. She explains that she is enroute to San Francisco.

8. Wainwright, Alaska

Miyax tries to rid herself of the need for a father and a friend in San Francisco. She tries to turn her back on non-Eskimo ways by pushing her sled back toward her friends in Wainwright and on into the wild. But Tornait dies, forcing her to give up her dreams of San Francisco and return to her father.

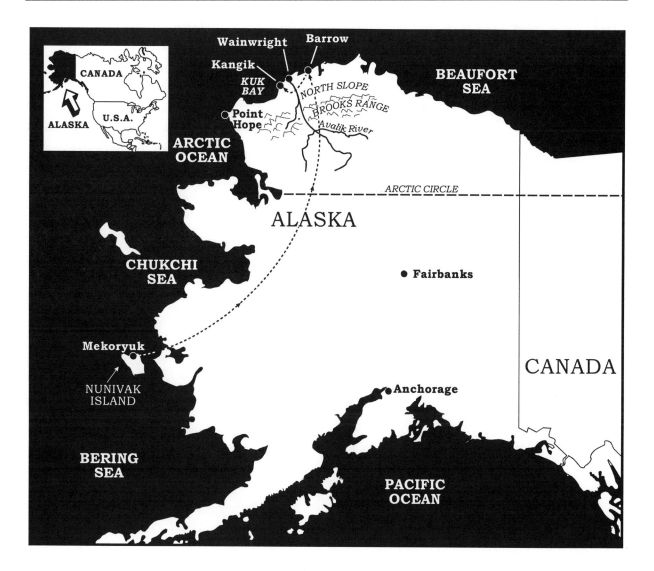

The Light in the Forest

BY CONRAD RICHTER

Young adult historical fiction, 1966

Geographical Summary: *The Light in the Forest,* set in Ohio and Pennsylvania in the last quarter of the eighteenth century, depicts the tragic circumstances that wrest True Son, born John Cameron Butler, the son of white settlers, from the village of his beloved Lenni Lenape (more familiarly known as Delaware) parents and thrust him back east to Paxton and his former identity as a white man. Traveling the frontier trail in both directions, True Son finds his lifestyle unacceptable in white culture and his allegiance to whites unwelcome among Indians. His alienation leaves him stranded in the middle, with no encouragement to move either west to his Lenni Lenape family's village on the Muskingum River in central Ohio or east to Paxton, north of Harrisburg, Pennsylvania.

Geographically, the novel takes place on historic territory marked by bloodshed between French and English conquerors and the Native American tribes who defended their lands from usurpation. True Son journeys east from Ohio, which has forests rich in deer, quail, squirrel, rabbits, and wild turkeys, and streams that are plentiful with bass, perch, and bluegills. In the southwestern quadrant of Pennsylvania, his escort party nears Fort Pitt, which was originally a French fur-trading outpost established in the mid-eighteenth century as Fort Duquesne. After it was captured by the English in 1758, the fort was renamed in honor of William Pitt, hero of the Seven Years' War (1756-1763). An outpost separating European settlements from the American wilds, Fort Pitt served as a command post and safety zone during troubled times between whites and Indians.

After the party leading True Son and other captives pushes into the rugged terrain that leads over the Allegheny Mountains and the Appalachian Mountains to the Susquehanna River, they pass through the seat of a six-tribe Indian confederation begun by Hiawatha and known as the Iroquois League. Envisioned about 1400 by Deganawida, an Iroquois shaman, and incorporated by the prophet Hiawatha a century and a half later, the league was initially composed of the Mohawk, Oneida, Cayuga, Onandaga, and Seneca. It fought Samuel de Champlain, founder of Quebec, who in 1609 joined with the Algonquin and Montagnais to assure French control of prime land in New France. The resulting ill will led to a century of wars. Joined by the Tuscarora in 1722, the Iroquois League aimed at settling internal differences and maintaining territorial control. A result of this powerful cabal was the gradual erosion of Delaware power and the migration of tribes east to Ohio, where they allied with the Shawnee and Wyandot. Delaware traditions from this period are preserved on a historical document, the *Walum Olum*, discovered in 1836 by a French anthropologist.

History records many instances of tribal adoptions of orphaned children. Some tribes rescued abandoned or parentless infants and brought them up according to Native American tradition. Most of these adoptions produced amicable, stable family and tribal relationships, even when the children were white. When authorities from white settlements reclaimed these adoptees, the children—who were more familiar with Indian customs, languages, and religion than with those of whites—were forced to relearn white ways and to suffer the disdain of whites who scorned their Indian upbringing.

Further Reading

Ferrell, Robert H., and Richard Natkiel. *Atlas of American History.* New York: Facts on File, 1987.

Patterson, Lotsee, and Mary Ellen Snodgrass. *Indian Terms of the Americas.* Englewood, CO: Libraries Unlimited, 1994.

Powers, William K. *Indians of the Northern Plains.* New York: Capricorn, 1973.

Vexler, Robert I. *Pennsylvania Chronology and Factbook.* Dobbs Ferry, NY: Oceana, 1978.

———. *Pittsburgh: A Chronological History 1682-1976.* Dobbs Ferry, NY: Oceana, 1977.

Waldman, Carl. *Atlas of the North American Indian.* New York: Facts on File, 1985.

Weslager, C. A. *Delaware Indians.* New Brunswick, NJ: Rutgers University Press, 1992.

Wolfson, Evelyn. *From Abenaki to Zuni.* New York: Walker, 1988.

Detailed Itinerary

1. Fort Pitt, Pennsylvania
As Colonel Bouquet's translator, Del Hardy leaves Fort Pitt near Pennsylvania's western border in October to march 100 miles west into hostile Indian territory. Colonel Bouquet's party is intent on recovering white captives living among the Lenni Lenape on the western fork of the Muskingum River.

2. Tuscarawa village on the forks of the Muskingum River in Ohio
In early November, 15-year-old True Son learns that white men are coming to reclaim him and other white captives of the Lenni Lenape and Shawanose. To avoid a return to his original family, he runs away from the Lenni Lenape village on the Muskingum River in central Ohio. But Cuyloga, his adoptive father, recovers True Son and thrusts him into the hands of white officials.

3. Allegheny River in Pennsylvania
On the march east, Half Arrow, True Son's cousin, and his friend Little Crane follow Colonel Bouquet's recovery party. They remain separate from the whites and spend the night on the far bank of the Allegheny River, which borders Fort Pitt on its north side. The next morning, the Indian followers turn west. True Son, unable to flee, crosses the river into white territory.

4. Fort Pitt, Pennsylvania
Settlers watch the group pass by and ask questions. True Son, who considers himself Lenni Lenape rather than white, remains sullen. The recovery party moves east toward Carlisle.

5. Carlisle, Pennsylvania

At Carlisle in south-central Pennsylvania, families identify their kin, leaving only True Son unclaimed. Mr. Butler, True Son's biological father, arrives and prepares to take him home to Paxton to the northeast. The colonel orders Del to accompany the Butlers and translate for True Son's family, who call him Johnny.

6. Blue Mountains, Susquehanna River in Pennsylvania

Arriving at the Susquehanna River southwest of Paxton and the Blue Mountains, Johnny urges his horse across the water and hides in underbrush on the opposite shore. However, Del and Mr. Butler capture Johnny and return him to his mount.

7. Paxton Township, Pennsylvania

At the Butler home in Paxton Township, Mr. Butler introduces Johnny to his younger brother Gordie, Aunt Kate, and Johnny's invalid mother, Myra Butler. That night, to avoid the stifling room, Johnny sleeps at the hearth in his bearskin. At a reception, he meets his disapproving uncles and is slapped by Uncle Wilse for impudence. Only Gordie seems able to accept Johnny.

After Del leaves Paxton, Johnny has no one with whom to speak Lenni Lenape. He visits the cabin of Bejance, the local black basket maker, who knows a few words of Lenni Lenape. By late winter, Johnny, spurned by a visiting minister and frequently punished and humiliated by his family, is miserably homesick for his Indian village on the Muskingum River.

8. Third Mountain in the Blue Mountains of Pennsylvania

In spring, Johnny and Gordie set out to meet Corn Blade, a reclusive Indian who lives on Third or Kittaniny, one of the Blue Mountains. Before they arrive at Corn Blade's residence, Johnny's father and uncle and a farmer overtake the pair and lead them home.

9. Paxton Township, Pennsylvania

As home conditions become more intolerable, Johnny suffers from fever. He learns that an Indian was shot at Mehargue's pasture. During the night, he climbs out his bedroom window and meets Half Arrow, who leads him to Little Crane's body in the pasture. The two bury Little Crane, who was shot from behind, and move on to the cooperage, where Johnny blames Uncle Wilse for Little Crane's murder. Wilse admits his crime, then tries to choke True Son. Half Arrow strikes Wilse; before an employee can intervene, Half Arrow and True Son escape northwest toward the Blue Mountains. Because True Son is sorry to part with Gordie, Half Arrow promises to take Gordie's place.

10. Across the Blue Mountains to the Ohio River

True Son and Half Arrow rapidly move northwest and cross four mountains. At the Allegheny River, the two steal a dugout from a trading post, float out of sight past guardposts at Fort Pitt, and move on to the Ohio River, which connects with the Allegheny as it flows across the Pennsylvania border into Ohio.

11. Muskingum River in Ohio

After bathing in the Muskingum River, True Son and Half Arrow arrive at their village on the west fork of the river and share a joyous reunion with True Son's sisters, Mechelit and A'astonah. Cuyloga conceals his emotions, but his eyes welcome his son. Villagers celebrate the return for several days, but Little Crane's relatives remain aloof.

Warriors, led by Little Crane's brother Thitpan, initiate a war party to avenge Little Crane's death. True Son disapproves of scalps taken from young children but accompanies the party to a part of the river frequented by whites. Dressed in an English boy's pantaloons and shirt and acting as a decoy, he pretends he can't swim and lures a flatboat to rescue him, but the resemblance of a white child to Gordie causes him to change his mind about the ambush, and he warns the white passengers of danger.

Even True Son is surprised at his behavior, which alienates him from Half Arrow. The outraged band binds him with creepers and treats him like a traitor. Cuyloga refuses to condemn True Son to death, yet accuses him of following the dictates of his white blood. Abandoning his son and refusing to accept him back, Cuyloga escorts him to a trail that leads to the white settlement. They part as enemies. True Son has little choice but to abandon his Lenni Lenape upbringing and accept his white family.

Lost Horizon

BY JAMES HILTON

Utopian novel, 1933

Geographical Summary: Hilton's *Lost Horizon*, a framework utopian fantasy that has twice served as a cinematic subject, covers several treks across eastern landscapes. The first journey involves the escape of four whites from an Indian revolution at Baskul in central India and the subsequent kidnapping of the foursome by Talu, a convert. He flies them northeast across the Himalaya Mountains to a concealed location near Kuen-Lun, Tibet, which bears the romantic name of Shangri-La. In the rarefied setting of a monastery, the four at first long to escape, then become attracted to Shangri-La's pleasant temperature and timeless existence. The central character, Hugh Conway, impresses the High Lama, Father Perrault, as a worthy successor to his post.

About the time of Perrault's death, gold is discovered, and Conway, who is named the monastery's leader, departs with several others on a 1,100-mile trek to the east. The grueling journey takes Conway from snowy Tibet to a mission hospital in Tatsien-Fu, China. After he joins Rutherford, the person to whom he narrates the book, on a voyage from Shanghai on China's east coast to Yokohama, Japan, to Honolulu, Hawaii, Conway's amnesia lifts. He unfolds to Rutherford his tale of a Tibetan paradise, then departs aboard a freighter for Fiji and ultimately passes through Kashmir on his way back to the mysterious monastery that once promised him a long, happy life.

Because the action takes place in the early days of commercial air travel, the need for refueling stops greatly complicates the High Lama's plans to restock the monastery with new converts. Against cross currents, altitude sickness, and poor visibility, Talu steers the hijacked plane into some of the Earth's most fearsome territory. His brief halt and rapid return to the coordinates land him near Shangri-La.

For Conway, the arrival at Shangri-La comes as a pleasant diversion, as a respite from turmoil in India and a release of the tensions he harbors from his experiences with murderous trench warfare in World War I. On China's southwestern border, rescued from the wrenching gales of a Himalayan snowstorm near the highest peaks on Earth, Conway and the other survivors look out on snow-capped declivities that soar more than 29,000 feet. The harsh environment serves as an ideal monastic retreat. Isolated from casual visits, international tensions, and commercialism, Tibet developed Lamaism, a type of Buddhism, in the seventh century. The fictional Blue Moon Valley serves as a welcome contrast to the yawning, icy crevasses over which Talu flies.

Further Reading

Ashvin, Mehta, ed. *Himalaya: Encounters with Eternity.* New York: Thames Hudson, 1985.

Bell, Charles. *Tibet: Past and Present.* Philadelphia: Coronet Books, 1990.

Fairservis, Walter A. *Asia.* New York: Harry N. Abrams, 1981.

Gibbons, Bob. *Himalayas.* North Pomfret, VT: Trafalgar Square, 1991.

Lail, J. S. *Himalaya.* New York: State Mutual Book and Periodical Service, 1981.

Tuccil, Giuseppe. *The Religions of Tibet.* Berkeley, CA: University of California Press, 1988.

Detailed Itinerary

1. Berlin, Germany

In spring 1932, three former schoolmates—Wyland, an embassy secretary; Rutherford, a novelist; and an unnamed neurologist, who is interested in amnesia—meet at Berlin's Templehof Airdrome, where Sanders, an English pilot, joins them and recounts the kidnapping of four airplane passengers in May 1931. Rutherford invites the neurologist to his hotel to hear more about one of the abducted passengers, a man named Hugh Conway.

2. Baskul, India, to Peshawar, Pakistan

On May 20, 1931, aboard a maharajah's luxury plane bound northwest from Baskul to Peshawar to avoid a revolution, Hugh "Glory" Conway, a 37-year-old British consul and former Oxford specialist in oriental history, disappears.

3. Chung-Kiang, China

Conway survives the skyjacking and resurfaces in China at a Chung-Kiang mission hospital.

4. Shanghai, China, to Yokohama, Japan, to Honolulu, Hawaii

During passage aboard a Japanese liner from Shanghai, China, northeast to Yokohama, Japan, and across the Pacific to Honolulu in the Hawaiian Islands, Conway reproduces a Chopin etude that he learned from Alphonse Briac, one of Chopin's pupils.

5. Fiji to Kashmir

According to Rutherford, who relates the tales of Conway's adventures to the neurologist, Conway begins to recover from amnesia, tells a fantastic story about a Tibetan paradise, and later disappears southwest aboard a freighter bound for Fiji, an island in the South Pacific. Eventually he heads northwest toward Kashmir, north of India.

6. Bangkok, Thailand

Three months later, Rutherford receives a manuscript from Bangkok, Thailand, that recounts Conway's kidnapping.

7. Baskul, India

According to Conway's manuscript, Talu, a Tibetan convert, kidnaps him and three other passengers—Roberta Brinklow, an Eastern missionary; Chalmers Bryant, an American swindler traveling under the alias of Henry Barnard; and Captain Charles Mallinson, a 24-year-old British vice consul.

8. Nanga Parbat, a mountain in the Himalayas

The pirated plane halts briefly for refueling, then sets out once more over treacherous Himalayan peaks, one of which Conway identifies as Nanga Parbat. The passengers begin to suffer high-altitude syndrome. After Talu points a pistol in their direction and continues toward an undisclosed destination, Mallinson becomes agitated. Conway, a sensible man who prefers to take no action rather than the wrong action, stays calm to set an example of rationality and fills the time writing S.O.S. notes in several languages to be dropped from the plane. A rough landing knocks Talu unconscious. Brinklow temporarily revives him with brandy. That night, the passengers survive uncertainty and bitter winds.

9. Kuen-Lun in the Himalayas

Conway surmises that the group has landed near Kuen-Lun, one of the highest peaks of the Himalayas in south-central Asia. The next morning, Talu dies just as rescuers clothed in yak skins arrive from a local monastery to retrieve the survivors.

10. Shangri-La, near Kuen-Lun, Tibet

The group's leader, a blue-robed Chinese man fluent in English, offers the four wine and luscious mangoes, then ropes them together for a steep ascent to Shangri-La, a verdant retreat marked by warm climate and lush greenery. The retreat offers buildings fitted with modern plumbing, central heating, oriental gardens and court-yards, and tasteful decor. The group gazes upward at a conical peak called Karakal (Blue Moon).

Chang, the host, provides a smattering of data, particularly regarding a return party to India. He avoids questions about how supplies enter the valley. Brinklow suggests petitioning mission headquarters for ministers to convert residents of Shangri-La. Barnard, a folksy Texan, seems content, but Mallinson, a short-tempered malcontent, insists that Chang arrange for immediate departure south to India. Conway conceals his fluency in oriental languages and observes the surroundings for clues to its mystery.

Chang indicates that the group may leave at any time but must traverse the treacherous mountain pass. He suggests a return trek in two months. Mallinson is outraged at so long a delay and notes that Shangri-La is not pinpointed on any of the monastery's charts.

Meanwhile, Conway observes Talu's funeral and realizes that the four are being watched. Unalarmed by Chang's elusive answers, Conway enjoys the keyboard skills of Lo-Tsen, a young Manchu harpsichordist who seems out of place as the lamasery's only female postulant. Conway learns that Talu volunteered to kidnap the party. He conceals his desire to remain at Shangri-La, where an excellent library and music collection fulfill his scholarly needs.

The High Lama surprises Chang by inviting Conway to his quarters. The delicate old holy man discloses his former identity as Father Perrault, a Capuchin monk in search of an obscure religious sect. Stranded in Shangri-La in 1719, he discovered tangatse, a local rejuvenating herb made into a delicate tea. Assisted by Henschell, an Austrian wayfarer, Perrault establishes a benign autocracy grounded on the principle of moderation. He warns Conway that world destruction worse than the last war lies ahead.

Conway, who values peace after service at the front during World War I, contemplates a five-year apprenticeship and a purging of human passions. He anticipates that, after initiation, he will reach full lamahood by age 100. Thus, he suppresses his love for Lo-Tsen and continues conferring with the High Lama, who grooms Conway as his successor. Gradually, Brinklow and Barnard lose their desire to return to the outside world. The missionary studies the Tibetan language; Barnard advises local gold miners, who trade ore for books and oriental *objets d'art*. Mallinson, the only holdout, grumbles over the lack of guides to take him back over the Himalayas to India.

On the night that Perrault dies, Conway is named High Lama. Mallinson, who has initiated a secret romance with Lo-Tsen, announces that he has hired bearers to lead them south over the mountains. Conway, shaken to learn that Lo-Tsen loves the young vice consul, realizes that she will die without regular use of Shangri-La's rejuvenating herb.

11. Tatsien-Fu, China

By convincing Conway that the old men of Shangri-La are like wizened spiders, Mallinson discredits Perrault's story, which depends on slender evidence—Briac's knowledge of unpublished Chopin etudes. Conway decides to join Mallinson and Lo-Tsen on the 1,100-mile journey southeast to Tatsien-Fu on the China border.

12. Delhi, India

The novel, composed in England at Woodford Green in April 1933, returns to a dinner party in Delhi in northern India, where the neurologist and Rutherford meet again.

13. China and Upper Siam

Rutherford follows the neurologist to his hotel and discloses why he made a 1,000-mile odyssey in search of Conway, which takes him across Asia as far as northern China and upper Siam (currently known as Thailand). Fragments of evidence concerning supply shipments, the pianist Briac, the location of the mountain known as Karakal, and the whereabouts of Barnard fail to complete the puzzle.

14. Chung-Kiang, China

The mission doctor reveals one tidbit: A fragile old Chinese woman led Conway to the mission on October 5, 1931. Almost immediately, she died. Conway departed February 3, 1932, to continue his search for Shangri-La. The neurologist wonders if Conway will ever return west to Tibet and the Valley of the Blue Moon.

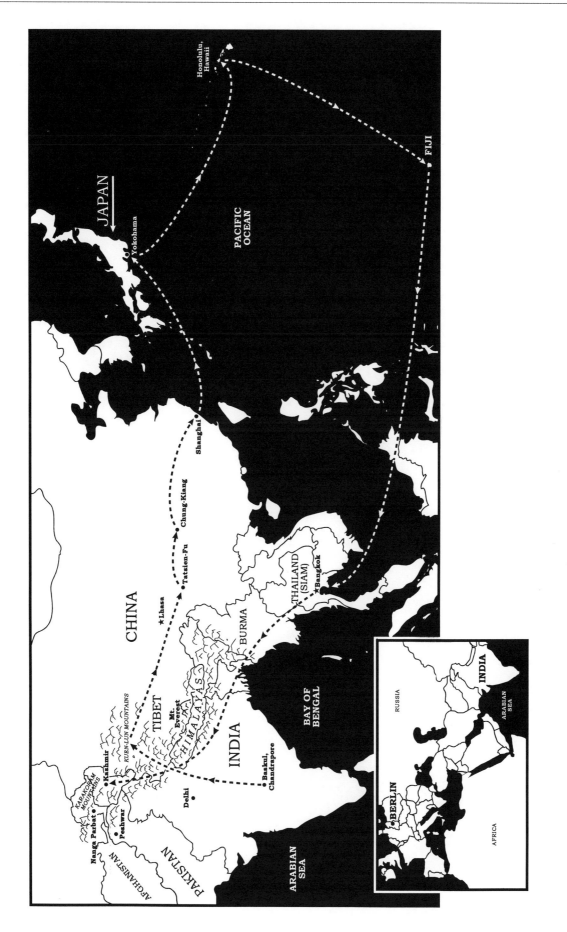

Night

BY ELIE WIESEL

Autobiography, 1960

Geographical Summary: *Night* is Wiesel's autobiographical account of his childhood experiences in two German concentration camps during World War II. It details the deportation of a Transylvanian Jewish community from Sighet on the Hungarian-Russian border northeast to Auschwitz, Poland, the notorious Nazi death camp, in June 1944. Elie, who remained with his father, describes the atrocities of travel in a densely packed cattle car; separation from his mother and three sisters; and starvation and forced labor at Auschwitz, the adjacent work camp at Buna, and Buchenwald. The grim documentary ends with the U.S. Army's liberation of Buchenwald on April 10, 1945, only two and a half months after Elie's father dies in his bunk.

Wiesel, a displaced or stateless person, was evacuated to Paris, France, where he studied at the Sorbonne and became a journalist for an Israeli newspaper. He settled in the United States, won the 1988 Nobel Peace Prize, and currently teaches humanities at Boston University.

Geographically, Elie Wiesel's autobiographical account moves over some of the most troubled terrain of the World War II era. Established in 1933, Hitler's death camps, staffed by the elite S.S. and fierce storm troopers, ran constantly under the skilled hands of *Reichsführer* Heinrich Himmler. Beginning with the establishment of Dachau, the systematic rounding up of suspected anarchists and rebels, gypsies, prostitutes, homosexuals, and known criminals expanded in 1939 to include Jews and prisoners of war. Likewise, invalids and handicapped inmates also were marked for extermination at Auschwitz, Treblinka, Bergen-Belsen, Sobibor, and Chelmno and at outlying Rumanian camps.

From the hill uplands of northern Transylvania, the Wiesels and their neighbors were transferred to Auschwitz, a Nazi death camp in south-central Poland where, from 1940 to 1945, gas chambers charged with Zyklon-B, a hydrocyanic gas designed as a pesticide, exterminated 2 million victims, most of whom were Poles and Jews. Scientifically and efficiently murdered by *Einsatzgruppen*, or extermination teams, the bodies were incinerated in crematoria run by inmates who were allowed to live as long as they had the strength to serve the Third Reich. Other relatively healthy individuals were selected for inhumane medical experimentation, such as tests to see how long the body could survive lethal doses of gas or bacteria.

From Auschwitz, Wiesel was marched to Buchenwald, a major addition to the Nazi concentration camp complex, which was established in 1937. Located near Weimar and headed by Colonel Karl Koch until 1942, when Lieutenant Colonel Hermann Pister took charge, Buchenwald also housed homosexuals, gypsies, and political dissidents, of whom 50,000 died. The inmate population rose rapidly after 1943 to 81,000 and supplied satellite camps at Laura, Ohrdruf, Dora, and Gustloff with slaves, some of whom helped assemble V-2 rockets. Populated beyond its capacity, Buchenwald lacked food, shelter, and sanitary facilities for the huge number of inmates, many of whom died of starvation, overwork, and disease. Others were murdered by guards or petty overseers or succumbed to heinous medical experiments with typhus toxins, phenol injections, and phosphorus burns.

Further Reading

The Apparatus of Death. New York: Time-Life Books, 1991.

Freedman, Samuel G. "Bearing Witness: The Life and Work of Elie Wiesel." *New York Times Magazine*, October 23, 1983, 6-9.

Friesel, Evyatar. *Atlas of Modern Jewish History*. New York: Oxford University Press, 1990.

Gutman, Yisrael, ed. *Encyclopedia of the Holocaust*. New York: Macmillan, 1990.

Lange, Nicholas de. *Atlas of the Jewish World*. New York: Facts on File, 1984.

Wiesel, Elie. "What Really Makes Us Free." *Parade*, December 27, 1987, 6-8.

Zentner, Christian, and Friedemann Bedurdtif, eds. *The Encyclopedia of the Third Reich*. New York: Macmillan, 1991.

Detailed Itinerary

1. Sighet (currently called Sighetul), Transylvania, on the Hungarian-Russian border

In 1941, 12-year-old Elie Wiesel, son of a Sighet grocer, maintains a fervid interest in Hasidic Judaism and studies Talmud, Torah, and Kabbalah with Moshe the Beadle, a minor parish official who works at the Sighet synagogue. Hungarian police arrest Moshe and other foreigners and deport them from the country. Months later, Moshe returns and tells of being the lone survivor of a group of deportees who had been transported north into Poland, forced to shovel their own graves, and shot. Moshe lay still among the corpses and escaped. His story is so bizarre that Sighet Jews dismiss him as a madman and maintain their optimism that the war will soon end.

In the spring of 1944, as Hitler's power appears to be crumbling, German soldiers enter Sighet and reside without incident among the Jews. But by Passover week, the atmosphere worsens as Jewish leaders are arrested and restrictive laws force Jews to relinquish gold and jewels and to stay in their houses. Relocated into two ghettos, the Jews try to lead normal lives.

The Saturday before Pentecost, Chlomo, Elie's devout father and a trusted local official, learns that local Jews are to be deported. At 8 A.M., some of the Jews are lined up, forced to abandon their valuables, and marched to rail cars. Elie's family is not selected for that trip, but three days later, on June, 20, 1944, Hungarian police herd the Wiesel family into the small ghetto. On Saturday, among the final convoy, the Wiesels board cattle cars and travel for three days, too cramped for space even to lie down.

2. Kaschau (currently called Kosice), Czechoslovakia

The deportees, unaware of their destination, recognize Kaschau in eastern Czechoslovakia. Wracked by the hysteria of Madame Schächter, they tolerate her shrieks, then tie and gag her to quell her insane visions of flames.

3. Birkenau, Poland

At midnight the convoy arrives south of the Vistula River at Birkenau, the reception center for Auschwitz. As Madame Schächter prophesied, the air reeks with the odor of burning human flesh. Armed guards separate men from women. Elie and his father never see Elie's mother or seven-year-old sister again. Dr. Mengele, the camp selection officer, examines the men to determine who will be allowed to live in work camps and who will be sent directly to the crematory. Elie is horrified to see a truck deliver small children and dump them into a flaming ditch.

Chlomo and Elie strive to stay together. After they are assigned to barracks, attendants shave their heads, disinfect their bodies, and issue work uniforms. Sadistic overseers regularly abuse them. Elie and his father, who are unskilled laborers, march for a half hour to Block 17, where a young Polish superintendent treats them humanely. The next day, attendants tattoo Elie with the number A-7713. Three weeks later, an inhuman overseer takes charge.

4. Buna, the factory segment of Auschwitz, Poland

The 100 laborers march east for four hours through the streets to Buna, the factory segment of the Auschwitz complex, where they are quarantined for three days. While a band plays march music, inmates plod to the warehouse. Elie eludes the camp dentist, who tries to remove his gold crown. A rabid overseer beats Elie for no reason. An unnamed Jewish French woman comforts the boy. (In later years he meets her in Paris, France, where the two reflect on their death camp experiences.) At the insistence of the foreman, the dentist extracts Elie's gold crown with a rusty spoon. Because he sees the overseer raping a young girl, Elie is beaten severely and collapses from pain.

One Sunday, for over an hour, American bombers pound Buna. The prisoners are forced to remove an unexploded bomb from the compound. The next week, they are lined up to observe the hanging of a camp thief. Three more hangings take place. Least bearable is the protracted execution of a young boy, who takes more than half an hour to die. A prisoner challenges God for failing to stop the torment.

During Rosh Hashanah that fall, Jews are still able to pray. But Elie has had his faith shaken by Nazi atrocities and can only accuse God of abandoning Jews. On Yom Kippur, Elie rebels against orthodox Judaism by refusing to fast.

The selection process intensifies as a means of ridding the camp of useless workers. Elie proves to Dr. Mengele that he is strong by running past him. Chlomo, summoned for a second examination, seems destined for the crematory. As a gesture of fatherly love and blessing, he bequeathes Elie his knife and spoon, significant treasures in the camp. That same day, Chlomo earns a reprieve. Akiba, a fellow inmate, recognizes that he is about to be executed and begs his friends to say funeral prayers in his honor. Three days later, his friends, struggling for survival, forget Akiba's request.

After the sole of his foot begins to swell in January 1945, Elie submits to an operation to drain the pus. The doctor promises that the boy will recover in two weeks. Two days later, Buna is evacuated after reports circulate that the Russian army is approaching.

5. Gleiwitz (currently called Gliwice), Poland

The next day, the inmates exit Buna and march east. Elie, wretched with pain in his foot, and Chlomo slog 42 miles through snow before taking a rest. Behind them, stragglers are shot. Chlomo forces Elie to remain awake so that he will not freeze. Eli and his father find shelter in a ramshackle brick factory, while other weary inmates die in the snow. Elie is disturbed that Rabbi Eliahou's son deserts his aged father and prays that he will never grow to resent Chlomo.

Prisoners, arriving at Gleiwitz more dead than alive, lie in heaps, nearly suffocating Elie, who struggles to the surface of a pile. One man, Juliek, is still energetic enough to play his violin but dies by morning. For three days inmates are given neither food nor water. Chlomo is again chosen for extermination, but Elie rescues him by dragging him through the confusion.

6. Buchenwald, Germany

Forced into roofless cattle cars 100 at a time, the inmates travel west into Germany for 10 days, surviving on snow. They grow so desperately hungry that they fight to the death for crusts of bread tossed into their midst by sadistic onlookers. Meir Katz and Chlomo rescue Elie from an attacker. On their arrival at Buchenwald in central Germany, only 12 inmates in their car prove to have survived the trip. Too weary to eat, they ignore cauldrons of soup and sink into stuporous sleep.

Elie awakens in panic that he has lost his father. He finds Chlomo weak and feverish from dysentery. Elie is weary of looking out for his father's welfare, but remains for a week at his bedside. Prisoners complain that the old man soils his bunk. The block leader urges Elie to save his strength and stop caring for Chlomo.

On January 28, 1945, an S.S. officer hits Chlomo on the head. The old man's last cry is "Eliezer." Elie, exhausted by his vigil, falls asleep in the upper bunk. The next morning, he finds a new inmate in the lower bunk. Ravaged by fatigue and hunger, Elie agonizes that he feels relief from the burden of protecting his father.

Sent to the children's block, Elie learns that the Germans plan to kill them all. On April 5, 1945, the inmates organize a resistance to roll call. For five days, 20,000 people are deprived of food. To survive, they eat grass and potato peelings. On April 10, 1945, camp rebels triumph. At six that evening, the gates open to American tanks, and the prisoners scramble for food.

On April 13, 1945, Elie falls ill with food poisoning. By the end of April, he is able to examine his reflection in the mirror, which reveals his cadaverous face.

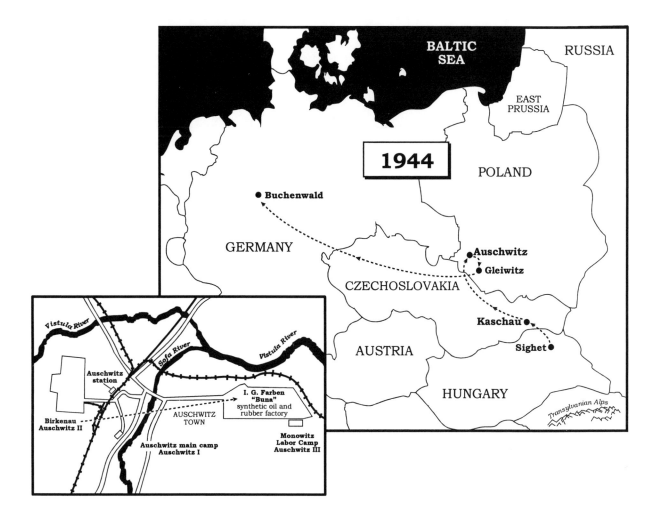

No Promises in the Wind

BY IRENE HUNT

Young adult fiction, 1970

Geographical Summary: During the Depression, Josh Grondowski, son of immigrants, joins his little brother Joey and his friend Howie and runs away from home. The trio travels south from Chicago's West Side, where Howie is killed while leaping onto a freight train. The Grondowski brothers continue south to Baton Rouge, Louisiana, and join the circus to find a place where they can feel welcome. On their way, the brothers join up with Lonnie Bromer, a fatherly Nebraska truck driver, who drives them to Baton Rouge and gives them his Omaha address to contact if they need him. After losing their circus job and hitchhiking into the Midwest, the brothers, plagued by hunger, cold, and illness, part in Nebraska. Josh ends up in Lonnie's Nebraska home; Lonnie locates Joey and reunites the boys. Josh eventually overcomes his resentment of his father and writes to his parents in Chicago. In better times, the boys travel north by train to their family.

The change in landscape and climate for the Grondowski brothers parallels the cultural and psychological stimuli that influence their maturity during the months away from their parents. From the severe winter of Chicago, which lies on the southwestern shore of Lake Michigan, they travel to the temperate, humid climate of Baton Rouge, the capital of Louisiana and a Mississippi River port city in the state's southeastern quadrant. From there, the pair hitchhikes north to the central plains states to reunite with Lonnie in Nebraska. Along the way, they pass through farm country, where barns offer temporary shelter and generous farm families share meager meals, warmth, and clothing.

Although the physical climate in Louisiana contrasts with the cold winds of the Canadian border states, the economic climate in that state bears a strong resemblance to the hunger and deprivation the boys hoped to escape in Chicago. The Depression, a severe economic decline that hit the United States after the stock market crash of 1929 ("Black Tuesday"), reached epidemic proportions in 1933, when incomes fell by 50 percent, banks collapsed, 14 million people were unemployed, and beleaguered debtors sold their goods and properties for as little as a tenth of their original worth. In November 1932, Franklin Delano Roosevelt was elected to his first presidential term on a platform offering hope through the National Recovery Administration, which promised minimum wages and fair distribution of employment, but the severe shock to American trust in capitalism was not alleviated until the end of the decade and the economic jumpstart of World War II.

Further Reading

Creigh, Dorothy W. *Nebraska: A History.* New York: W. W. Norton, 1977.

Culhane, John. *The American Circus: An Illustrated History.* New York: Henry Holt, 1989.

Ferrell, Robert H., and Richard Natkiel. *Atlas of American History.* New York: Facts on File, 1987.

Gray, James. *Illinois.* Champaign, IL: University of Illinois Press, 1989.

Israel, Fred L. *Franklin D. Roosevelt.* New York: Chelsea House, 1985.

Ogden, Tom. *Two Hundred Years of the American Circus.* New York: Facts on File, 1993.

Rothstein, Arthur. *Depression Years as Photographed by Arthur Rothstein.* New York: Dover, 1978.

Taylor, Joe G. *Louisiana: A History.* New York: W. W. Norton, 1984.

Detailed Itinerary

1. Chicago, Illinois

On a chill October morning in 1932, 15-year-old Josh Grondowski, oldest son of Stefan (a Polish immigrant) and Mary (an Irish immigrant 18 years younger than her husband), wakes up to begin a three-hour paper route to supplement his family's income. Family finances are strained, because Josh's father's skimpy salary as factory foreman ended with the loss of his job the previous February. Josh feels like a burden to his family, particularly to his mother, a skilled pianist who earns a small amount by ironing for other people. A student of music for seven years until the Grondowskis had to sell their piano, Josh intends to make her proud by playing for the assembly at Penn High School.

Josh, a shy youth who shares a love of musical improvisation with his friend Howie, longs to continue his piano lessons, but Stefan considers music an unacceptable skill for a working man. Repeated family arguments about money increase the tensions between father and son. Mary tries to intervene by reminding Josh that his father is a good man made desperate by hard times. Josh decides that his mother thinks he would be better off leaving home. Josh, Howie, and Joey, Josh's frail 10-year-old brother, run away with only a cardboard suitcase, matches, blanket, and Howie's banjo. The first day, they beg bowls of oatmeal from the Salvation Army kitchen, panhandle, and earn 78 cents on the street by singing and playing.

2. Traveling west in boxcars

Journeying by streetcar, the trio travels to the freight yards, hops on a freight train, and intends to escape Chicago's winter cold. They try to steer clear of railroad detectives and angry locals, who force them and other hobos out of town. As Howie leaps for the train, Josh catches his banjo, but Howie is thrown down on the tracks in front of an express train. Josh faints.

The two Grondowski brothers encounter a group of hobos who invite them to share a meal. The boys weep for Howie and hunch their bodies against the cold. Josh considers sending Joey back to Chicago but knows that he must continue his escape from Stefan. They spend the night at an abandoned farmhouse and chase a rooster, which they cook for dinner. When Ben, the owner of the house, and his wife approach the boys, Josh pretends that he and Joey are traveling to their grandfather's house in Montana. Ben tells the boys that bank foreclosures and tight money make him hope that Franklin Roosevelt wins the next presidential election so he can help the country recover from the Depression.

The couple offer the boys a bag of potatoes to live on as they continue their journey. Joey and Josh depart the next morning in dry weather. A gang of young thugs steals their blanket, potatoes, and extra clothes, but discard the banjo. A kind policeman lets them spend the night at the jail.

The boys travel the midwestern United States for several weeks and locate pitiful meals in garbage cans. Joey looks so appealing that people offer him warm clothes.

3. Nebraska

At a farmhouse door in Nebraska in November, the boys beg for food. One night, when Josh ponders going to sleep and not waking up, he stops at a small farmhouse. There the boys receive food, a bath, long underwear, and a night's stay from a kind woman who makes them write to their parents.

4. New Orleans, Louisiana

A truck driver, Lonnie Bromer, offers to drive the boys southeast toward New Orleans, Louisiana, on the Gulf of Mexico. After Josh tells of his family situation, Lonnie compares him to his son David, who died of appendicitis in 1927. When Lonnie stops for lunch, he asks Josh to play the cafe piano. Customers applaud the performance.

The waitress gives Lonnie the name of her cousin, Pete Harris, who owns a circus in Baton Rouge in east-central Louisiana and might be interested in hiring a piano player. That night, Lonnie notes that Josh is bitter toward his parents. Lonnie, who recognizes the destructiveness of ill feelings, admits that he blames himself for David's death.

5. Baton Rouge, Louisiana

Over the days that the three travel together, Lonnie assesses Josh's character. He drives the boys to the carnival in Baton Rouge. Both he and Pete agree that neither one knows how long the boys will have jobs. Pete offers Josh $5 per week plus food and lodging to play the piano. Edward C. Kensington, a gentle dwarf, and Emily, who plays Bongo the clown, welcome Josh and Joey. Lonnie says goodbye and leaves his name and an Omaha address so Josh can repay him for the boys' meals. The boys scrape together $4 after their first two weeks of employment and send the money to Lonnie.

Josh falls in love with Emily, a tall, attractive mother of three boys, who holds the show together. At Christmas, Josh buys Joey a shirt and candy bar; Joey buys Josh a wallet containing an identification card. Josh writes Lonnie Bromer's name in the space indicating the person to notify in case of accident. Because Pete Harris plans to marry Emily to give her sons a home, Josh faces the bitter fact that he will never have Emily for himself. He keeps to himself and broods over her. Joey embarrasses him by being rude to her.

Winter weather drives away carnival-goers, and an untended oil heater catches fire and destroys tents and the piano. With the source of their employment gone, Josh and Joey depart with the banjo, intending to return to Lonnie. On the way out, Pete gives them $2; Emily offers molasses cookies, pecans, a wool blanket, and her address. Edward C. is too sad to say goodbye and expresses his thanks in a note.

6. Seventy miles north of Baton Rouge

On their way to Omaha, the boys walk 20 miles north and travel 50 miles by truck. A few days later, they share rabbit stew with hobos who discuss Franklin Roosevelt, who has been elected president. A bootlegger named Charley gives the boys a lift in a shiny Cadillac. Charley buys them a meal and intends to leaves a large tip for the waitress, but he has no small bills, so Josh exchanges his earnings for Charley's $20 bill.

The boys rent a bed and travel the next day on foot. Josh stops to buy Joey overshoes. The owner of the shop and the sheriff cheat Josh out of his $20 bill by claiming that it is counterfeit. The boys are left with cookies, pecans, and the $4 in change that Joey earned. They spend the night in a heated country schoolhouse. For weeks, the boys push on against winter winds. Suffering from exposure and malnutrition, Josh develops a cough and spends precious coins for cough syrup.

7. Nebraska

By the last week in February, Josh and Joey are forced to beg bones from a butcher. They find a poor man who will cook the bones into broth. The man also lines their shoes with cardboard and gives them heavy socks. A poor, feverish woman chases them away, then runs to fetch them. She waters down soup for the Grondowskis, herself, and her six children. When Josh's strength wavers, he scolds Joey, then slaps him for giving half a loaf of fresh bread to the feverish woman. Joey dejectedly leaves. Josh stumbles wearily after his brother, leaving behind the rest of the bread. Fearful that he will die, Josh sinks into unconsciousness.

8. Omaha, Nebraska

Because he has Lonnie's name on the card in his wallet, Josh awakens at Lonnie's house in Omaha. Janey, Lonnie's 14-year-old niece, helps her uncle tend Josh, who mourns the absence of his brother so deeply that he has no will to live. Lonnie promises to find the boy and notifies the state police.

Lonnie's mother washes Josh; Janey visits to brighten his convalescence. To fulfill a classroom assignment, Janey and Josh listen to President Roosevelt's inaugural address on the radio on March 4, 1933. The president warns people that "the only thing we have to fear is fear itself—nameless, unreasoning, unjustified terror."

While visiting Josh, Janey fills in information about Lonnie's losses. She regrets the separation of her uncle and aunt after Davy's death. Although Janey is less beautiful than Emily, Josh feels affection for her and wishes that he could give her earrings like Pete gave Emily at Christmas.

Lonnie has no news of Joey from the police or Pete. He writes to the Grondowskis to inquire whether the boy hitchhiked home. Mary Grondowski replies and encloses a note telling Josh how much his father and sister miss him and how much she loves him and wants him home again. Her best news is that she is giving piano lessons to a gangster's wife.

An Omaha radio broadcast describes the collapse of a barn on three homeless boys, two from Des Moines and one from Chicago. Lonnie departs and returns with Joey, who was claimed by the Arthurs, a prosperous family who return Joey's belongings plus books, toys, clothes, and food. Lonnie informs the Grondowskis and Pete that Joey is safe.

With the Arthurs' help, Josh and Joey get a job at a restaurant and use the proceeds from performances on the piano and banjo to repay Lonnie for their lodging and the cost of his search for Joey. The boys send money home and correspond with Emily, who is happy to have Pete as her husband and father to her boys. She urges Josh to make peace with his father and return to Chicago.

Josh gives a last performance at the restaurant, performing Stefan's favorite Polish folk song. At last the boys decide to return to their parents. The restaurant owner gives Josh a letter of recommendation to a restaurateur in Chicago. The boys say farewell to the Arthurs and Lonnie and Janey. Josh declares that Janey is his girl.

9. Chicago, Illinois

In the coach on the train to Chicago, the boys eat in comfort. The conductor inquires if they have been on vacation. Upon arrival, the brothers tensely reunite with their parents and sister. Josh sees age and strain on his father's face, but Stefan is glad to have the boys home again.

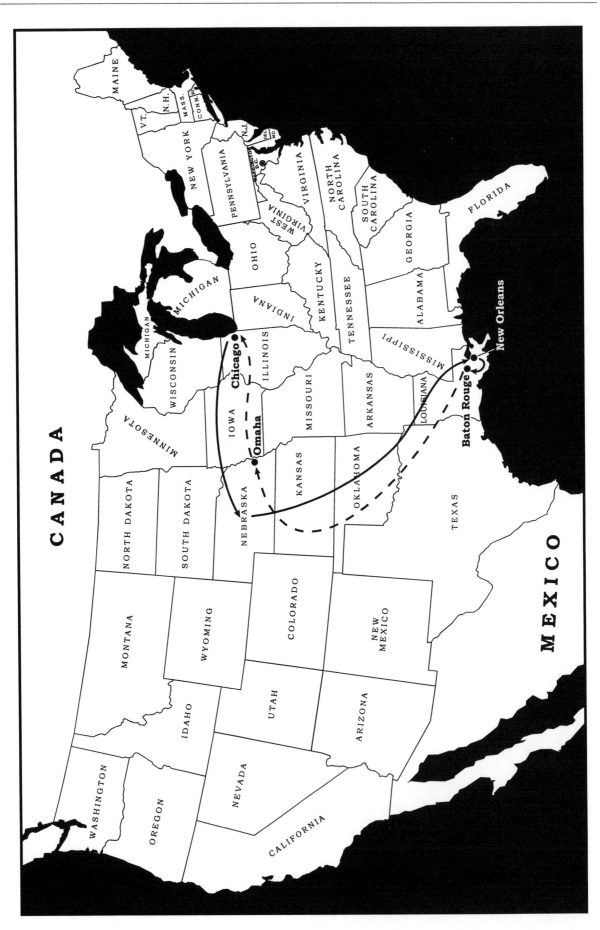

Shoeless Joe

BY WILLIAM PATRICK KINSELLA

Fantasy novel, 1982

Geographical Summary: A whimsical blend of reality and fiction, *Shoeless Joe* is the basis of the movie *Field of Dreams*. It takes Iowa farmer Ray Kinsella on a 1,500-mile odyssey from his land near Iowa City through the ballparks of five major northeastern cities to the Vermont home of J. D. Salinger, a reclusive novelist who was a popular cult figure in the 1950s and 1960s. Their trip to a baseball game at Boston's Fenway Park concludes with Salinger joining his genial kidnapper on a trip to the Baseball Hall of Fame in Cooperstown, New York, and a fact-finding mission through Chisholm, Minnesota. The information they obtain on Archibald Graham helps re-create a magic moment after ghost players convene at Ray's baseball field on his Iowa farm.

Written by Canadian teacher and writer W. P. Kinsella, the story captures a significant part of Americana—the deification of baseball. According to legend, Abner Doubleday created the game in Cooperstown, New York, in 1839, although references in eighteenth-century American children's books suggest that the term and game are at least a century older and may have evolved from an English game called rounders. Whatever its origin, by the beginning of the twentieth century, baseball had earned national devotion. In the first World Series, played in 1903, Pittsburgh lost to Boston by a two-game margin. Significant to *Shoeless Joe* is the "Black Sox" bribery scandal of 1919, which cost eight members of the Chicago White Sox permanent expulsion from organized play for deliberately losing the World Series.

Twenty years after the debacle, the National Baseball Hall of Fame and Museum opened in Cooperstown. Among displays of memorabilia, statistics, photographs, and artifacts are bronze plaques honoring great baseball stars, including Connie Mack, John McGraw, Casey Stengel, and Pee Wee Reese, whom veteran ballplayers honored for their skill, honesty, character, and sportsmanship. In addition, the Baseball Writers' Association of America named such figures as Ty Cobb, Cy Young, Lou Gehrig, Rogers Hornsby, Dizzy Dean, Joe DiMaggio, and Jackie Robinson to the Hall of Fame. A third committee on the Negro Leagues added such stars as Satchel Paige, Buck Leonard, and Monte Irvin to the honor roll, which numbers more than 225 stars.

Further Reading

Allen, Ethan N. *Baseball Play and Strategy*. Melbourne, FL: Krieger, 1985.

Angell, Roger. *Late Innings: A Baseball Companion*. New York: Ballantine Books, 1983.

Appel, Martin, and Burt Goldblatt. *Baseball's Best: The Hall of Fame Gallery*. New York: McGraw-Hill, 1980.

DeLorme, David. *Minnesota Atlas and Gazetteer*. Freeport, ME: DeLorme, 1990.

Fargo, O. J., ed. *Iowa Geography*. Creston, IA: Green Valley Area Education Agency, 1988.

Gilbert, C. L., ed. *Vermont Odysseys: Contemporary Tales from the Green Mountain State.* New York: New American Library-Dutton, 1991.

Lundquist, James. *J. D. Salinger.* New York: Ungar, 1978.

Detailed Itinerary

1. Johnson County, Iowa

The story opens on the midwestern farm of Ray and Annie Kinsella, parents of toddler Karin, near Iowa City in the spring of 1979. Ray, a former life insurance salesman, attempts to re-create the golden age of baseball and to make up for the wrong done an innocent player, Shoeless Joe Jackson, who was accused of defrauding the public in the Black Sox scandal during the 1919 World Series.

2. Deer Lodge, Montana

Ray Kinsella and his twin, Richard, were born in Deer Lodge, Montana. At maturity, the boys separated. Richard, a drifter, ceased to keep in touch with his family.

3. University of Iowa, Iowa City

After completing his education at the University of Iowa, Ray marries Annie, whose mother and brother ridicule his dreams. Although he knows nothing about farming, Ray leases land from Eddie "Kid" Scissons, an elderly retired farmer who claims to be the oldest living former player for the Chicago Cubs. Ray leads the conventional life of a corn farmer until a mystical voice urges him to put his energies into the construction of a baseball stadium. With Annie's concurrence, Ray covers an area adjacent to their home with grass and jeopardizes his tenuous finances by purchasing a lawn tractor to tend the infield. The spirit of Shoeless Joe Jackson appears and practices regularly on the new diamond.

4. Des Moines, Iowa

A subsequent disembodied messenger presses Ray to "ease his pain." Ray surmises that the "his" refers to J. D. Salinger. Again, with Annie's blessing, Ray drives his battered Datsun 100 miles west to Des Moines, Iowa, and purchases a gun from a pawnshop to take on the trip.

5. Chicago, Illinois

After studying the United States map, Ray departs for I-80 northwest to Chicago. He braves the dangers of South Chicago streets to take in a White Sox game at Cominsky Park.

6. Cleveland, Ohio

Following I-80 east to Cleveland to watch the Indians play at Municipal Stadium, Ray witnesses a failed restaurant robbery at a cafe near his hotel.

7. Pittsburgh, Pennsylvania

Ray takes a dreary motel room near Pittsburgh, then drives northeast to New York City.

8. New York City, New York

In New York on a warm day, Ray watches a game at Yankee Stadium before heading northeast to Boston, on the coast of Massachusetts overlooking the Atlantic Ocean.

9. Boston, Massachusetts

Ray prepares for his meeting with Salinger by buying two tickets in advance for Section 17 behind the Red Sox dugout at Fenway Park in Boston.

10. Holyoke, Massachusetts

As Ray passes through Holyoke, Massachusetts, toward Salinger's home, he grows more tense and thinks about growing up in Montana.

11. Windsor, Vermont, on the New Hampshire border

In the woods outside Windsor, on the New Hampshire border, Ray follows the road toward the "Private Property" sign at Salinger's home. Ray bargains Salinger out of self-imposed exile by offering him Shoeless Joe's baseball, threatens him with a fake gun, and invites him to the game in Fenway Park. Salinger introduces himself as Jerry.

12. Claremont, New Hampshire

In Claremont, a police officer stops the car. Jerry has an opportunity to escape, but he indicates his partial compliance by remaining silent about the abduction.

13. Boston, Massachusetts

Jerry and Ray eat at a Greek restaurant, then attend the Red Sox game at Fenway Park. During the game, a signboard lights up with information about Archibald "Moonlight" Graham, a player for the New York Giants who completed only one inning, left baseball, and died in Chisholm, Minnesota, in 1965. Salinger hears the mysterious voice command: "Go the distance" and "Fulfill the dream." On an errand for more orange soda, Ray runs into a steel girder. Jerry drives Ray's car out of Boston as Ray recuperates.

14. Windsor, Vermont

On the night drive north to Jerry's home, the writer indicates that he once had Ray's passion for baseball. The two share their mystical experience with the voice and discuss the scoreboard. They decide to search for more information about Archie Graham.

15. Cooperstown, New York

To gather data, Ray and Jerry stop at the National Baseball Hall of Fame and Museum in Cooperstown, New York, southwest of Schenectady. They then take I-90 west across Ohio, Indiana, and Illinois.

16. Chisholm, Minnesota

The Datsun travels north to the Iron Range in the upper regions of Minnesota. Along the way, Salinger fears that fans will recognize him and destroy his anonymity, but no one bothers him. (One person falsely identifies him as Truman Capote.) In Chisholm, the mining town where Moonlight Graham practiced medicine for 50 years, the editor of the *Chisholm Free Press* shares Graham's obituary, an editorial eulogizing his kindness and altruism, and a framed photograph of him dressed in a New York Giants uniform. Jerry and Ray collect quotations from friends and former patients who recall Graham's generosity to needy children.

As Jerry sleeps in the motel, Ray follows Graham's ghost back in time to his office. Ray tricks Doc into revealing the date—June 1955. The ghost returns to his wife Alicia; Ray and Jerry leave Chisholm without resurrecting Moonlight for their team. But on the road out of Chisholm, they pick up a hitchhiker—the young Archie Graham.

17. Minneapolis, Minnesota

The trio travels west into Minnesota and halts in Minneapolis for a Twins game. Ray and Jerry learn that Archie, a North Carolina rookie, hasn't yet earned the nickname "Moonlight."

18. Bloomington, Minnesota

From Minneapolis, the men drive south. After taking a room near the ballpark in Bloomington, the home of the Minnesota Twins, the three force a lock and enter the empty stadium, where Archie impresses them with his strong pitch. Archie looks forward to reaching Iowa and a chance to realize his ambition.

19. Iowa City, Iowa

On the way west to Ray's stadium, the three travelers stop at the Bishop Cridge Friendship center in Iowa City to pick up Eddie and drive him to Ray's farm. Ray starts his lawn mower and immediately begins grooming the field and plucking weeds.

Mark, Annie's greedy brother and a professor at the University of Iowa, has joined Abner Bluestein, a grasping pseudointellectual, in snapping up prime farmland. To complete a sizeable parcel, they need Ray's acreage. Annie and Ray visit the registry of deeds and learn about the land-grabbing plan. Eddie, who was once in league with Mark, abandons the scheme and becomes involved in the ghostly baseball team that has appeared at Ray's private stadium.

Richard, now a seedy carnival barker, arrives at the farm but cannot see Ray's fantasy team. The men remain indoors and play hearts until Shoeless Joe returns with the ghost players, who include Ray's father, Johnny, as catcher. Karin announces the team's arrival. As the stadium lights brighten, Eddie proclaims baseball's virtues. On July 28, he lays himself out on the company bed in Ray's guest room and dies. The ghost team helps Ray bury him on the diamond. Salinger offers Ray enough cash to pay outstanding installments on the farm mortgage; Ray refuses his money.

Ray visits the carnival and encounters Gypsy, Richard's girlfriend. She brings Richard to Ray's stadium and enjoys the ghost game, but Richard, who lacks imagination, is unable to see it. Eventually, however, Richard tunes in to the mystical voice. Ray and Richard introduce themselves to an incarnation of their father, 25-year-old Johnny Kinsella.

Mark and Bluestein threaten to destroy the playing field, so Ray hurls orange soda on Mark. Annie assaults her brother's shins. Ray retrieves his pistol from the Datsun and brandishes it at Mark. Unable to remove the safety, Ray appears to shoot at the same time that a fly ball breaks a stadium light.

At that moment, Karin falls from the bleachers and nearly chokes on a hot dog. Graham, who long ago chose medicine over sports, abandons "Moonlight" and becomes "Doc" to save Karin from suffocation.

The stadium is already drawing fans and begins to earn enough money to save the farm. When their job is done, the team withdraws into fantasy, taking Jerry with them into the corn rows.

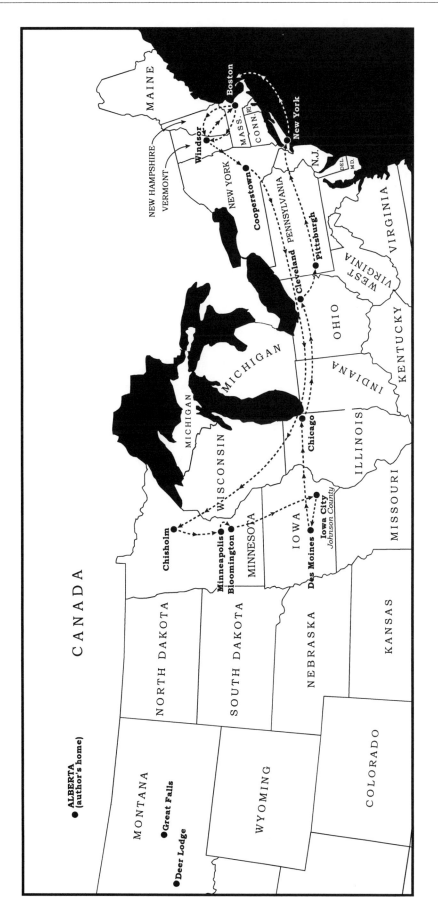

Sing Down the Moon

BY SCOTT O'DELL

Young adult historical fiction, 1970

Geographical Summary: *Sing Down the Moon* is a fictional retelling of the Long Walk, a military action led by Colonel Christopher "Kit" Carson in June 1863. The novel depicts the resettlement of thousands of Navajo and Apache through the eyes of Bright Morning, a courageous young Canyon de Chelly native who has been kidnapped from her northwestern Arizona home. Escaping enslavement as well as hunger, maltreatment, and despair, she eludes pursuers on her way home. After she rejoins the tribe at Canyon de Chelly, soldiers force the Navajo out of the hills into east central Colorado across the Pecos River near Fort Sumner. With the help of her husband, Tall Boy, Bright Morning leaves Bosque Redondo (southeast of Santa Fe, New Mexico), gives birth to a son on their long journey north through Elk Running Valley, and returns to the hidden cave, high in the cliffs, of her family's ancestral home south of Four Corners (the place where Utah, Colorado, New Mexico, and Arizona meet).

Four Corners is the site of several historic landmarks and events, particularly Anasazi cliff dwellings (which were once common in the Four Corners area and are preserved at the Canyon de Chelly National Monument in Arizona) and the Pueblo defeat of Hispanic settlers, who fled south to Juarez, Mexico, in 1680. This rugged canyon was also the beginning point of the Long Walk, a brutal forced march of Navajos from Arizona to Bosque Redondo, after white settlers tried to usurp choice pasturage to the east at Canyon Bonito. The Navajo signed a truce in 1861, but according to Chester Arthur, a Navajo chronicler, the prophet Nahtahlith saw in a vision that white solders would force his people to make the Long Walk.

Following a riot over a rigged horse race, after which cavalry artillery turned howitzers against the Navajo, Kit Carson received a commission to prepare this unstable area for white settlement by transporting local tribes 300 miles east to an unpromising piece of land on the Pecos River. Officials ordered a voluntary migration by June 23, 1863. After the Indians ignored the ultimatum, Carson organized a forced march, preceded by the slaughter of Navajo livestock and the destruction of fruit trees and vegetable gardens in Canyon de Chelly so that inhabitants would have to leave or starve. Led by Carson and superintended by Mexican, Apache, and Ute hirelings, the journey began in March 1864 and concluded with four years' imprisonment of 8,491 Apache and Navajo.

A native contingent under Manuelito, a rebel chief who refused to yield to Carson's troops, led 4,000 Navajo to western strongholds, but by September 1, 1866, they surrendered at Fort Wingate, New Mexico. Two years later, Manuelito and a fellow chief journeyed to Washington, D.C., to petition for Navajo rights. Upon signing a new treaty in the fall of 1868, the Navajo were allowed to return to Fort Defiance, Arizona, and migrate on foot across the Chuska Mountains on the Arizona-New Mexico border to their sacred homeland, Canyon de Chelly.

Further Reading

The American Southwest. New York: Prentice Hall Press, 1990.

Johnson, Broderick H. *Navajo Stories of the Long Walk Period.* Tsaile, AZ: Navajo Community College Press, 1975.

Kelly, Lawrence C. *Navajo Roundup: Selected Correspondence of Kit Carson's Expedition Against the Navajo.* Ann Arbor, MI: Books on Demand UMI, 1992.

Patterson, Lotsee, and Mary Ellen Snodgrass. *Indian Terms of the Americas.* Englewood, CO: Libraries Unlimited, 1994.

Waldman, Carl. *Atlas of the North American Indian. New York: Facts on File, 1985.*

Detailed Itinerary

1. Canyon de Chelly, Arizona

On the high mesas above Canyon de Chelly in the northeastern corner of Arizona, a 14-year-old Navajo (or Navaho) girl, Bright Morning, tends her mother's sheep. The job is a mark of pride to her tribe. The community weaves blankets from the wool and also grows peaches, melons, and squash.

At Spider Rock and Lost Sheep Mountain, Bright Morning watches the fine spring weather change to snow. In alarm, she leaves the sheep and returns to the hogan. Bright Morning's mother humiliates her for abandoning the herd by caring for the flock herself, refusing to speak to her daughter, and denying her the job of herder. However, the next spring, Bright Morning, along with White Deer and Running Bird, returns to the mesas to herd sheep. The girls discuss marriage and children. Bright Morning expects to marry Tall Boy, but White Deer and Running Bird imply that Tall Boy may choose a Ute bride when he rides west the following day.

The next morning Tall Boy leads 12 tribesmen to the west on a raid against the Ute. Bright Morning's mother disapproves of his arrogance. At noon, the three girls, again watching sheep, hear gunfire and see 10 soldiers from Fort Defiance, south of Canyon de Chelly on the Arizona-New Mexico border. The men, armed with bayonets, guard the peace promised by Old Bear, the village spokesman. The next day on the mesa, two Spanish slavers ask directions to Corn Mountain, then grab Bright Morning and Running Bird.

2. Lowlands below the Dawn Trail in Arizona

The kidnappers force the girls on horseback down the Dawn Trail to the lowlands. After four nights of hard travel, the party arrives at a white settlement. An old Jicarilla Apache woman sells them dog meat stew. The slaver gives Running Bird to the Apache and deposits Bright Morning in the care of a white woman, the wife of a soldier. Bright Morning works in the kitchen with 12-year-old Rosita, a Navajo captive from White Mesa, and is assigned sleeping quarters, two Navajo blankets, two dresses, and a pair of red shoes with buttons.

The next morning in the market, Nehana, a Nez Percé slave, warns Bright Morning that Rosita cannot be trusted and tells her that Running Bird is in the second house in the market. Nehana and Bright Morning plan to escape during Easter services, but Bright Morning's mistress stays too close for her to get away. The following night, Bright Morning fakes a headache and climbs over the wall. She and her dog rendezvous with Nehana and Running Bird at the church. During the service, when candles are put out, the girls steal three horses and ride north, stopping only for snatches of rest.

On the trail the girls encounter Tall Boy and his friend Mando. The boys are overtaken by the Spaniards and hear their complaints that the girls stole horses. Tall Boy hurls his lance into a Spanish pursuer, then is shot in the shoulder. He rides the rest of the way tied to the saddle so he won't fall off.

3. Canyon de Chelly, Arizona

On the third day of the escape, the group places Tall Boy on a travois for the return trip to Canyon de Chelly, where Bright Morning helps nurse him. Despite treatment from the medicine man, Tall Boy's right arm remains paralyzed. Bright Morning admires and defends him, while others pity him and treat him condescendingly as though he were a woman.

While running during the four-day Womanhood Ceremony, Bright Morning slows down for Tall Boy. He interprets her act as public humiliation for a handicapped male and shouts that he did not follow the kidnappers just to rescue her. Because of his swaggering bravado, she pities his useless arm even more.

4. High country in the Four Corners area

That winter, with help from enemy Ute, the Long Knives (U.S. cavalry soldiers) force the Navajo out of Canyon de Chelly. Tall Boy defies the authorities' written orders by shredding them and tossing the bits into the river. To escape the soldiers, Bright Morning's father leads the tribe farther north to the high country. They conceal flocks in a secret canyon and, carrying only a week's supply of food, climb slabs of stone up the cliffs. Tall Boy joins the tribe by dragging himself up the steep slope; he hones an iron lance point to use against his enemies.

5. Canyon de Chelly, Arizona

The next morning, soldiers on the land below destroy the Navajo village by burning hogans, cutting their peach trees down to stumps, and trampling the garden. They garrison the village and starve the tribe out of the hills. Old Bear dies from the ordeal. As the Navajo return, Tall Boy attempts to hurl his lance at a soldier, but humiliates himself further by failing.

6. The road southeast to Fort Sumner, New Mexico

The Canyon de Chelly Navajo join a band from Blue Water Canyon. That spring, others swell the band until many Navajo are marching the 300 miles southeast toward a prison camp outside Fort Sumner in central New Mexico. On the month-long march, Bright Morning helps Little Rainbow manage her two small children. As the soldiers round up thousands of Indians, Little Rainbow becomes separated from her baby girl, Meadow Flower. Old and young die of hunger as food becomes scarce. They are hastily buried by the wayside.

7. Bosque Redondo, northeast of Fort Sumner, New Mexico

At noon of the third day, at the bend of the Pecos River river near Bosque Redondo, 8,491 captives halt and construct makeshift driftwood shelters, where they chafe at idleness and oppression. Bright Morning comforts Little Rainbow about the deaths of both her children. Competition for limited food between several hundred Apache and the Navajo makes life miserable.

8. Sand Creek, Colorado

In 1864, rumors of J. M. Chivington's massacre of 300 Cheyenne and Arapaho at Sand Creek, on the east-central border of Colorado, cause greater tension.

9. Bosque Redondo, New Mexico

That winter, Tall Boy, who has bartered for a horse, marries Bright Morning and helps her construct a willow and soil lean-to next to her parents' shelter. When she is four months pregnant, she stores up food for a return to Canyon de Chelly. She trades her turquoise bracelet to obtain blankets for the trip. Tall Boy goes to prison for fighting and breaking the arm of an Apache.

In spring, Tall Boy escapes prison through a garbage hole in the wall and returns to Bright Morning. He shows little interest in returning to the old village, but his wife insists that they try. Impelled by her enthusiasm, he joins her for the escape northwest across the New Mexico-Arizona border to Canyon de Chelly.

10. Elk-Running Valley, New Mexico

On the seventh day of the trek north, Tall Boy changes direction and moves northward into the forested piedmont. They build their shelter beside a pond in Elk-Running Valley and spend the summer there. Bright Morning gives birth to a son. The family spends the winter busily preparing skins for clothing, strengthening their shelter against the winter snow, and hunting for food. Bright Morning cannot stop thinking about her sheep in Canyon de Chelly.

11. Canyon de Chelly, Arizona

The trio arrive at the old village and move into a cave above the canyon near a plum grove. Bright Morning recovers a sheep and a lamb and looks forward to returning to the old life. She breaks a toy spear and laughs with her son as a pleasant rain falls.

12. Four Corners area

Four years later the surviving Navajo prisoners, minus the 1,500 who died of smallpox and other diseases, are released and resettle in the Four Corners area.

Slave Dancer

BY PAULA FOX

Young adult historical fiction, 1973

Geographical Summary: Jessie Bollier, a sensitive young Southerner, is kidnapped from New Orleans and forced to serve as fife player aboard a slave ship bound for the Bight of Benin on Africa's west coast. Returning from Africa via the Cape Verde islands to Cuba, where the cargo is to be traded, he witnesses the dumping of slaves into shark-infested waters. Battered by a storm that sinks the ship, Jessie and Ras, the only slave to survive, wash ashore on the Gulf of Mexico in Mississippi. Jessie returns west to New Orleans, then moves northeast to Rhode Island to become an apothecary. During the Civil War, he is captured and serves time in Andersonville Prison in southwest Georgia. His life is so marred by the memories of slavery that he never again enjoys music.

Historically, American slave trading dates to 1619, when Dutch ships imported the first black indentured servants, who were listed on a Jamestown, Virginia, census along with European settlers. By 1761, more than 600,000 slaves had been transported over the Atlantic route from Africa. To supply entrepreneurs with field workers to cultivate and harvest tobacco, rice, and indigo, Portuguese navigators combed Africa's west coast. Working in conjunction with African kings and kidnappers, these merchants surveyed the human merchandise, made their trade, and loaded their goods on ships by whatever method would produce the greatest profit.

The slaver's route, known as the trade triangle, brought ships to principal exporting points on the Gulf of Guinea, especially the Ivory Coast, the Gold Coast, and the Bronze Coast. Likely blacks, judged by the health of their teeth, skin, hair, eyes, and musculature, were rounded up and restrained in holding pens before boarding. The journey west to American markets took place under insufferable conditions. Male and female slaves were chained, stowed horizontally like cord wood on crude shelves, and fed and watered like animals. Sporadic exercise, known as slave dancing, involved bringing a small group of prisoners up on deck for fresh air, rhythmic movements to drum or fife, and stretching. Before being returned to the dank, foul-smelling hold, women and boys were often allotted to the crew as sexual diversions.

Large numbers of slaves died during the Middle Passage. It was not uncommon for a slave ship to lose half its store of captives or for disease to spread to the crew. To prove to black inmates the might of the ship's crew, a captain might brand or maim an unruly captive or slaughter a few to impress the others with the importance of obeying orders. Many died of smallpox, diphtheria, diarrhea, malnutrition, injury, suffocation, murder, intertribal fighting, or suicide; others arrived so traumatized that they were useless to overseers. Unloaded in West Indian training complexes, the best of the lot were broken like wild beasts before being transported to auction centers in North or South America in exchange for lumber, flour, whale oil, and livestock.

The triangle continued with shiploads of linen, lumber, iron, tobacco, rice, and indigo traded to Europe and rum to Africa to pay for more slaves. Officially, the United States ended the slave trade in 1808, yet merchandising of African flesh continued until 1861. The value of trade goods produced by slave labor, which enriched industrialists as well as plantation owners, increased the value of slaves, particularly the skilled and semiskilled, such as seamstresses, cooks, ironworkers, farriers, masons, bricklayers, and carpenters, who might be sold for as much as $2,000. By 1860, more than half the populations in parts of Texas, Louisiana, Mississippi, Alabama, Georgia, South Carolina, North Carolina, and Virginia were slaves.

Further Reading

Asante, Molefi K., and Mark T. Mattson. *Historical and Cultural Atlas of African Americans.* New York: Macmillan, 1992.

Cantor, George. *Historic Landmarks of Black America.* Detroit: Gale, 1991.

Evitts, William J. *Captive Bodies, Free Spirits: The Story of Southern Slavery.* Englewood Cliffs, NJ: Julian Messner, 1985.

Ferrell, Robert H., and Richard Natkiel. *Atlas of American History.* New York: Facts on File, 1987.

Foner, Eric, and John A. Garraty, eds. *The Reader's Companion to American History.* Boston: Houghton Mifflin, 1991.

Low, W. Augustus, and Virgil A. Clift. *Encyclopedia of Black America.* New York: Da Capo Press, 1981.

Ploski, Harry A., and James Williams, eds. *The Negro Almanac: A Reference Work on the African American.* Detroit: Gale, 1989.

Walvin, James. *Slavery and the Slave Trade: A Short Illustrated History.* Jackson, MS: University Press of Mississippi, 1983.

Wilson, Charles Reagan, and William Ferris, eds. *Encyclopedia of Southern Culture.* Chapel Hill, NC: University of North Carolina Press, 1989.

Detailed Itinerary

1. New Orleans, Louisiana

The grandson of a Frenchman named Beaulieu, Jessie Bollier lives in Pirate's Alley with his sister Betty and his widowed mother, who supports them by sewing for rich women. Jessie dreams of his father, who drowned in the Mississippi River, and grows up hating slavery.

2. Vieux Carré, New Orleans

In 1840, on an errand into the Vieux Carré (the French Quarter, New Orleans's oldest section) to borrow candles from an aunt, Jessie is kidnapped by Purvis and Claudius, two sailors who had paid him to play his fife in the marketplace. The men march him through marsh and sand to Lake Bourgne and a stinking slave vessel, *The Moonlight*, bound on a four-month voyage for Whydah in the Bight of Benin on Africa's west coast. It is manned by Captain Cawthorne, his mate Nick Spark, and 10 sailors. Jessie's captors tell him that his mother said he could join the crew to play his fife for "royalty." Jessie is not fooled by their lies.

3. Whydah on the Bight of Benin in Africa

On the long voyage east over the Atlantic Ocean to Africa, the Captain, a greedy profiteer, flies various national flags to deceive enemy ships. Arriving at noon at the Bight of Benin on Africa's west coast, *The Moonlight* makes its way to Whydah, but remains offshore. Four nights later, the Captain trades for nearly 100 men, women, and children, who are shackled at the ankles and dragged aboard from canoes. Jessie learns that local chiefs lock them in a barracoon and sell them for cash, rum, and tobacco.

4. Cape Palmas, Liberia, off the windward coast of Africa

The Captain hears news of American cruisers patrolling Cape Palmas, west of Whydah, and worries that British informers have given away his location.

5. Säo Tormé

Quickly traveling south, *The Moonlight* makes for the Portuguese island of Säo Tormé, off Gabon, to load water and food. Bad weather causes seasickness, and filth reduces the decks to muck and stench. The crew has nothing to eat but wormy meat. Captain Cawthorne drowns a mutinous mate and a tormented black woman. Disease kills a crewman and six blacks, whose corpses are heaved overboard. More deaths cause Purvis to swear off future voyages on slave ships. Jessie, despairing over the wretched voyage, befriends an African boy about his own age.

6. Cape Verde Islands

On the passage northwest to Cape Verde, off Senegal, the slaves are brought on deck and "danced" to Jessie's pipe music every day to keep them healthy. He grows so distraught by the slavers' vile treatment of the Africans that he refuses to play. Cawthorne has him beaten.

Stout deliberately drops Jesse's fife into the slave hold. While being lowered after the instrument, Jessie sees a young African with his fife. Although Jesse is weakened by visiting the miserable hold, he returns to his post and dances the slaves before retreating below, sickened with fear and disgust. Purvis offers Jessie a cup of tea and encourages him to do his best to survive the final three weeks of the voyage.

7. Havana, Cuba

Under a Spanish flag, *The Moonlight* anchors in Cuban waters south of Florida. When a Spanish trader and his tongueless slave board to make final arrangements for buying the slaves and marching them to Havana, Jessie is dispatched to the Captain's quarters for a trunkful of fancy garments. The crew dresses the slaves in lace and frills so they can dance to Jessie's pipe while the sailors get drunk on rum and enjoy the show. An English ship interrupts the festivities. Quickly the crew conceals their illegal activities by tossing overboard the hatch covers, shackles, and cauldron. Cawthorne recognizes the ship as American and panics, ordering the hoisting of an American flag and the dumping of slaves into shark-infested waters. Jessie is traumatized by the inhuman events.

8. Mississippi

A storm interrupts the action. *The Moonlight* founders on a reef and capsizes. Jessie and his African friend survive and arrive on land near a shack owned by Daniel, an escaped slave. He feeds the boys, who get to know each other better. Jessie learns that the African's name is Ras. Parts of *The Moonlight* wash ashore, but no other passengers have survived. Jessie relives his horror of his father's death by drowning. Ras believes that sharks ate the human remains.

The boys part, Ras leaving with men who speak his language; Jessie, after telling Daniel the story of his kidnapping and the voyage to Africa, obtains directions for his walk west to Louisiana. As Jessie departs, he promises not to tell anyone of Daniel's home. In four days, Jessie walks from Mississippi to Louisiana, returning home with bloody feet. He embraces Betty and his mother and stays up into the night telling of his adventures.

9. Orleans Bank Canal, Louisiana

In the years after his return, Jessie looks with concern and kindness at local blacks to identify signs of a terrifying voyage or mistreatment. He finds work on the Orleans Bank Canal connecting New Orleans and Lake Pontchartrain. The work does not suit him, but he is thwarted in trying to find a job that does not promote slavery.

10. Rhode Island

Through a friend of his Aunt Agatha, Jessie obtains an apprenticeship with an apothecary and moves northeast to Rhode Island, where his mother and sister eventually join him. He often dreams of the languorous life near the Vieux Carré.

11. Boston, Massachusetts

One day, Jessie thinks he spots Ras in Boston, on the shore of Massachusetts, but he is mistaken.

12. Andersonville Prison, Georgia

Jessie fights for the Union army and spends three months in Andersonville Prison, 10 miles northeast of Americus, Georgia, before he returns to civilian life. He deals with wartime imprisonment better than the experience aboard the slave ship and forever avoids music, which makes him remember the tormented Africans whom he once danced aboard *The Moonlight*.

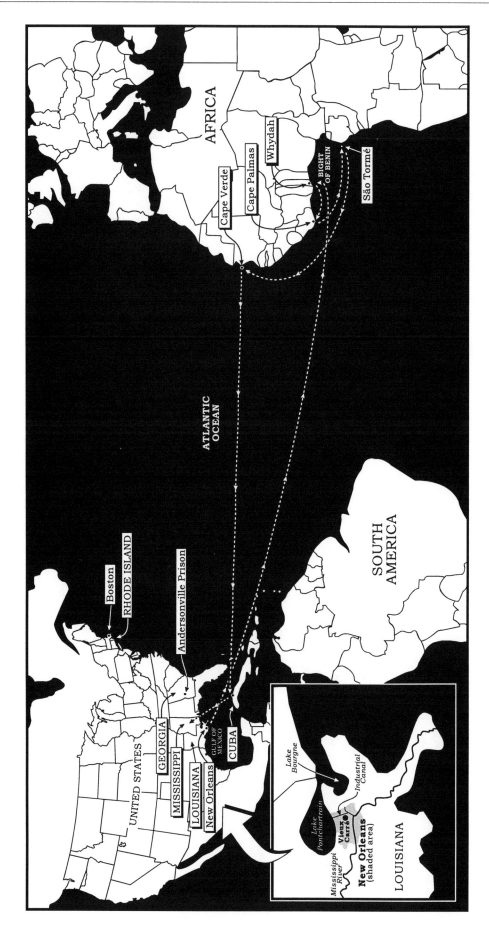

Streams to the River, River to the Sea

BY SCOTT O'DELL

Young adult fictional biography, 1986

Geographical Summary: In this book, Sacagawea, or "Bird Girl," one of history's most prominent Native Americans, completes a 19-month journey from a Mandan village in North Dakota westward over the Rocky Mountains to Washington and the Pacific Ocean and back by a different route, which swings south along the Yellowstone River. Traveling on foot, by cart, and by canoe, she aids her husband and their companions, Lewis and Clark, in surveying a vast expanse of uncharted territory that President Thomas Jefferson purchased from France in 1801. While acting as guide, translator, cook, and nurse, she still manages to care for her infant son, who is born at the beginning of the expedition.

Historically, President Thomas Jefferson initiated the Lewis and Clark expedition as a surveying mission following the Louisiana Purchase of 1803, ostensibly to search for the Northwest Passage, a waterway leading from the Mississippi River to the Pacific Ocean. Led by William Clark and Meriwether Lewis, two experienced soldiers, a surveying party of 50 followed the Mississippi River to the Rocky Mountains, then moved west to the Columbia River. After leaving St. Louis, Missouri, on May 14, 1804, the explorers journeyed to a Mandan village in South Dakota, where they engaged Toussaint Charbonneau as a translator and guide, although it was his wife, Sacagawea, who had the true knowledge. The party traveled by water and portage to Fort Clatsop on the Oregon-Washington border, which they sighted on November 7, 1805. Varying their return route, they arrived at their starting point on September 23, 1806. Although the Lewis and Clark expedition did not discover a water link between the Mississippi River and the Pacific Ocean, the group's report contained valuable information about plants, animals, and Indian tribes in the northwest United States, particularly the Flathead, Nez Percé, Clatsop, and Shoshone.

Sacagawea (1786-April 9, 1884), the expedition's Shoshone interpreter and explorer, was born in the Rocky Mountains. In 1799, she was kidnapped by the Minnetaree, who took her to North Dakota. According to legend, Sacagawea became the slave of a Hidatsa chief, who staked her as the prize in a betting match. The chief lost, and Sacagawea became the property of Toussaint Charbonneau, a 40-year-old French trader who lived with the Mandan. In 1804, she and her husband were chosen to accompany the Lewis and Clark expedition from Fort Mandan, North Dakota, to the Pacific Ocean and back.

Following the birth of her son, variously known as Pompey or Jean Baptiste Charbonneau, on February 11, 1805, Sacagawea carried him in a cradleboard on her back as she translated native languages and helped trade for horses. Lewis and Clark were also benefited by the fact that tribes were less suspicious of a group that included a female. According to expeditionary records, she reunited with her brother, Chief Cameahwait, in southwestern Montana on August 17, 1805, and arrived at the

Pacific Ocean on November 7, 1805. Sacagawea's husband earned $500 for his part in the expedition; she received nothing.

Further Reading

Ferrell, Robert H., and Richard Natkiel. *Atlas of American History.* New York: Facts on File, 1987.

Jassem, Kate. *Sacajawea.* Mahwah, NJ: Troll, 1979.

Patterson, Lotsee, and Mary Ellen Snodgrass. *Indian Terms of the Americas.* Englewood, CO: Libraries Unlimited, 1994.

Seibert, Jerry. *Sacajawea.* Boston: Houghton Mifflin, 1960.

Snyder, Gerald S. *In the Footsteps of Lewis and Clark.* Washington, DC: National Geographic Society, 1970.

Sturtevant, William C., ed. *Handbook of North American Indians.* Washington, DC: Smithsonian Institution Press, 1984.

Waldman, Carl. *Atlas of the North American Indian.* New York: Facts on File, 1985.

———. *Who Was Who in North American History.* New York: Facts on File, 1990.

Wolfson, Evelyn. *From Abenaki to Zuni.* New York: Walker, 1988.

Detailed Itinerary

1. Missouri River, south-central Montana

Minnetaree Indians capture 13-year-old Sacagawea, an Agaidüka Shoshone gathering blackcaps on an island in a stream. They burn her village, kill her mother, and take her on horseback north to the village of Metaharta in North Dakota. She fears her captors, who had twice in her girlhood raided her people, killed the men, and kidnapped the women, and hopes that her father and two brothers will return from their buffalo hunt and reclaim her.

2. Near Fort Mandan, North Dakota

Living with Chief Black Moccasin's family, Sacagawea attracts the attention of Red Hawk. Before their romance can blossom, Tall Rock kidnaps her to the village of Hidatsa, where the deceptive Le Borgne is chief. Sacagawea escapes by boat on the Missouri River and lands on an island, where she prepares for winter.

A French-Sioux trader, Toussaint Charbonneau, rescues her, returns her to Metaharta, and claims her as a second wife. Red Hawk declares previous rights to Sacagawea and challenges Charbonneau and Le Borgne in the Hand Game. Charbonneau wins the match and Sacagawea. After their marriage, he departs on a trading mission to St. Louis. Left behind, Sacagawea prepares for the birth of her baby.

Having completed Fort Mandan to protect the Minnetaree, white explorers, led by Merriwether Lewis and William Clark, arrive by boat. Clark selects Sacagawea to accompany the expedition as an interpreter of the Shoshone language to help them barter for horses. Before they depart, she undergoes a painful childbirth, which Clark relieves with a native remedy. She calls her newborn son Meeko, which means Little Brown Squirrel; Charbonneau names him Jean Baptiste. Clark nicknames him Pompey.

On Sunday, April 7, 1805, Charbonneau and Sacagawea, with Meeko on a cradleboard, depart Fort Mandan with the expedition in a boat, six canoes, and two pirogues, going west toward the Pacific coast. Although Charbonneau mistreats her and tries to convince Clark that she wants to turn back, Sacagawea likes traveling with the expedition and enjoys cooking roots for the men.

Near the Minnetaree village, the pirogue capsizes. Sacagawea rescues Captain Clark's journal and a wooden box containing his compass. Clark kisses her and rewards her with a blue beaded belt of antelope hide.

3. White Bear Island, at the fork of the Missouri and Maria's rivers (currently called Marias River)

At the eastern border of Montana, Lewis debates whether to take the north or south fork of the Missouri River. During a two-week hiatus while he explores the south fork, Sacagawea makes new clothes for the men. In Blackfoot country, she pushes herself too hard and gets sick. Lewis proposes sending her back to Fort Mandan; Clark replies that they should cure her so that she can continue serving as their ambassador to the Indians. Because Lewis has found the Great Falls, the group cache the canoes and travel on land by cart and on foot.

4. Great Falls, Montana

The expedition travels 18 miles toward Great Falls in central Montana, where a flood engulfs them, followed by hail and snow. Sacagawea loses Meeko's cradleboard in the flood and makes a sling to carry him.

5. Beaverhead in Montana

By July 15, 1805, the expedition enters Shoshone territory in southern Montana, which lies west of Great Falls and near the Shining Mountains. After a voice speaks to her, Sacagawea recognizes the area where she was kidnapped in girlhood. A week later, the group reaches Beaverhead.

6. Camp Fortunate in Montana

In another week, Sacagawea reunites with her old companion Running Deer and her brother, Chief Cameahwait. Man Who Smiles, who once courted Sacagawea, claims her. Captain Clark gives her the opportunity to choose a mate; despite her distaste for her husband's abuse and tyranny, Sacagawea selects Charbonneau. Cameahwait recommends that the expedition turn back, but Sacagawea elects to continue. She prays for an omen in an inner chamber of the sacred cave and hears the sound of a swift river, a sign from the Great Spirit that she should continue toward the Pacific Ocean.

7. Traveler's Rest in Idaho

The expedition travels in a northwesterly direction to a Flathead village on the east border of Idaho, which the group names Traveler's Rest. Charbonneau marries Alone in the Clouds, a beautiful native princess, then deserts her when the party pushes on.

8. Camp Canoe on the Snake River in Idaho

The group leave their horses with the Nez Percé at Camp Canoe and travel by water down the Snake River into central Idaho Territory.

9. Columbia River on the border between Washington and Oregon

Soon after buying supplies, the expedition swings northwest on the Snake River and, at the border separating Oregon and Washington, reaches the Columbia River. Captain Clark disappoints Sacagawea by trading her blue beaded belt for an otter robe. They follow the widening river on its curving path to the sea.

10. Camp Disappointment on the Pacific coast

The explorers recognize ocean tides as they reach the estuary of the Columbia River, inhabited by Clatsop Indians. Severe rain hampers their approach to the Pacific. On the coast at Camp Disappointment on December 3, Clark carves his name on a pine tree. Sacagawea carves "Janey," the nickname he gave her, beneath his name. Using beads, trinkets, and garments, the leaders trade with local tribes.

11. Fort Clatsop on the Pacific coast

Members of the expedition build a stockade on the north bank of the Columbia River and name it Fort Clatsop. The Indians report the beaching of a great fish. Sacagawea accompanies Clark to the shore and sees dolphins and sea otters and a whale.

12. Traveler's Rest in Idaho

On the return trip, the expedition, beset by hunger, cold, disease, and fatigue, returns through Lolo Pass in northern Idaho Territory. At the Flathead village, Charbonneau claims Alone in the Clouds and escorts her to camp. The princess returns to her people; in frustration at the loss of his bride, Charbonneau punishes Sacagawea.

13. Beaverhead in Montana

Sacagawea shows the way east through familiar Shoshone territory in southern Montana and helps Clark recover the hidden canoes at Beaverhead.

14. Three Forks, Montana

Traveling rapidly downstream over 97 miles, the group arrives at Three Forks in the southwestern corner of Montana in three days. Clark takes Sacagawea and her family east toward the Rosebud and Powder rivers at the mouth of the Yellowstone River in southeastern Montana, where Clark names a rock "Pompey's Pillar" in honor of Meeko. Lewis leads his party to the Missouri River in northern Montana. Clark's group fails to rendezvous with Lewis. A half day later, his men report that Lewis was accidentally shot in the back while hunting deer. However, Lewis quickly recovers.

15. Fort Mandan, North Dakota

At Fort Mandan, North Dakota, the expedition reunites with the Minnetarees at the end of 19 months. Charbonneau collects $500 in wages and quickly gambles it away. Sacagawea, who receives no pay for her part in translating and guiding, refuses Clark's offer to educate her son or to send her to school. She prefers that Meeko grow up according to Shoshone traditions.

Sadly taking her leave of Clark, whom she has come to love, Sacagawea accepts the gift of his dog Scannon. At Charbonneau's threats that the dog would make good food, she packs to leave her husband. As Captain Clark departs, she sets out west with Meeko toward the Shoshone village.

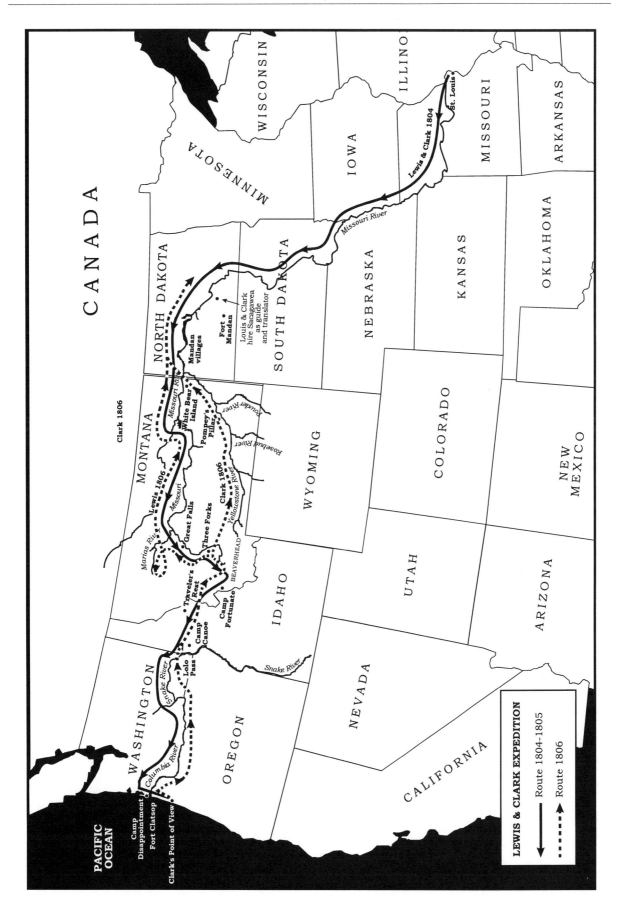

Their Eyes Were Watching God

BY ZORA NEALE HURSTON

Fiction, 1937

Geographical Summary: The story of Janie Mae Crawford Woods carries the heroine only a short distance on the map of Florida, but over a rough patch of emotional terrain. Born to a former slave who deserts her, Janie is reared by her grandmother in West Florida and marries a farmer. Janie leaves him for an ambitious politician and developer who makes her life miserable by forcing her to fit his notion of the ideal mate. Escaping to the love of a drifter nicknamed Tea Cake, she joins migrant workers who harvest beans on "the muck" of the Everglades among Seminoles and Bahamians along the shores of Lake Okeechobee on the Florida peninsula. Janie enjoys two years of contentment before being displaced by a hurricane. Then she is forced to shoot her husband when he contracts rabies and attacks her. Afterward, she returns north to Eatonville, the black town that her second husband helped develop.

Like her central character, Zora Neale Hurston (January 7, 1891-January 28, 1960) knew well the lifestyle of Florida blacks. Born in Eatonville, the United States' first incorporated black town, she listened to stories and conversations on the front stoop of Joe Clark's store and evolved these bits of black Americana into a lifetime's work. As folklorist and writer, she polished her trade in New York before returning to the south to gather more material. On a visit to the Caribbean, she completed *Their Eyes Were Watching God*, which critics consider her most mature work.

The Florida Everglades, the central setting of the novel, is the semitropical, marshy expanse south of Eatonville. It covers 4,000 square miles of shallow, slow-moving water and stretches south from the Kissimmee River Basin and Lake Okeechobee to the Florida Keys and the Gulf of Mexico. Drained by a network of canals, pump stations, dams, and dikes, "the muck" provides rich, peaty soil for vegetable farming. With a perennial fringe of saw grass and stands of cypress, palmetto, mangrove, and pine trees, the Everglades supports plentiful wildlife, including manatee, cougars, alligators, snakes, opossums, rabbits, raccoons, herons, eagles, and ospreys.

For 2,000 years, the Everglades have sheltered Native American tribes, such as the Seminole and Choctaw, who fished, hunted, and gathered food and craft materials from the region and lived in elevated chickees (shelters) to protect themselves from dangerous reptiles. Because of the forbidding nature of the place, with its shallow waters, thick mud, poisonous snakes, and stinging insects, explorers and developers left the area alone until the end of the nineteenth century. With the coming of fruit-growers, cattle ranches, and sugarcane plantations, the land began to change as entrepreneurs imported cheap migrant labor from the Caribbean to plant and harvest crops. By the time of Hurston's novel, drainage of low-lying waters had uncovered habitable land for work crews, who subsisted in shanties that frequently collapsed during tropical storms.

Further Reading

Asante, Molefi K., and Mark T. Mattson. *Historical and Cultural Atlas of African Americans.* New York: Macmillan, 1992.

Banford, Hal. *Florida History.* St. Petersburg, FL: Great Outdoors, 1984.

Bowe, Richard. J. *Pictorial History of Florida.* Chuluota, FL: Mickler House, 1970.

Ferrell, Robert H., and Richard Natkiel. *Atlas of American History.* New York: Facts on File, 1987.

Foner, Eric, and John A. Garraty, eds. *The Reader's Companion to American History.* Boston: Houghton Mifflin, 1991.

Low, W. Augustus, and Virgil A. Clift. *Encyclopedia of Black America.* New York: Da Capo Press, 1981.

Ploski, Harry A., and James Williams, eds. *The Negro Almanac: A Reference Work on the African American.* Detroit: Gale, 1989.

Smith, Jessie Carney. *Notable Black American Women.* Detroit: Gale, 1991.

Toops, Connie. *The Everglades.* Stillwater, MN: Voyageur Press, 1989.

Wilson, Charles Reagan, and William Ferris, eds. *Encyclopedia of Southern Culture.* Chapel Hill, NC: University of North Carolina Press, 1989.

Detailed Itinerary

1. Eatonville, Florida

In 1921, in the incorporated black town of Eatonville, north of Orlando in central Florida, the recently widowed 40-year-old Janie Crawford Woods strides back to the house in which she used to live as wife of Mayor Joe "Jody" Starks. Dressed in overalls, she wears her hair loose, to the consternation of local gossips. Phoeby Watson, Janie's best friend, hurries to console her by listening to her story. Phoeby suggests that Janie halt neighborhood talk by reporting that she married Tea Cake, the younger man with whom she left Eatonville two years earlier. Janie dispatches Phoeby to spread the truth.

2. West Florida

Nanny, Janie's maternal grandmother, reared her in west Florida after Janie's mother Leafy left home. Janie, nicknamed Alphabet, sees her likeness next to Eleanor in a photo and realizes for the first time that she is not white like the Washburns. When Nanny spies Johnny Taylor kissing Janie, she recognizes the danger that lured Leafy into bearing an illegitimate child. To prevent Janie from a similar mistake, she arranges a marriage with a well-off farmer, Logan Killicks, who owns 60 acres, a house near the road, and the town's only organ.

Janie bridles at her lack of choice in the matter and begs for more time. Nanny slaps her, then presses her close to relate some of life's bitter truths and to confess that she longs to see Janie married to a man who will spare her the sufferings of poverty.

3. Savannah, Georgia

Nanny recalls Civil War times when she belonged to Marse Robert Washburn and Mistis, his wife, near Savannah, an Atlantic port on Georgia's eastern coast. The

Washburns lost a son in the Battle of Chickamauga, over the border of Tennessee in northwestern Georgia. The concubine of Marse Robert, Nanny gave birth to Leafy a week before General William T. Sherman of the Union Army captured Atlanta, Georgia.

Marse Robert pauses on his way to join Confederate troops driving Northern soldiers back to Tennessee. Jealous because her husband said his final goodbyes to Nanny at her cabin, Mistis Washburn demands to view the gray-eyed, blond-haired infant girl. She hits Nanny and threatens to sell the baby by the time it is a month old. She orders the overseer to tie Nanny in a kneeling position at the whipping post and lash her.

Still in bed after giving birth, Nanny forces herself to wrap Leafy and flee through the swamp by the Savannah River, which divides Georgia and South Carolina. After leaving Leafy tied to a tree, Nanny hurries to the sounds of cannon near the Savannah landing, where Sherman made his way to the boats. The uproar celebrated the end of slavery. Nanny joins other slaves in an unspecified place.

The war ends and Confederate soldiers are forced to bury their weapons at Moultrie in southern Georgia to symbolize the end of the fight over slavery.

4. West Florida

Settled among good white people in west Florida, Nanny purchases a small piece of land and rejects suitors so that Leafy can get an education and become a teacher. Nanny cannot foresee Leafy's tragedy—rape by the schoolteacher. Leafy reacts to the trauma by drinking and running wild. After giving birth to Janie, Leafy disappears, leaving Nanny to tend Janie, work her small piece of land, and pay Janie back for Leafy's shame.

Janie gives in to her grandmother and marries Logan Killicks. The couple move to a dismal house on his 60 acres. Two and a half months after the wedding, Janie visits Nanny to ask why her marriage lacks love. Nanny insists that Janie should appreciate security. Janie retorts that she hates going to bed with a man who doesn't wash his feet or "talk pretty."

That night, Nanny prays that God will take charge of Janie. A month later, Nanny dies.

5. Lake City, Florida

Before departing to Lake City in northern Florida, Logan assigns Janie the chore of cutting seed potatoes and sets out to trade for a mule so she can help plow. Janie works in the barn as Joe Starks, a flashy urbanite, whistles on his way past the house. To draw his eye, she jerks on the pump handle and shakes loose her hair. Starks asks for a drink and tells Janie that he is going to a town inhabited only by blacks.

For two weeks, Joe and Janie meet secretly in the scrub oaks near the farm. That night, Janie awakens Logan to complain of their lifeless marriage. Logan claims that Janie is "powerful independent" for a person of her background and blames her childhood spent with whites.

The next morning, Logan demands that Janie help him move a manure pile. She remains in the kitchen stirring cornmeal dough. Logan threatens to kill her with an ax. Janie placidly continues making hoecake. On her way out the front gate to rendezvous with Joe, she tosses her apron on a bush.

6. Green Cove Springs, Florida

Joe hires a buggy to take them to Green Cove Springs, on Florida's upper eastern coast. After their wedding that same day, they spend the night in a local boarding house.

7. Maitland, Florida

Traveling by train the next day, they arrive at Maitland, northwest of Orlando. Joe hires a buggy to take them east to Eatonville.

8. Eatonville, Florida

Early in the afternoon, they arrive at the town, where Amos Hicks greets them. Joe, surprised that the town is still undeveloped, asks for the mayor and learns that not only is there no mayor, but also that the town is not properly named. Joe buys 200 acres and returns to the town, where he learns that Apopka, west of Eatonville, is the best place to buy wood for the Starks' house. Joe puts house plans on hold so that he can build a community store. The next day, with Tony Taylor as chairman, Joe announces the construction of a crossroads and spreads the word that Eatonville is ready for more citizens. Six weeks later, 10 families move to town.

On the day that the store is complete, Janie, dressed in rustling wine-colored silk, is the star attraction. Tony, commenting on her beauty, nominates Joe for mayor and asks that Janie make a speech. Joe silences her. Janie pretends not to be hurt.

The next day, while Janie tends store, Joe buys a street lamp. The placement of the light results in a neighborhood barbecue. Janie hopes that the uproar will soon end, but Joe chills her with his plans to make her a privileged mayor's wife. Joe continues to upgrade Eatonville and to belittle Janie. She remains quiet.

In looking for pickled pig's feet, Lum discovers that Janie has improperly checked in a bill of lading, which she fails to post. Joe degrades her as though she were an animal or child. Janie feels herself growing cold to Joe and his pompous, mean-spirited treatment.

At 35, Janie resents Joe's self-aggrandizement and despises his fat body. He compensates for his age and deterioration by ridiculing her body. Because of a disparaging remark about his manhood, Joe hits her and drives her from the store. From that time on, the Starks sleep apart.

In their twentieth year, Joe's kidneys weaken. To spite Janie, he spurns her food and hires a cook. Joe calls in root-doctors from Altamonte Springs, west of Eatonville, and keeps Janie out of his room. Janie terrifies Joe by divulging that he is going to die. She vilifies him for mistreating her and for his egotism, then watches as square-toed Death takes Joe, whose hands writhe in fear. Janie smooths his hands over his corpse, removes her head-rag, and calls the community to witness his death. Beneath the trappings of the bereaved widow, she is glad to be free of him.

Janie closes the store from lack of customers while most of the neighbors watch a baseball game in Winter Park, a few miles south of Eatonville.

A stranger walks seven miles from Orlando to the store and requests cigarettes. His name is Vergible "Tea Cake" Woods. With Janie's permission, he escorts her home. All the next week, Janie thinks over the 12-year difference in their ages. One night, she discovers him waiting for her. They fish most of the night at Lake Sabelia and return at daylight. The store clerk scolds Janie for being seen with a drifter.

The next evening Tea Cake returns to her porch with a gift of fresh trout. They spend the evening playing the piano and singing. The next morning, Tea Cake knocks on the door and awakens Janie. He leaves her in bed so that he can return to his job. For four days, she hears nothing from him. Growing fearful that she has lost him, Janie is reassured on Saturday when he drives up to take her to the Sunday School picnic.

9. Jacksonville, Florida

Janie takes the train northeast to Jacksonville on the Atlantic coast, where Tea Cake has been promised a job. After their wedding, they live in his rented room. While she sleeps, Tea Cake takes her money and leaves without telling her but returns with his guitar, which he had pawned. To experience how it feels to be wealthy, Tea Cake had gone north to Callahan and bankrolled a chicken and macaroni supper for his friends. With only $12 of her money left, he justifies his actions by explaining that his railroad friends are too common for a woman of Janie's background. She replies that she is his wife. On Sunday, he returns at daylight from gambling all night and bleeds from a razor wound, which Janie tends.

10. The muck, between Clewiston and Belle Glade, Florida

Tea Cake repays the $200 he took from Janie and suggests that they move to "the muck," the section of the Everglades that lies between Clewiston and Belle Glade, northeast of Lake Okeechobee. The couple move within sight of the dike, where Tea Cake works for the Boss picking beans. Tea Cake goes east to the coast to buy a rifle, shotgun, and pistol in Palm Beach. He helps Janie learn to shoot. At night they hunt by boat in the 'glades for alligators so that they can sell their hides and teeth. Friendly migrant workers flock to the Woods' house. That fall, at the conclusion of the picking season, the Woods remain behind as other migrants depart. Janie meets Mrs. Turner, an ignorant busybody who denigrates dark-skinned blacks.

11. Palm Beach, Fort Myers, and Fort Lauderdale, Florida

That winter, Tea Cake and Janie withdraw to Palm Beach, Fort Myers, and Fort Lauderdale for fun.

12. The muck, between Clewiston and Belle Glade, Florida

The other migrants return for the season. Mrs. Turner deliberately sets up a meeting between Janie and her brother. Tea Cake makes an example of his manhood by whipping Janie, then petting her. To get even with Mrs. Turner, Tea Cake sets up a fight at her eating place. Mrs. Turner and her family depart the muck for more civilized company in Miami on Florida's southeast tip.

One afternoon, a band of Seminoles departing for Palm Beach warn that a hurricane is coming. The next day, more Indians move east; darkness falls. Tea Cake tries to locate transportation while Janie stitches their insurance papers in an oilcloth pouch.

Lake Okeechobee bursts the dike as 200 mph winds buffet them. Janie and Tea Cake run and swim to a bridge. She is swept into the flood by the wind and clings to a cow's tail, trying to evade a dog on the cow's back as it makes its way to shore. Tea Cake knifes the dog with a switch blade. Before he kills it, the dog sinks its teeth into his cheek.

13. Palm Beach, Florida

After reaching Palm Beach, the next day Janie and Tea Cake spend a portion of their savings for a room. Two days later, white guards commandeer Tea Cake for a Red Cross burial detail. Janie, who does not see him go, worries about his absence.

14. The muck, between Clewiston and Belle Glade, Florida

Tea Cake slips away, rejoins Janie, and goes back to their shack. Within four weeks, he is too ill to swallow water. Janie summons Doctor Simmons, who diagnoses rabies and sends to Miami for serum. He warns Janie to stay out of Tea Cake's bed. Janie removes the pistol Tea Cake has hidden under his pillow and empties the chambers so that she can escape if he tries to shoot her.

Tea Cake menaces her with his pistol and fires, so Janie kills him with a single rifle shot. She cradles him as he bites her forearm, then dies. Accused of murder, she spends three days in jail, but the jury deliberates only five minutes before finding no fault against her.

15. Palm Beach, Florida

Janie orchestrates an elaborate Palm Beach funeral and buries Tea Cake in a vault rather than in the wet ground of the Everglades. She is so grief-stricken that she forgets to remove her overalls for the service.

16. The muck, between Clewiston and Belle Glade, Florida

For two days the community turns against Janie, then accepts her version of the shooting. They invite Janie to stay, but she cannot enjoy the Everglades without Tea Cake.

17. Eatonville, Florida

As soon as she arrives in Eatonville, Janie tells her story to Phoeby. Alone in her house, Janie finds strength in the memories of her marriage to Tea Cake, who lives in bright, happy visions. She embraces peace.

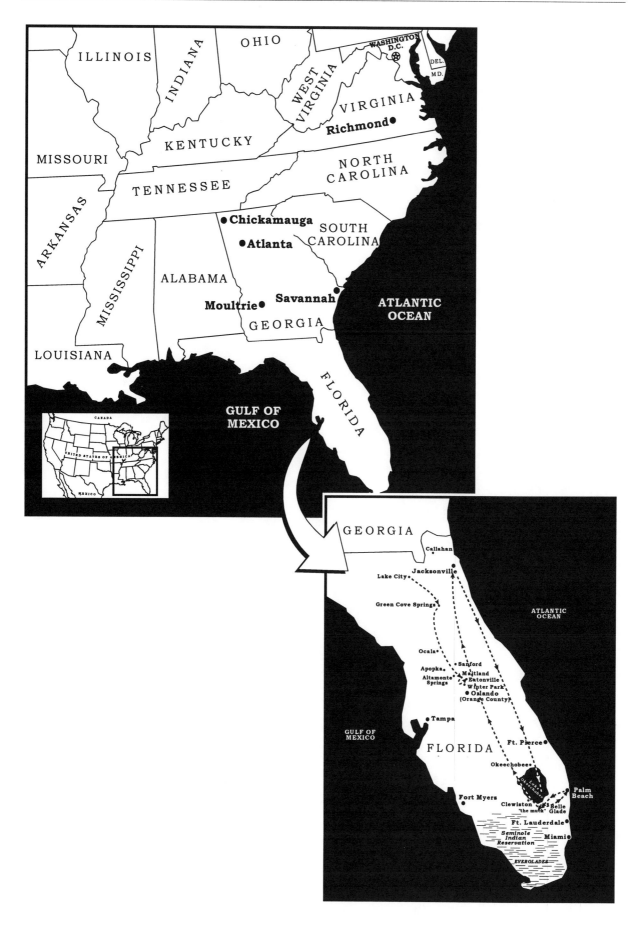

To Sir, with Love

BY E. R. BRAITHWAITE

Autobiographical novel, 1959

Geographical Summary: The teaching experience of Ricardo Braithwaite, a native of British Guiana, (now known as Guyana), in South America, takes him to the grittier parts of London, England, and the homes of students who suffer from poverty, neglect, abuse, and racism. As a black man, Braithwaite meets the challenge of teaching unwanted students by introducing them to a more expansive world, particularly the Caribbean island of Aruba, British Guiana, and other parts of the British Empire where black skin is not uncommon. By insisting on courtesy and escorting his students to parts of London where they can practice good manners, he increases their self-esteem and earns their respect and the nickname "Sir."

For Braithwaite, the problem of blending into white society is shared by many British colonials who, over the twentieth century, looked for advancement in England, particularly London. By the end of World War II, the influx of immigrants from the Caribbean, South Africa, Hong Kong, India, Pakistan, and other parts of the British Commonwealth significantly altered the city's racial makeup. Despite attempts by conservative elements to stem the flow in 1962, the settlement of nonwhite people in London has continued, causing tensions in schools and industry; charges of racial discrimination against the police, immigration officers, and public officials; and consternation among many whites.

Braithwaite, a native of British Guiana reflects the complex lifestyle and high standards of literacy in this South American coastal country. His hometown, Georgetown, is the seat of a national university, several technical training schools, and a technical institute. Having grown up in an ethnically diverse populace of Africans, Chinese, South American Indians, Portuguese, and British and a religious mix of Hinduism, Islam, animism, and Christianity, he has a cosmopolitan attitude toward race, which he conveys to his students. In contrast to his East End students' ignorance and superstitions about blacks, Braithwaite's willingness to overlook skin color and to judge people on the basis of character and behavior forms a major segment of the book's theme. In the 1967 Columbia film version of this novel, Sidney Poitier portrays Braithwaite's suave, sophisticated character against a backdrop of dreary public school squalor; staff apathy; and student discontent, capriciousness, and violence.

Further Reading

Braveboy-Wagner, Jacqueline A. *The Venezuela-Guyana Border Dispute: Britain's Colonial Legacy in Latin America.* Boulder, CO: Westview Press, 1984.

British Tourist Authority Staff. *London Map.* Cincinnati, OH: Seven Hills Books, 1991.

Fermor, Patrick L. *The Traveller's Tree: A Journey Through the Caribbean Islands.* New York: Viking Penguin, 1991.

Guyana. New York: State Mutual Book and Periodical Service, 1984.

Hall, Gus. *Fighting Racism.* New York: International Publications, 1985.

Huttenback, Robert A. *The British Imperial Experience.* Westport, CT: Greenwood Press, 1976.

Detailed Itinerary

1. Hornchurch, Essex

Twenty-eight-year-old Ricardo Braithwaite, a black teacher, grew up in Georgetown, British Guiana, a country on South America's northeastern coast, and attended school in a shady wooden building in Georgetown. He worked at the Standard Oil Company in Aruba for two years, and served as an airman for the R.A.F. in England during World War II.

Braithwaite met the Belmonts, an older couple at Hornchurch in Essex, near Brentwood, northeast of London, and kept in touch with them during World War II. He honors them by calling them Mom and Dad.

In 1945, Braithwaite returned to live with the Belmonts. After a vacation at Torquay on the southwest coast of England, he searched for work, but was often rejected because of his race.

2. St. James's Park, London

Seated at the lake in St. James's Park, Braithwaite chats with an old man who comments on how lonely London can be. He warns that a survivor must fight to enjoy the big city. Braithwaite retorts that people set up barriers against blacks. The old man suggests that Braithwaite get a job as a teacher in East End London, the toughest part of the city. From this conversation comes Braithwaite's job at Greenslade School.

3. Greenslade School, London

On a May morning, a bus traveling past Aldgate in London's East End carries a few women and a depressed Braithwaite. Divisional Office has assigned him a teaching position at Greenslade School, where he will teach upper-grade students math, health, and geography.

Gossip about the departure of his predecessor warns Braithwaite that teaching underprivileged students will be a challenge, not only because of unemployed parents and poor nutrition, clothing, and housing, but also because of their spiritual and moral inadequacies. Braithwaite becomes annoyed at their faults: bad language, smoking, and discourtesy. Turning his attention to the faculty, Braithwaite meets Gillian Blanchard, who reminds him of an island beauty he met in Martinique, a Caribbean island north of Georgetown.

Early for the first day, Braithwaite is introduced at assembly. In class, he sizes up his 46 students, who are sullen, unkempt, wary, and not eager to study reading or weights and measures, their initial lessons. The day is so wearying that he chooses not to eat with the other teachers. Students try several ploys to bait him, first silent, then noisy, then crude.

Braithwaite changes tactics by becoming courteous and treating the students as adults, in part because they have only six more months of school and will soon enter the adult phase of their lives. The students respond enthusiastically and engage in a discussion about getting along with others.

The students test Braithwaite during gym, where Denham, a student, engages him in boxing. He strikes at his teacher; Braithwaite jabs him in the gut, and Denham collapses. Braithwaite leaves Denham to pick himself up. From that point on, the students respect him.

4. Victoria and Albert Museum, London

With Gillian's assistance, Braithwaite escorts his class to the Victoria and Albert Museum, in the west part of London, at the end of his second month at Greenslade. The students reciprocate by giving him a vase of flowers and by taking notes, asking questions, and demonstrating their enthusiasm for the field trip and for their teacher.

5. Greenslade School, London

Braithwaite introduces a human skeleton and answers questions about anatomy, flora, and fauna. The students question him about his race. He tells them about British Guiana and explains that it is the only British colony on the continent. The discussion turns to Jamaica and Nigeria. The students want more information about Demerara, one of three large territories in British Guiana.

Questions about the color of citizens of South Africa lead Braithwaite to an important lesson—the fact that people can be natives of a country and belong to different races.

6. East End, London

A tobacconist and his wife welcome Braithwaite to the East End and suggest a place where he might rent a room nearer the school. Upon presenting himself to the landlady, Mrs. Pegg, she rejects him as a "darky." But her daughter Barbara identifies him as "Sir," the students' name for Braithwaite. He is so discouraged by the episode that he decides to continue commuting from the Belmonts' home rather than to find a person willing to rent a room to a black tenant. Mrs. Pegg visits Braithwaite and tries to make amends, but he chooses not to move closer to London. To ease Barbara's concern that he is angry, he promises that if he does change his mind, he will seek the Peggs' place first.

7. Soho, London

Braithwaite takes Gillian to a movie and dinner in Soho, in the heart of London's theater district, and begins a regular pattern of dates. During the August holiday, Braithewaite reads and enjoys exhibitions, theater, ballet, and concerts with Gillian.

Gillian, a resident of Chelsea (north of the Thames River on the west side of London), comes from Richmond in northern England and frequently returns to visit her parents.

8. Kent, England

When classes resume, half of Braithewaite's class remains in Kent to work the hop fields with their parents, then straggles in late.

9. Greenslade School, London

In the final three months of school, Pamela Dare, who has grown more mature and observant, begins showing special attention in Braithwaite and challenges other students for asking him about his color. The others accuse her of having a crush on

"Sir." Braithwaite consults Grace about Pamela's confused feelings. Grace attributes the crush to his courtesy, good grooming, and handsome features.

The arrest of Patrick Fernman for knifing another boy prompts criticism of Greenslade, which authorities condemn as a "breeding ground for delinquents." Braithwaite and Gillian visit the Fernmans; Gillian surprises him by speaking Yiddish.

Braithwaite attends Patrick's court hearing. The verdict begins with a condemnation of liberal practices at Patrick's school and concludes with a year's probation.

Braithwaite continues to encourage good manners and community awareness by organizing trips to the ballet, the theater, and an exhibition game by the Harlem Globetrotters. In October, he talks with Pamela and visits her widowed mother, who describes how her daughter returned unexpectedly from a visit with relatives and found her mother sleeping with a man. Braithwaite requests that Pamela treat her mother with courtesy.

10. Piccadilly Circus, Soho

On November 18, his birthday, Braithwaite escorts Gillian to a film, a walk through Piccadilly Circus, and dinner at the Poisson d'Or in Soho. The couple receive rude treatment; Gillian insists on leaving. At her apartment, she screams at Braithwaite for refusing to stand up to racism. They agree that they love each other, yet Gillian fears the racism that he accepts as part of life for a black man living in London. Gillian makes up with him and promises to write her mother that they will visit the family in Richmond the following weekend.

11. Greenslade School, London

A fight between teachers and students provokes ill feeling. Larry Seales notes that nobody pushes Braithwaite around. Braithwaite rebuts his statement and comments that weapons and fighting are not the answer to differences of opinion. An incident with a newspaper causes more dissension after Braithwaite refuses to pose as black teacher to white East End students.

The climax of Braithwaite's experience with his students occurs after Larry's mother dies. The students collect money for a wreath but refuse to visit the biracial family. Braithwaite is so provoked by their refusal that he leaves the room. On Saturday, Braithwaite takes the wreath and arrives at the Seales' home. To his surprise, his class stands dressed in their best, penitent for their insensitivity. Braithwaite loves them even more.

12. Richmond, England

Braithwaite and Gillian spend time with her parents, who ask the usual questions of a man seeking to marry their daughter.

The conversation turns to Aruba. Braithwaite claims to speak Papiamento, the island patois. Mr. Blanchard embarrasses Braithwaite by commenting on the long lines waiting for Aruban prostitutes.

On Sunday afternoon, Mr. Blanchard speaks frankly about his preference that Gillian marry a white man so that her children will be accepted. Braithwaite retorts that he plans to have children and regrets that biracial grandchildren would inconvenience the Blanchards. Blanchard requests that he and Braithwaite part as friends.

13. Greenslade School, London

The school year ends with the senior class party. Pamela asks for a special dance with "Sir." He devotes most of his dances to Gillian, then allows Pamela her fox trot to a special recording of "In the Still of the Night." The next day, the class cheers for their teacher and teases him about dancing with Gillian. Pamela presents a wrapped gift labeled "To Sir, with Love."

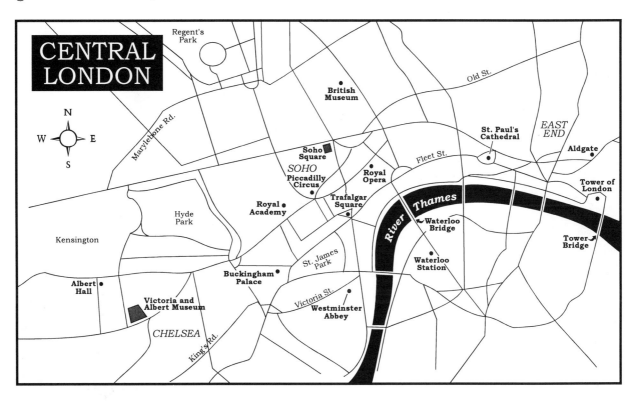

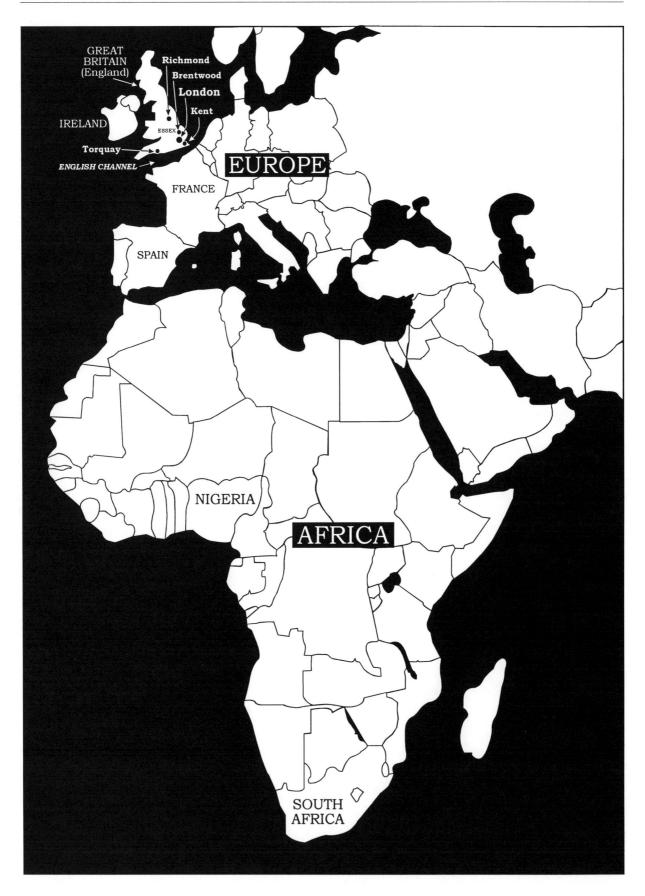

True Grit

BY CHARLES PORTIS

Western novel, 1968

Geographical Summary: This story is set during the winter of 1878, when Rutherford B. Hayes is president. Mattie Ross, a resident of Dardanelle, Arkansas, on the Arkansas River, only 70 miles east of a haven of crime in Indian Territory, journeys west to Fort Smith and into the lawless realm beyond to bring Tom Chaney, her father's murderer, to justice. Moving expertly aboard her pony Blackie, she accompanies Federal Marshal Rooster Cogburn and LaBoeuf, a Texas Ranger, to McAlester and a robbers' hideout in the Winding Stair Mountains. A quarter of a century later, she journeys to Memphis, Tennessee, and Jonesboro, Arkansas, in search of Rooster, who saved her life.

Mattie's trek to Fort Smith, Arkansas, takes her dangerously near the edge of civilization. Named for General Thomas A. Smith, the original fortress contained a federal commissary and jail. At this western seat of justice, which was established to settle tribal squabbling among the Comanche, Osage, Shoshone, and Quapaw, U.S. marshals, by various means of coercion and transport, return outlaws for trial or their corpses for burial. The town's frequent hangings drew an appreciative audience. The town of Fort Smith, which in Mattie's day bore some resemblance to its destiny as a prosperous mining community on the Oklahoma border, was incorporated in 1842. In the 1969 Paramount Pictures version of *True Grit*, the bustle and authority of Fort Smith prefigures its later prominence in the state of Arkansas.

Located adjacent to Fort Smith and extending north to Nebraska and south to Mexico was Indian Territory. A portion of this broad expanse of unsettled land became Oklahoma, which obtained statehood in 1907. In its early years, Indian Territory provided the lawless with a quick escape from the authorities and a convenient hiding place until U.S. marshals, under orders of federal courts, began collaring and returning brigands, murderers, rustlers, train robbers, and horse thieves for trial, prison, or execution.

By the end of Portis's story, much change had affected these lands. In 1893, the Dawes Act allotted land to members of the Five Civilized Tribes—Cherokee, Chickasaw, Choctaw, Creek, and Seminole—and supplanted tribal courts with U.S. judicial districts. By 1901, after these Native Americans achieved full citizenship, the era of banditry and segregation of Indians came to a close.

Further Reading

Ashmore, Henry S. *Arkansas: A History.* New York: W. W. Norton, 1984.

Berry, Fred, and John Novak. *The History of Arkansas.* Little Rock, AR: Rose Publishing, 1987.

Ferrell, Robert H., and Richard Natkiel. *Atlas of American History.* New York: Facts on File, 1987.

Foner, Eric, and John A. Garraty, eds. *The Reader's Companion to American History.* Boston: Houghton Mifflin, 1991.

Steckmesser, Kent L. *Western Outlaws: The 'Good Badman' in Fact, Film, and Folklore.* Claremont, CA: Regina Books, 1983.

Underhill, Lonnie E. *Outlaws in the Indian Territory.* Tucson, AZ: Roan Horse Press, 1985.

Detailed Itinerary

1. Dardanelle to Fort Smith, Arkansas

According to 14-year-old Mattie Ross (resident of Dardanelle in Yell County in central Arkansas), her father Frank hired Tom Chaney, a no-good bachelor from Louisiana, to help him move livestock he intended to purchase. In the winter of 1878, the two traveled 70 miles due west to Fort Smith, in Sebastian County, on the Arkansas border of Indian Territory, to buy stock from Colonel Stonehill, a dealer in Texas cow ponies. At Fort Smith, Ross and Chaney roomed at the Monarch boardinghouse and bought four geldings, leaving Ross $150 of his original bankroll. That night, Chaney got into a card game and lost his wages. When he returned to his room for his rifle, Ross tried to stop him from shooting the card sharks. Instead, Chaney shot Ross in the forehead; robbed him of his horse, cash, and two California gold pieces; and rode off bareback. The townspeople took no action to apprehend the killer.

2. Dardanelle to Mount Nebo to Mount Magazine, Arkansas

In the absence of the Ross family lawyer, who is trying a lawsuit in Helena, Montana, Mattie aims to reach Fort Smith to obtain justice herself. Accompanied by a trusted black hired hand, Yarnell Poindexter, she leaves her family and journeys from her home on the Arkansas River to identify her father's remains. Along the way, the pair pass Mount Nebo, where the Ross family owns a small summer house, and Arkansas' highest point, Mount Magazine. The train is packed with sightseers intent on reaching the Federal Courthouse in Fort Smith for a spectacular triple hanging, conducted under the watchful eye of Judge Isaac Parker, famed for his role in frontier justice.

3. Fort Smith, Arkansas

With information extracted from the sheriff of Sebastian County, Mattie and Yarnell fill in gaps in their understanding of the crime. After viewing the hangings, Mattie identifies Frank's body and pays the undertaker to process and ship the remains to Dardanelle. Yarnell informs Mattie she has been cheated, but she is too intent on vengeance to outmaneuver the undertaker. Leaving Yarnell to supervise the handling of her father's coffin, she moves on to the sheriff's office and learns that he will take no action because he lacks jurisdiction in Indian Territory, the direction in which Tom departed. The sheriff surmises that Chaney intends to join Lucky Ned Pepper, who robbed the mail that Tuesday due west of Fort Smith near the Poteau River.

Mattie sends Yarnell home on the train with Frank's body and spends the night at Mrs. Floyd's Monarch boardinghouse. From Mrs. Floyd, Mattie obtains her father's knife, Colt dragoon, brass watch, and other belongings and avoids personal questions about family business. Because the boardinghouse is full, Mattie rooms with an old woman.

The next morning Mattie goes to the Federal Courthouse on the sheriff's recommendation to hire an overweight, hard-drinking, one-eyed marshal named Reuben "Rooster" Cogburn. Mattie selects him because he appears to be a man of true grit. Until his arrival, Mattie spends the time returning the ponies to Stonehill, a sour-tempered auctioneer who reluctantly reimburses Mattie $325.

Rooster, an uncompromising lawman, impresses Mattie with his toughness. She offers him $50 to capture Chaney and joins him for dinner in the back of Lee's Chinese grocery store, which he shares with his cat. Rooster insists on a fee of $100. Mattie agrees and advances him $25, then, sick with a cold, grows impatient with the drunken Rooster and returns to the Monarch, where she remains in bed two days to recover.

4. Waco, Texas

On the second day, a jaunty, spurred Texan named LaBoeuf appears and identifies Tom Chaney as Theron Chelmsford, who shot Senator Bibbs four months earlier in Waco, Texas, in an argument over the killing of a bird dog. LaBoeuf offers to join Rooster in capturing Chaney.

5. Fort Smith, Arkansas

While awaiting Rooster's return from Little Rock, Mattie receives a message from Lawyer Daggett concerning her father's funeral, collects her money from Stonehill, and bandies words with the cocky LaBoeuf. Finding Rooster still in bed at 10:00 A.M., Mattie concludes her deal with him and announces that she intends to ride along on the manhunt. She pays for supplies and purchases one of the cow ponies from Stonehill. It is a shy animal she names Blackie. LaBoeuf, anticipating rewards from the governor of Texas and the Bibbs family, joins the duo.

After spending the night in a bunk in Stonehill's office, Mattie rides out to the ferry to await Rooster. He and LaBoeuf board and, rejecting Mattie, depart. They inform the ferryman that Mattie is a runaway. She is left to swim Blackie across the Arkansas River.

6. Choctaw Nation, Indian Territory

On the way toward the Choctaw Nation, west of Fort Smith in Indian Territory, in what is now Oklahoma, Mattie canters at a sharp clip. LaBoeuf tries to intimidate Mattie by hurling a rock at her and spanking her. Rooster intervenes and invites her to ride with them. Heading south off the Fort Gibson Road as snow begins to fall, the trio stops at a river store and makes two boys quit abusing a mule and ferry them across the river.

7. San Bois Mountains, Indian Territory

Rooster learns that Ned Pepper, Haze, and a Mexican have been spotted near the railroad at McAlester's store, 60 miles to the southwest. The gang is believed to be headed to their hideout in the Winding Stair Mountains. Through nearly seven inches of snow in the San Bois Mountains, Mattie endures her part of the discomfort and shares her cheese with Rooster and LaBoeuf.

At a dugout in a V-shaped valley near the Texas Road, Rooster and LaBoeuf use a jacket to block the chimney and smoke out Emmett Quincy and Moon Garrett. As Mattie stands in the background, Quincy suddenly chops off four of Moon's fingers with his bowie knife. Moon shoots Quincy, and Rooster shoots Moon. Mattie, spattered with blood, hides on the dirt floor. Rooster and LaBoeuf check on her safety before interrogating Moon, the only living prisoner. Before his death, Moon divulges that Ned and Haze are on their way to Wagoner's Switch to rob the *Katy Flyer* and will return before morning to fresh mounts corraled in the cave out back.

Rooster and LaBoeuf arrange an ambush. While LaBoeuf guards the north slope, Mattie follows Rooster to the opposite crest and keeps warm by asking about his travels. She tells him that her grandfather lives in Monterey, California. Roster replies that he once worked for a supplier in Denver, Colorado; fought in the Civil War; was blinded in one eye by Lone Jack; and rode with Captain Quantrill, a renegade officer rumored to have ravaged parts of the Midwest following the Civil War. Later, Rooster bought the Green Frog cafe in Cairo, Illinois, and married Nola, who left him and returned with their son Horace to her first husband. Rooster, who was not sorry to part with Horace, migrated to Fort Smith and signed up as deputy marshal under Columbus Potter, a trusted friend and war buddy.

Shortly before dawn, six bandits ride up. With a Sharps rifle, LaBoeuf kills Haze, a boy named Billy, and Pepper's horse. Mattie is mesmerized by the swift and bloody action and does not fire a shot. Ned jumps in the saddle of a gang member, who is unseated from his horse, and departs with the Original Greaser Bob, a Mexican gambler. Rooster, on Haze's horse, locates two sacks of jewelry, cash, checks, and other loot from the train holdup.

8. McAlester, Indian Territory

With the four outlaws' bodies, Rooster, LaBoeuf, and Mattie ride to J. J. McAlester's store. Rooster asks Captain Boots Finch to bury the corpses and returns the sacks of goods to the railroad agent. The trio enjoy a good meal; a medic treats LaBoeuf's wound. Before their departure, Finch reports that a man Rooster testified against and imprisoned, Odus Wharton, escaped from the Fort Smith jail by hiding in a barrel. Rooster attempts to leave Mattie with Mrs. McAlester, but Mattie refuses to abandon the trail of her father's killer.

9. Winding Stair Mountains, Indian Territory

The trio travels to a mountainous ridge. Mattie grows testy at the sight of Rooster drinking himself into a stupor. At a stream where Mattie fills containers with water, she surprises Tom Chaney and shoots him in the side. Chaney recovers enough to take Mattie hostage and threatens to kill her. Rooster pretends not to care about the girl's fate. Ned orders Rooster and his partner to ride over the northwest ridge. Mattie fears that Rooster has abandoned her.

Ned, Greaser Bob, and Harold and Ferrell Permalee divide the cash and loot from a stolen mailbag. Unable to cash a counter check, Ned forces Mattie to forge bank notes and leaves her in Chaney's custody. She throws boiling water at Chaney's face; he strikes her on the head with a pistol barrel.

After LaBoeuf arrests Chaney, Mattie regains her pistol. In the meadow below, Rooster confronts Ned and promises to kill him or see him hanged. Ned kills Rooster's horse and threatens the lawman with a revolver. From 600 yards away, LaBoeuf aims his Sharps rifle and drops Ned. Chaney takes the initiative and claps LaBoeuf on the head with a rock.

In the act of shooting Tom in the head, Mattie is knocked backward into a snake pit by the pistol's recoil. Wedged in above a coil of hibernating rattlers, she is unable to hold on and defend herself because her arm is broken. Grabbing for a support, she pulls the upper arm bone from a skeleton and fends off the snakes. Rooster loops a rope about his waist and descends far enough to grasp Mattie, but not before she is bitten by a small snake. Rooster slices the fang marks, chews a cud of tobacco, and places it over the wound to draw out the venom.

10. Fort Smith, Arkansas

Mounted on Blackie, Rooster cradles Mattie and gallops toward Fort Smith. Pushed to the limit, Blackie drops dead. Mattie faints. Rooster, with Mattie on his back, jogs to the Poteau River and commandeers a wagon and team at gunpoint. Changing to a buggy at farmer Cullen's home, he reaches Fort Smith late that night. Days later, as Mrs. Ross and Lawyer Daggett watch, a doctor amputates Mattie's blackened arm above the elbow. Before parting from Mattie, Rooster reports that LaBoeuf climbed down the pit, recovered Chaney's body, and rode toward Texas with it. Daggett, at first angry over Mattie's role in the manhunt, pays Rooster and presents him a check for $200 as reward for his bravery.

11. Dardanelle and Russellville, Arkansas

For the next 25 years Mattie remains unmarried, cares for her invalid mother, supports the Presbyterian church, and works for a bank in Dardanelle and Russellville. She hears through Chen Lee about Rooster, who got into trouble in Fort Gibson, Oklahoma, while rearresting Odus Wharton.

12. San Antonio, Texas

Forced to surrender his badge, Rooster took a widow southwest to San Antonio, Texas, and set up as a cattleman. The venture fell through. Rooster departed once more on his own.

13. Memphis, Tennessee

From a clipping sent by her brother in May 1903, Mattie learns that Rooster is employed by a Wild West show in Memphis, northeast of Arkansas, and takes the train to find him.

14. Jonesboro, Arkansas

On a Pullman car, Mattie encounters Frank James and Cole Younger, aging former outlaws. Younger claims that Rooster died a few days earlier in Jonesboro, Arkansas.

15. Dardanelle, Arkansas

Mattie journeys southwest to Jonesboro and transfers Rooster's remains to Dardanelle, where she honors him with a marble Confederate headstone engraved with the dates 1835-1903.

Walkabout

BY JAMES VANCE MARSHALL

Young adult novel, 1959

Geographical Summary: *Walkabout* is a story of endurance and learning. Peter and Mary, two American children, survive a plane crash on Sturt Plain in the north-central Outback of Australia. Stranded 1,400 miles from their destination, they launch an ambitious trek south across harsh desert land to their uncle, who lives at Adelaide on the island continent's southern coast. Through their acquaintance with a teenage Aborigine, the children learn to use nature to supply them with food and water as they learn about trust between races. Their guide dies, leaving Peter and Mary to complete the journey alone.

Set on Sturt Plain, which was named for Charles Sturt (Australia's greatest explorer and discoverer of the Murray and Darling rivers), the story takes place in a region first explored by Europeans in the mid-1800s and marked by a hot, dry climate and a desert rich in flora and fauna, including marsupials, insects, reptiles, and fish. The action places the two American children in an alien environment nearly devoid of human habitation. Their chance meeting with a wandering bush boy, one of about 500 tribes of Australian Aborigines, introduces them to a type of desert survival and subsistence that requires guidance and explanation. Without words, the three youngsters manage to live off the land until Peter and Mary can reunite with white residents.

Traditionally, adaptable indigenous people like the bush boy have lived a semi-nomadic life hunting and gathering, living in small camps, traveling to water holes, and sheltering in temporary huts or near windbreaks. Burdened by few possessions, the Aborigines use spears, boomerangs, and cultivation tools or digging sticks. Frequently naked or wrapped in skins, they manage well against the elements of a desert climate by studying nature and applying their knowledge to hunting, shelter, and finding sparse water supplies. A significant part of the aboriginal adaptive skill derives from ritual, such as the walkabout, by which young tribe members learn the discipline that will sustain them in a harsh environment.

Further Reading

Australia. New York: Time-Life Books, 1985.

Berndt, Ronald, and Catherine H. Berndt. *Man, Land and Myth in North Australia: The Gunwinggu People.* East Lansing, MI: Michigan State University Press, 1970.

Goldberg, S. L., and F. B. Smith, eds. *Australian Cultural History.* New York: Cambridge University Press, 1990.

Lewis, Brian. *The Naked Australian: Australia, Her People, and the Way They Live.* San Jose, CA: Australian American Publishing, 1987.

Shaw, John, ed. *Australian Encyclopedia.* Boston: G. K. Hall, 1989.

Tindale, Norman B. *Aboriginal Tribes of Australia.* Berkeley, CA: University of California Press, 1974.

Detailed Itinerary

1. Sturt Plain, Australia

Far from their home in Charleston, South Carolina, 13-year-old Mary and Peter, her 8-year-old brother, survive the crash of a transport plane in the desert of north-central Australia while on their way south to Adelaide to visit their Uncle Keith. That night, Mary dreams of the crash and blaze from which she and Peter escaped and in which the pilot and navigating officer were killed by fire. The next morning, following a bath in a creek, the children begin their walk across the great desert of Sturt Plain, 1,400 miles away from Adelaide.

The children realize they are being watched and are approached by a bush boy, a 13- or 14-year-old member of an Australian aboriginal desert tribe. He is on a walkabout, which is a six- to eight-month period where he has to survive alone in the desert as proof of his manhood. Mary and Peter are the first white people he has ever encountered, and, in amazement, he touches their skin and light hair. Conditioned by southern prejudice toward black males, Mary is shocked at the boy's familiarity. More than his touch or stare, his nakedness alarms her, as she is entering adolescence. Peter, who is too immature to perceive the cause of his older sister's unease, accepts the bush boy's attentions and delights him by sneezing. The bush boy laughs spontaneously, then flinches when Peter snaps the elastic in his shorts to demonstrate the need for clothes.

The boy asks questions in his native language, then wanders away. Peter insists on following the bush boy and calls for the stranger to wait for them. In sign language, Peter indicates their need for water and food. The bush boy, graceful and sure in his home territory, leads them to water, builds a fire, then bakes a wallaby for them to eat.

2. Waterfall on the Sturt Plain

Mary grows uneasy that Peter, who is thoroughly entranced by the bush boy's survival skills, no longer depends on her. The next morning, after a swim, the three share a yam-like root called *worwora.* Peter emulates the bush boy by shedding his shorts. Mary forces him back into his clothes and gives the bush boy her underpants to wear. Unaware of the lacy edge on the garment, he is intrigued by elastic and whirls in a celebratory dance that simulates combat. His joy yields to terror when he concludes that Mary has foreseen his death.

According to tribal custom, the bush boy prepares to die. His bizarre behavior causes Peter to cry. The bush boy wanders helplessly away, then stops when Peter confronts him. By drawing ritual rings, he wards off the Spirit of Death, then determines to continue his walkabout to the Valley-of-waters-under-the-earth to save Peter and Mary from dying of hunger and thirst.

3. Salt pans on the Sturt Plain

The trio walk toward the barren salt pans, then stop by a water hole for a drink. By the end of the day, they have gone 15 miles. The bush boy kills a bustard and, respecting his tribe's understanding of sex roles, hands it to Mary to carry. At nightfall, Mary, still fearful of the stranger, asks Peter to sleep near her on the opposite side of the fire from the bush boy. In the distance, she sees the boy standing on one foot, staring into the valley, waiting for death.

On the fourth day of their journey, the trio eats fresh-caught fish. The bush boy, infected by Peter's nasal congestion, begins to sweat. He grows more fearful that death is near. The next morning, he refuses to eat and appears to have fallen into a trance. He worries that the children will not know how to construct a burial table where his corpse will be safe from evil spirits.

4. Hill country of the Australian Outback

The trio arrives at the hills. The bush boy grows weaker and trembles as though with cold. By morning, he lies sleeping when Mary takes her turn at the pool. The bush boy awakens and goes in search of her, startling her so badly that she threatens him with a rock. He withdraws, confused and depressed.

Mary extinguishes the fire and presses Peter to move on. Peter insists that they remain with the dying bush boy. Mary relents and holds the bush boy's head in her lap. At dawn, he dies. Peter christens the corpse before they bury him at the water hole. Following the bush boy's last directions, Peter and Mary trudge toward the other side of the hill.

5. Valley-of-waters-under-the-earth in the Australian Outback

On the ninth day of their ordeal, brother and sister arrive at a pool, where they drink cool water and feast on crayfish. Refreshed, they press on to the Valley-of-waters-under-the-earth. On their third day in the valley, a baby koala shreds Mary's dress, which she discards. She is comfortable with her nakedness, which is partially obscured by her waist-length blond hair. They walk confidently through the forest, eating whatever foods they can find and drawing their dreams in clay pictures on lake rocks.

The next day, the children see smoke. With a branch, they signal three approaching black figures—a man carrying a three-year-old boy on his shoulders, a woman with a dingo puppy draped around her neck, and a slender girl Mary's age. Peter chats with them haltingly in the aboriginal language; they exchange bauble nuts for yams.

The man recognizes Mary's picture of a house and points toward the far side of the valley. Through pantomime and drawings, he describes a two-day journey to the east over the hills and by a lake. On the third day, he predicts that they will arrive at a house like the one in the drawing. Peter, who has gained maturity through his desert experience, bids the Aborigines farewell and leads the way toward the lake.

When the Legends Die

BY HAL BORLAND

Psychological novel, 1963

Geographical Summary: *When the Legends Die,* a fictional account of initiation and alienation, describes how Thomas Black Bull, a Ute Indian, faces an identity crisis while attempting to accommodate both his ethnic heritage and his desire for fame on the rodeo circuit. The story covers a four-part journey, from his boyhood on Bald Mountain in southwestern Colorado to an inhospitable reservation school, which Tom escapes with the help of Red, a rodeo rider. Tom becomes a professional rodeo rider, competing throughout the United States and Canada under the name Tom Black. Following a serious injury at Madison Square Garden in New York, he recuperates in a hospital and returns to his homeland, where he convalesces while herding sheep. In the wilderness setting where he grew up, Tom makes peace with the complex person he has become.

Tom's people, the Ute, a native tribe of stocky hunter-gatherers, farmers, and raiders of the Rocky Mountains and parts of the Northwest, followed the ancient Fremont and Anasazi tribes into the western basin of the Colorado River. The Ute, whose name means "people at the mountaintops," hunted elk and deer in the tablelands adjacent to the Wasatch Mountains and became famous for their equestrian skills. For a time, they used their remote location to dominate the area northwest of Santa Fe, New Mexico. Taking naturally to animals, Tom applies understanding and patience to the complex task of managing wild, unpredictable horses, a skill that brings him fame.

The rodeo circuit, a uniquely American sport popular in Florida, the West and Southwest, Canada, and New York, has its roots in local displays of cowboys' skills, particularly bareback riding, bronc riding, bull riding, calf roping, steer wrestling, and bulldogging (subduing a calf by tying its feet). The first rodeo organized purely for entertainment took place in Prescott, Arizona, in 1888. From early days, these colorful events contained parades, pageantry, trick riding, clowns, and barrel racing. A major thrill for the audience is the timed ride on an unbroken horse, or bronc. The horse is provoked to buck wildly, attempting to unseat the rider from its back. To survive on the grueling rodeo circuit, competitors must stay healthy and win prize money often enough to pay their expenses as the show moves from town to town. Low pay, travel expenses, frequent falls, broken bones, and internal injuries usually shorten the time a contestant can remain competitive.

Further Reading

Dictionary of Daily Life of Indians of the Americas. Newport Beach, CA: American Indian Publishers, 1981.

Martin, Chuck. *Rodeo Cowboy.* South Yarmouth, MA: John Curley, 1988.

Mauskoff, Norman. *Rodeo: Photographs.* Altadena, CA: Twelvetrees Press, 1985.

Norbury, Rosamond. *Behind the Chutes: The Mystique of the Rodeo Cowboy.* Missoula, MT: Mountain Press, 1992.

Patterson, Lotsee, and Mary Ellen Snodgrass. *Indian Terms of the Americas.* Englewood, CO: Libraries Unlimited, 1994.

Pettit, Jan. *Utes: The Mountain People.* Boulder, CO: Johnson Books, 1990.

Sturtevant, William C., ed. *Handbook of North American Indians.* Washington, DC: Smithsonian Institution Press, 1984.

Waldman, Carl. *Atlas of the North American Indian.* New York: Facts on File, 1985.

Detailed Itinerary

1. Arboles, Colorado
In the summer of 1910, Bessie and George Black Bull and their young son Tom live near Arboles, a Ute reservation in southwestern Colorado near the border of New Mexico.

2. Horse Mountain, near Pagosa, Colorado
The first week in July, Bessie and George join a hunting and fishing expedition to Horse Mountain on the Piedra River.

3. Piedra and Pagosa, Colorado
The Ute party visits Piedra Town, then continues gathering berries and smoking meat for the winter. To make amends for illegal hunting, they live in nearby Pagosa for two months to save money for their return to the reservation. However, the family is trapped for two years by debts to the company store. George tries to save enough to pay his debts, but his money is stolen. By August, George has saved $15; again, the money disappears. George kills the suspected thief and escapes to the mountains. That evening, Bessie takes her small son and, making certain she isn't observed, follows her husband.

4. Horse Mountain, near Pagosa, Colorado
The Black Bull family reunites on Horse Mountain and builds a traditional Ute lodge. In the second winter, George dies under a snowy avalanche. Bessie and and Tom continue living at the lodge. She goes into Pagosa to trade baskets at Jim Thatcher's store for an axehead, ammunition, and a knife.

Bessie returns alone to town to trade two baskets for calico and a coat for the boy. The next summer, she returns to trade four baskets for a red blanket for Tom. That winter, she dies; her son places her body in the cave beside his father's remains. In spring, Tom befriends an orphaned bear cub and names himself Bear Brother.

In July, Tom and his cub go to Jim's store in Pagosa to trade three baskets for a red blanket. Blue Elk, an Indian who victimizes his own race, is paid to trail the boy to the lodge on Horse Mountain and to persuade him to return to the reservation.

5. Ignacio, Colorado
At the reservation school, Tom is unhappy because he and the bear are unwelcome. Three days later, Blue Elk returns Tom to Horse Mountain and forces him to abandon the bear. Blue Elk returns Tom to Ignacio. For two days, Tom reluctantly attends the reservation school, then runs away to Horse Mountain to look for the

bear. Because his lodge has been burned, Tom unhappily returns to the school, where he is assigned to herd horses and tend sheep for Albert Left Hand.

6. Bayfield, Colorado

Tom and Albert Left Hand go north to Bayfield to trade hides. Because of his skill with horses, Tom accepts a job breaking broncs on Red Dillon's ranch near Blanco, New Mexico.

7. Red's Ranch near Blanco, New Mexico

In New Mexico, southeast of Blanco near the San Juan River, Tom arrives at his new home and meets Meo, Red's Hispanic cook, who raises his own beans and chiles. Tom learns to ride Red's broncs and masters basic rodeo skills, including how to lose.

8. Aztec, New Mexico

When he is ready, Tom competes in his first rodeo. Red makes him lose the final round so that he can manipulate the betting and win more money. Tom rides a horse to its death. The crowd realizes that Red is a fraud and forces him to leave Aztec.

9. Blanco, New Mexico

On the road home, Red stops in Blanco for whisky and gets drunk. He maps out a rodeo course for Tom, beginning with Bernalillo and on to Carrizozo, where Tom falls and injures his shoulder. Red ends up in jail. He and Tom elude a posse and return home.

10. The rodeo circuit

For a year, Red and Tom follow the rodeo around New Mexico, Oklahoma, Colorado, and Texas. The pattern of their lives remains about the same, with Red frequently drunk. In north Texas near the Oklahoma border, Tom breaks his leg.

11. Red's Ranch near Blanco, New Mexico

Tom and Red return home to Meo and a brief rest at the ranch. By August, Tom has recuperated and is able to ride professionally again.

12. The rodeo circuit

The next season takes Tom and his manager to Colorado, Arizona, and Texas and north to Idaho, Wyoming, and Utah. Tom reaches the end of his patience in Uvalde County, Texas, where he rebels against Red's tyranny and fraud. Under the name Tom Black, he competes honestly and becomes a rodeo star.

In September, Red dies in a hotel in Aztec, New Mexico. Tom pays for the funeral. He is named best first-year man on the circuit, then breaks his arm and ribs in a bad fall.

13. Red's Ranch near Blanco, New Mexico

Tom drives home to Red's ranch and discovers that Meo has died. After two weeks of brooding, Tom burns the ranch.

14. The rodeo circuit

At a rodeo in Wolf Point, Montana, Tom earns the name "Killer Tom Black." He competes in California; Odessa, Texas; and Calgary, Alberta. After following the rodeo circuit to Chicago, Philadelphia, and Los Angeles, Tom goes to New York City. At a show in Madison Square Garden, a big roan horse rolls over his hips, breaking his pelvis, femur, and some ribs; puncturing a lung; and causing a concussion. For two days Tom clings to life in a private hospital room, then recovers.

15. Pagosa and Piedra, Colorado

Tom takes the bus to Pagosa, the only place that feels like home. He accepts a job as shepherd in Piedra, then settles in sight of Bald Mountain and Horse Mountain. He builds a lodge, dresses Indian style, hunts for food, and finds peace in the traditional Ute lifestyle.

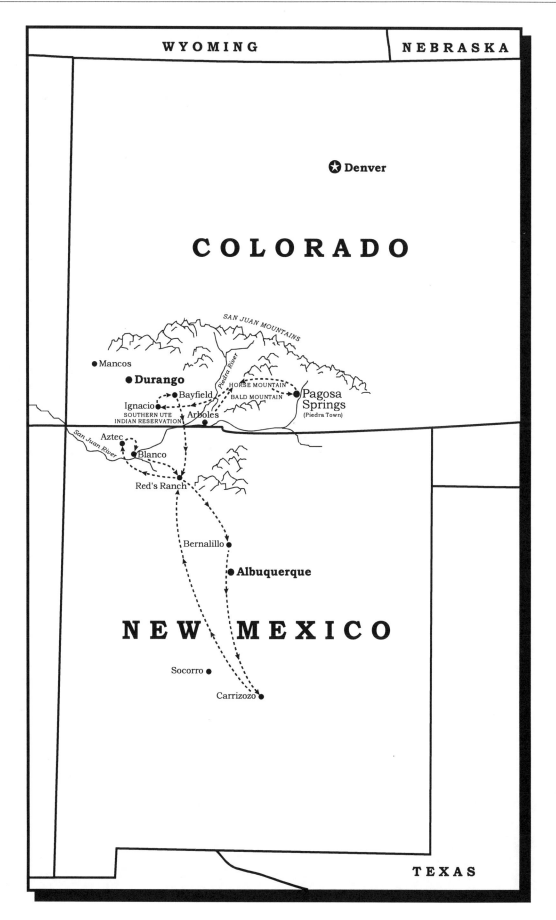

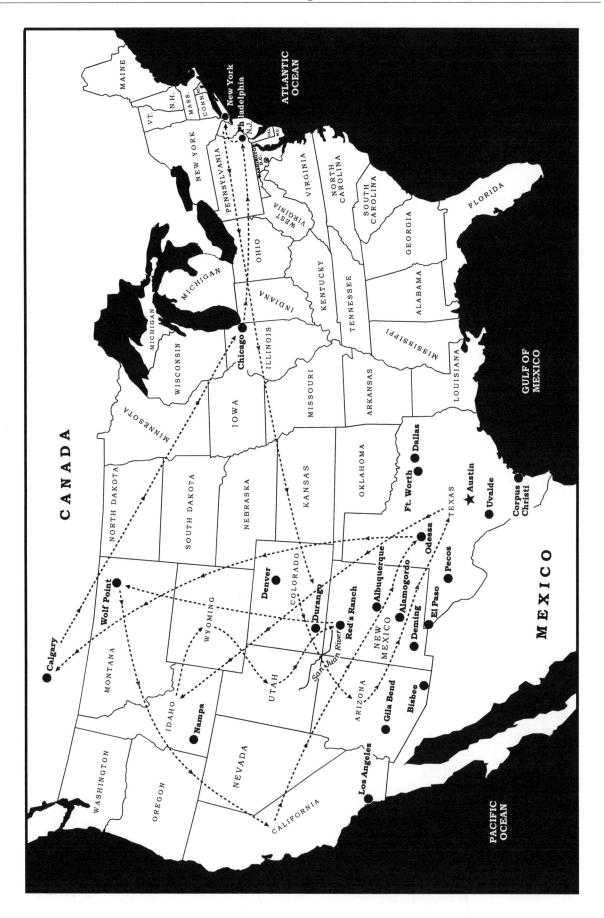

The Witch of Blackbird Pond

BY ELIZABETH SPEARE

Young adult historical fiction, 1958

Geographical Summary: Far from her home in Barbados, an island of the West Indies, Katherine "Kit" Tyler makes her way north by ship to the port of Saybrook and upriver to Wethersfield, Connecticut, to live with her mother's sister. In the constraining culture of Puritan Connecticut Colony, Kit avoids the dismal atmosphere and harsh chores by escaping to the great meadowland, where Hannah Tupper, a banished Quaker, lives. Local witch-hunters drive Hannah out of her home and lock Kit in the constable's tool shed to test her for witchcraft. Although Kit is tempted to return to Barbados, she agrees to marry Nat Eaton, whose ship the *Witch* sails from Barbados to New England, thus joining the only two homes she has known.

Geographically, Kit Tyler makes a vast change in social and religious background, climate, and topography when she migrates to Connecticut from Barbados, a paradise in the Windward Islands of the Caribbean. After English settlers began colonizing Barbados in 1624, the island was quickly subdivided into prosperous sugar plantations that, for the next two centuries, were farmed by African slaves. Owners extended their investments by producing molasses and rum, both useful trade items for the trade triangle, which bartered rum with West Africans in exchange for more slaves.

Leaving white sandy beaches, fresh fish and fruit, exotic flowers, refreshing swims on hot days, and gentle breezes on temperate nights, Kit discovers the cheerless, bitter winters in Connecticut. Among the sour, joyless, suspicious Puritans who settled Connecticut's river colony, she fares poorly because of her delight in pretty, feminine clothing and her openmindedness. In 1688, a period when hysteria brought about the deaths of suspected witches in Salem, Massachusetts, Kit endangers herself with her headstrong ways and her refusal to give in to the behavior expected of a young, marriageable, Christian woman.

One event that occurs during her tenure in Wethersfield is the arrival of Sir Edmund Andros, New England's governor general, who demands that the residents of Hartford hand over the charter originally granted by England's Charles II. This legendary event was connected with the famous Charter Oak, a tree in Hartford where rebels are thought to have concealed the document.

Further Reading

Barbour, Hugh. *The Quakers in Puritan England.* Richmond, IN: Friends United, 1985.

Ferrell, Robert H., and Richard Natkiel. *Atlas of American History.* New York: Facts on File, 1987.

Kent, David L. *Barbados and America.* Austin, TX: C. M. Kent, 1980.

Summers, Montague. *The Geography of Witchcraft.* New York: Carol Publishing Group, 1973.

———. *The History of Witchcraft in the United States.* New York: Hippocrene Books, 1990.

Taylor, John M. *Witchcraft Delusion in Colonial Connecticut.* Bowie, MD: Heritage Books, 1989.

Taylor, Robert J. *Colonial Connecticut: A History.* Millwood, NY: Kraus International, 1979.

Tree, Harold. *A History of Barbados.* Woodstock, NY: Beekman Publications, 1979.

Detailed Itinerary

1. Saybrook, Connecticut Colony

On her arrival aboard the brigantine *Dolphin* at Saybrook, Connecticut, on the Connecticut river, in mid-April 1687, 16-year-old Katherine "Kit" Tyler stands on the forecastle deck. She enjoys the first sight of land in her five-week voyage from the West Indies. Nathaniel "Nat" Eaton, first mate and son of the captain, points out his father's shipyard and compliments Kit on being a sturdy sailor. She begs to go ashore on the longboat with Nat's mother, who has kept her company on the trip north.

On land, Kit meets the disapproving stares of two tattered Puritan women, who glare at her silk gown. She boards the longboat with other passengers. Prudence Cruff, daughter of a prim Puritan mother, loses her doll overboard. Kit impulsively dives into the cold water to retrieve it. Nat, unaware that she is a skilled swimmer, plunges in after her.

Kit returns unharmed to the longboat. She introduces herself to passenger John Holbrook and explains that she is going upriver to Wethersfield to live with her mother's sister, Mistress Rachel, whom Kit has never met.

2. Barbados, West Indies

Holbrook is curious where Kit learned to swim. She replies that she learned in early childhood in Barbados, where her grandfather owned a plantation. Holbrook indicates that he is traveling to Wethersfield to study for the ministry. At mealtime, Nat assigns Kit to the table of Goodwife Cruff, who believes that Kit must be a witch, as witches are known to float on water.

3. Wethersfield, Connecticut Colony

For nine days, the crew sails and tows the longboat toward Wethersfield. Along the way, John divulges his disappointment in not having the money to attend Harvard University; Kit relates her parents' drowning on a pleasure sail to the island of Antigua, which is north of Barbados. Kit and Nat exchange hostile words after she complains of the *Dolphin's* horsy smell. He retorts that the stink is better than the smell of a slave ship, which brought human cargo to Barbados. John, also disapproving, questions Kit's wide range of reading material, especially plays, which he considers unseemly. Captain Eaton, who escorts her from the wharf, is surprised that Kit has traveled to Wethersfield without contacting her relatives first.

4. High Street, Wethersfield

Rachel Wood, standing in her doorway, identifies Kit because she looks like her sister. Welcomed into a bright kitchen, Kit meets Judith and Mercy, her cousins, who admire her elegant clothes and embroidered gloves. Mercy is limited in movement because of a severe disformity in her spine. Kit's explanation of her abrupt visit surprises Matthew, Rachel's husband: Her grandfather died after being cheated by his overseer, and Kit sold her slave to pay passage so that she could escape a 50-year-old suitor who offered to keep up the family property and marry her.

Matthew, a bitter man since the death of his young sons, returns Kit's gifts of bright clothing, which he declares unsuitable for Puritans. He only allows a shawl for the crippled Mercy. Judith resents sharing her bed with her cousin and complains that Kit is poor help in the kitchen. Kit overhears, ascends to the loft, and weeps into her pillow.

5. Meeting House, Wethersfield

Against her religious custom, Kit is coerced into attending Sunday meetings both morning and afternoon. Along the way to Wethersfield's Meeting House, she notes the pillory, stocks, and whipping post. The service is ruled over by a stern minister and a disciplinarian with a pole. At the door, Kit meets the Reverend Gershom Bulkeley, who comments raspily on her poverty. Rachel urges Bulkeley to invite John, his pupil, to Thursday dinner.

Over the meal, Bulkeley engages Kit in conversation about the islands and her loyalty to the British crown. Matthew bridles at the suggestion that he is disloyal for his distaste for Governor Andros, the colonial authority appointed by King James. The visit ends with Matthew's revolt against being chastened in his own house.

On other days, William Ashby, a likely suitor, comes to call, as does John Holbrook. Kit disdains William's persistence.

While pulling weeds in the onion field, Kit learns from Judith about Hannah Tupper, who lives near Blackbird Pond. To earn real wages and help the family, Kit joins Mercy in teaching a dame school in the Wood kitchen. After Mercy's reading of dour Puritan verses, Kit adds sprightly, original couplets, which delight the 11 young pupils.The class acts out a story, but the schoolmaster and Reverend John Woodbridge interrupt their noisy activity. Kit is fired for play-acting a scene from the Bible.

6. Blackbird Pond, Wethersfield

Humiliated, Kit runs away to the meadow, where Hannah Tupper comforts her. At Hannah's house, Kit accepts a blueberry corn cake and goat's milk and warms to Hannah's cat. A bit of coral introduces the subject of Kit's homesickness for Barbados. Hannah shows Kit a scarlet blossom springing from a small African bulb and urges her to listen to her heart.

7. High Street, Wethersfield

Kit tells Mercy that she asked the headmaster for a second chance and startles Rachel with the news that she visited Hannah. Rachel warns Kit that others shun Hannah because she is a Quaker who, along with her husband Thomas, was branded and driven from Massachusetts.

8. Blackbird Pond, Wethersfield

On a return visit to Hannah, Kit exults that she faced the headmaster and returned to the dame school. Hannah, who spins flax to earn enough to pay taxes on her land and fines for not attending meetings, welcomes Nat, a frequent visitor, who has just come from Charlestown, South Carolina, far to the south on the Atlantic coast. Hannah is glad that both Kit and Nat have turned to her in friendship and need.

9. High Street, Wethersfield

Prudence Cruff, who is not allowed to attend dame school, delivers flowers to Kit in secret. Kit rewards her with a hornbook, which Prudence must leave behind to avoid being caned by her mother. Kit invites Prudence to visit Hannah's house, where the child can learn to read and write without fear.

10. Blackbird Pond, Wethersfield

Carrying a bit of apple tart from Rachel, Kit returns to Hannah's house and finds Nat chopping wood. Having rowed out from the longboat, becalmed to the south at Rocky Hill, Nat is eager to help Hannah by rethatching the roof. Kit assists by gathering grass. Nat tells of Hannah's dismal past, when Puritans jailed her, branded her forehead, tied her and her husband to a cart, and flogged them out of Massachusetts.

11. High Street, Wethersfield

Nat escorts Kit home and takes the blame for her tardiness. Matthew forbids her to return to Blackbird Pond. John reports Dr. Bulkeley's opinion on witches like Hannah. Kit retorts that John should think for himself instead of expecting Bulkeley to do it for him.

John admits to Kit that he prefers Mercy to Judith. At Kit's urging, he tries to ask for Mercy's hand but is maneuvered into asking for Judith. Mercy conceals her disappointment and wishes them both well. William proposes to Kit, but Kit is not ready for matrimony. William agrees to wait.

12. Wethersfield wharf

On a brief return trip of the *Dolphin*, Nat gives Kit a package of wool cloth to deliver to Hannah. He is jealous of William, whose parcel of window panes will adorn the home of his bride. Nat assumes that the bride is Kit. Judith scolds Kit for befriending a common river man like Nat.

13. High Street, Wethersfield

In the angry flurry surrounding Governor Andros's visit, William joins Matthew in protecting the charter, which William steals from the meeting house when the lights are extinguished. On All Hallow's Eve, rivermen place jack-o-lanterns in William's windows.

14. High Street, Wethersfield

For their prank, three *Dolphin* crewmen are confined to the stocks, smeared with mud, and pelted with garbage. Nat is proud of being a part of the mischief that costs him several hours in the stocks, a fine of 40 shillings, and banishment from Wethersfield. He urges Kit to leave the street before the rowdiness gets out of hand. She hurries home.

15. Blackbird Pond, Wethersfield

Kit carries the wool cloth to Hannah and pours out her unhappiness at Nat's confinement and humiliation. Hannah questions whether it would be wise of Kit to marry William just to escape her uncle's house.

16. High Street, Wethersfield

Kit, Judith, and Mercy come down with fever. Against Matthew's objections, Bulkeley, a physician, attends Mercy and applies an onion poultice to her chest. A group of vigilantes summon Matthew to help them drive out the witch who caused the fever. Matthew declines to join a witch hunt, but when the group leader implicates Kit in Hannah's purported witchcraft, Matthew forces her out of the house.

17. Blackbird Pond, Wethersfield

To rescue Hannah from the witch-hunters, Kit rushes through the shed door at the back of the house and down Broad Street and South Road. She forces the old woman to abandon her house. From a hiding place in the brush they see townspeople burning Hannah's house.

18. Connecticut River near Wright's Island

Kit swims out to the *Dolphin* and begs Nat to help Hannah. Nat returns to rescue Hannah's cat and begs Kit to sail south with them to his grandmother's house. Kit insists on returning to nurse Mercy.

19. High Street, Wethersfield

Kit slips back into the house without notice. The witch-hunters, led by Goodwife Cruff, display the hornbook that Prudence left at Hannah's house and take Kit into custody as Hannah's accomplice. Goodwife Cruff signs a charge of witchcraft against Kit.

Kit is locked in a shed and receives a quilt and food from the constable's wife. She longs for William to rescue her.

20. Town House, Wethersfield

Escorted to trial the next morning, Kit hears the charge. Matthew protests the absurd evidence of witchcraft. Goodwife Cruff produces Prudence's hornbook with her name written repeatedly. Nat appears with Prudence, who testifies that Kit taught her to read. Prudence reads a Bible passage. On the strength of her reading, Kit goes free. Goodwife Cruff turns her fury on Nat and demands that he be lashed. Prudence whispers to Kit that Nat has slipped away in a boat.

21. Hartford, Connecticut; Hadley, Massachusetts; and Deerfield, New Hampshire

That winter, two militiamen return with news of an Indian attack on the colonial detachment. Only 8 of 20 returned to Hartford, having been ambushed south of Hadley, Massachusetts, on their way northwest to Deerfield, New Hampshire. John, who had been studying with the troop doctor, was captured. Late that winter, John stumbles through the door and drops before Mercy. That April, William and Judith are pledged to marry, as are Mercy and John.

22. Wethersfield wharf

In May, Kit, determined to escape her uncle's house even if she has to sell her dresses to pay passage back to Barbados, waits for the *Dolphin* to come back. Nat returns and displays his own ketch, proudly named the *Witch*. He promises to take Kit aboard.

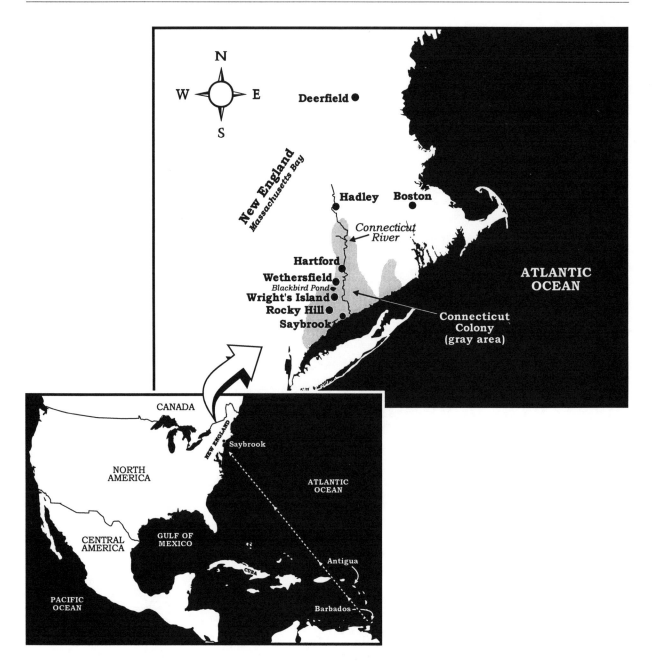

Location Index

Note: Maps are listed in **bold**.

Subject Index

Note: This index contains authors, titles, and topics mentioned in the text. Maps are listed in **bold**.